GLORIOUS UNCERTAINTY

THE AUTOBIOGRAPHY OF JENNY PITMAN

GLORIOUS UNCERTAINTY

THE AUTOBIOGRAPHY OF JENNY PITMAN

written with Sue Gibson

WILLOW BOOKS
Collins
Grafton Street, London
1984

Willow Books
William Collins Sons & Co Ltd
London · Glasgow · Sydney
Auckland · Toronto · Johannesburg

First published in Great Britain 1984

Front cover photograph: Bob Thomas
Back cover photograph: Gerry Cranham

Pitman, Jenny
Glorious uncertainty
1. Pitman, Jenny   2. Racehorse training – Biography
3. Horse-racing – Great Britain
I. Title
636.1′092′4   SF336.P/
ISBN 0 00 218110 X

Filmset in Imprint by
Ace Filmsetting Ltd, Frome, Somerset
Printed and bound in Great Britain by
William Collins Sons & Co Ltd, Glasgow

THIS BOOK IS DEDICATED TO MY FAMILY
AND FRIENDS, WITHOUT WHOM THE STORY
WOULD NEVER HAVE BEEN WRITTEN

CONTENTS

INTRODUCTION

Jenny Pitman began her professional training career in 1975. I began my own professional writing career in the same year: Jenny Pitman was my first assignment for the *Sporting Chronicle*, and my article on her published early in 1976. She was, by that time, enjoying her first fruitful season, and her yard produced 12 winners from just 12 horses: a remarkable achievement for a first season.

I have watched Jenny's career with great interest over the intervening years, and I have also watched her handle the very public traumas of her personal life with the utmost dignity and outward calm. It has been my privilege and pleasure to interview her several times, and I was truly delighted when I was approached with the idea of collaborating on her first autobiography.

Our careers seem to have run a parallel course: Jenny won her first National (apart from the victory 'by default' at Uttoxeter which is explained within these pages) at Chepstow in the same year that my first book, a small paperback, was published. She won her supreme prize, the Grand National, for the first time – never doubt for a moment that she will win another – in 1983, coinciding with my own first major book assignment, and it is fitting that the assignment should be Jenny's book. As Jenny very aptly puts it: 'This book is your personal Grand National'.

Collaborating with Jenny has been, above all, fun. No one I ever interviewed before made me laugh so much; no one was more keen than Jenny to co-operate to the utmost degree. Without her dedication to the cause, none of this could have appeared in print. I now look forward with great interest to the possibility of being asked to help her write Part Two. Jenny is, after all, still a comparative youngster in the world of racehorse training, and the next 30 years ought to be even more riveting than the last! All this is really to say, in short: thank you, Jenny.

Sue Gibson
Hurstpierpoint, 1983

1
PROLOGUE

This is it, I thought to myself. Yet again. Here I was, with another Grand National about to begin and three of my horses out there ready to join the fray. Three of my horses and three of my jockeys, all at the point of no return. There was no calling them back. No turning the clock back an hour and changing my mind. The horses and the jockeys lined up at the start of the 1983 Grand National now had to take their chances with the 40 other runners and riders in that headlong gallop down the narrow channel to the first two fences. After the third I might begin to relax a little. When the horses settled down and there would be more space to gallop and jump.

Why, I asked my family, do I do it? They were all about me, as usual, supportive and caring and keyed-up almost as much as me. Why is it, I thought, that I spend all the year waiting for this race, only to get to Aintree, where England's most prestigious – the world's most prestigious – steeplechase takes place every April, and wonder the same thing. Am I mad? What on earth possesses me to bring horses to jump round these huge fences over four-and-a-half miles of track?

All I could possibly care about at that moment, and all I care about at the same moment before every Grand National, is the safety of those horses and their riders. I suddenly find I am very religious and pray like mad. I make all sorts of promises which of course remain unfulfilled the rest of the year. Just get my horses round safely and I'll give up swearing, or smoking, or whatever, and I don't care whether they come first, middle, last, or don't even finish the race . . . please God, don't let any of them get hurt. I know how it feels to lose horses, and especially good horses like the ones that end up running at Aintree.

Then the starter climbs up onto his rostrum and my heart is trying to escape from between my teeth. If you are afraid of flying, you will understand what it's like: the second when the plane puts the engines on full power and starts shuddering, just before it moves down the runway for take-off. No escape. It's do or die, so let's get it over! The starter's red flag goes up into the air, and I watch my jockeys trying to position the horses as I asked them. I've been over it with them. They know how I want them to run the race. Keep Corbiere and Artistic Prince to the inside, I'd said to two of the jockeys. Keep Monty Python on the wide outside, I'd said to the other. Try and keep out of trouble. Be lucky. Be safe.

It's a moment of relief when the field of 40 runners finally surges forward, as it is when that plane takes off after all the waiting. They're away and over the first fence and now I can settle down and read the race in a more professional manner. That is, watch my horses negotiate the course, safely over each fence – I always pick my horses out from miles away, just by the way they gallop. Mentally – and sometimes out loud – I'm encouraging them, telling them to watch for a particular loose horse, or steer clear of a horse which is tiring in front of them. Tired horses and loose horses are like landmines: they can stop dead in front of a jump and, if you're in their slipstream, you stop dead with them. If they fall at the point where you are landing, you fall with them. Even the top class horses get put out of the Grand National this way.

Artistic Prince gets carried out of the race by another horse, but he's not hurt. He'll live to fight another day. Monty Python comes to an abrupt finish before the end of the first circuit. But Corbiere! He's jumping like a stag. He's never out of the first three. He's eating up the ground, hacking over the old Aintree turf as though he were on a gentle canter through the woods on a Saturday afternoon, instead of flying over the most famous jumps in racing history. He heads for the second circuit looking as fresh and cheeky as he did earlier in the morning when we brought him out of his box. Bouncing up and over, with young Ben de Haan sitting perfectly in position. Ben is giving him a fantastic ride. Drawing up his reins as he approaches each fence, keeping Corbiere straight, checking him gently back onto his hocks so he's in the best possible position to jump, just as a cat sits back on its haunches ready to spring into the air. It's beginning to look as though Corbiere can win the 1983 Grand National, but I don't allow myself to think about it just yet.

He's going to win it, Jenny, cries my brother. Oh, don't say that yet, I plead with him; but it's a comfort, having him there, having my family there. Over the Canal Turn, over Valentine's, and Ben de Haan points my horse for home. The horse's owner, Brian Burrough, and his parents, we can all of us hardly bear to watch. Over the third from home, second from home and the opposition is now fading, with the exception of a bay with a funny-shaped white blaze: Greasepaint. A horse with an exceptional turn of foot, and my only worry from now on. Ben begins to niggle at Corbiere, asking him for a little bit more. He flies the last and I watch Ben go for the whip for the first time. Just a tap, just a reminder that there's a long run-in to go. Greasepaint is sitting a couple of lengths back, going ominously easily. My mind flashes back to another Grand National.

Richard Pitman and I were still married at that time. Richard was riding Fred Winter's great steeplechaser, the Australian-bred Crisp, and there they were, in the same position as Corbiere now: in front and looking all over the winners. Then Crisp had started rolling. He was tiring, and galloping up on his tail was a bay horse. That horse was Red Rum, and he caught Crisp and my husband on the line and beat them. No disgrace to Richard or to Crisp, for Red Rum won the Grand National twice more after that. But having a race like that snatched away from under our noses, when victory was just a hair's-breadth away, was a bitter pill. I couldn't talk about it for over six months. If someone started asking Richard about losing the Grand National, and I was around, I simply left the room or went off by myself. It hurt me that much. It still isn't a moment I particularly like to remember, even now, all these years later.

And it wasn't a nice moment on that Saturday afternoon in April to think in terms of defeat. This was Corbiere's day and as the sun shone on his back and on the thousands watching the last throes of the 1983 National, there was only one winner. But as the gap shrank between the last fence and the finishing post, and the end came nearer, Greasepaint began to close. Oh God no, I prayed. If only my horse can hold on for a few more strides.

My horse held on. Not only held on, but, as he sensed rather than heard Greasepaint – the crowd is making a terrible roaring noise and it's hard for a horse to hear anything out there – he put down his head like a true champion racehorse, and began to run on. He suddenly realized his race was not quite in the bag, and as Greasepaint's shadow loomed up on his outside, he must have thought: oh no you don't. He drew on all his courage and found just one more gear. That was all it needed to keep Greasepaint behind. Three-quarters of a length, he won by. The two horses swept over the line close together, but I knew my horse had got it. Corbiere had made it. He had fulfilled the dream of a lifetime. For a split second, time stood still. I had to drag myself back into reality. He had won. The owners had won. The jockey had won. I had won. The first woman ever to train a Grand National winner. Brian was the youngest owner we could remember, Ben the youngest jockey. A hundred dreams were suddenly put in our hands. This was it. I just *couldn't* believe it.

Even now I find it hard to describe my feelings at that moment. I had never experienced such a thing in my entire life. It was, and remains, indescribable. But I had to come back to earth. I had a

Grand National winner and I had things to do. My horse had won the greatest steeplechase in the world, but he had to be attended to just like any other horse after a race. He still had to be unsaddled, the jockey had to weigh in. The formalities were the same, even though the roof of the grandstand was still lifted off by the crowds and the people shouting my name. 'Well done, Jenny', 'Good old Jenny' – people I did not even know.

I felt as though I was floating. I have heard the saying 'It feels like a dream' many times before. It is uncannily accurate to describe such an experience like that, because I really did feel that it was nothing to do with me. It was as though I was an onlooker to a scene in which I had no part. It was a peculiar sensation. If someone had told me that I had just died, and I was a ghost looking on, then I wouldn't have been surprised. It was a strange feeling as well as a marvellous one, and I think you would need to experience something like it in order to understand. Seeing yourself from outside. All sorts of memories came into my mind, such as the year before Corbiere's National, in 1982, when a photographer asked to take a picture of me standing in the eye of the white horse carved in chalk on the Downs near our home in Lambourn. He had done some research into the horse and it was supposed to be lucky to stand in the eye of the chalk figure and make a wish. I remember saying: 'Please let me win the Grand National' as I stood there.

I had been dealt my share of bad luck, too, in 1982. Though the tides turned in 1983, I still remembered the year before, when I had lost one of my best horses on the gallops at home. Lord Gulliver, one of my National hopes for the 1982 race, had suffered a heart attack only about seven weeks before the race. It was a terrible thing to watch . . . three horses heading round a bend at somewhere around 40 mph, when one collided with the others and I found myself running hell for leather towards them. My sister Mandy was riding Lord Gulliver that morning, and as he hit the other horses, there was such force in the impact that she was catapulted out of the saddle to safety. Lord Gulliver went straight across the dirt track and collided with a concrete post before he collapsed and lay still.

Mandy was still for quite a long time, too. Then she began staggering to her feet, helped up by Colin Brown, who was riding one of the horses they had collided with. Though she had a black eye, she would live. But Lord Gulliver was dead. He just lay there on the ground, and from the truly handsome racehorse he had been just a few seconds before, a strikingly good-looking animal, he looked like any old moke as he was now. The sight was quite horrible. Because Mandy was sobbing her heart out, I had to be

very hard. It was no use my crying and breaking down in front of
everyone else; I had to put up a front and tell her to pull herself
together. I sat her in the Land Rover, took her home and made a
cup of tea, and then I had a good cry myself. It's never easy, working
closely with horses the way we do, to lose one. It's like losing a
friend. Even if one gets injured, it's upsetting.

And I remembered Roll of Drums, who had won the last leg of
my first treble at Worcester, and who had gone to Sandown a week
later, only to have a heart attack and drop dead in the middle of the
racecourse. Mrs Bealby, his owner, was dreadfully upset, but I had
to stay calm and handle the situation firmly. As a trainer, with
thousands of onlookers, you cannot be seen to break down and cry
about these things. I had Artistic Prince to saddle for the next race.
People think I'm tough, but I have to carry on doing my job – and,
as with Lord Gulliver, I had to save my tears for when I got back
to the privacy of my own home.

But on this sunny April day Corbiere was heading for the unsaddling enclosure and, for once, I allowed myself some public
tears. I could feel them rolling down my face – and the video of the
race proves it! Some of my lads like to call me the Iron Maiden,
because they see only the business side of me most of the time. I'm a
tough person to deal with on the outside – I have to be, a woman in
a man's world – but one or two of them sidled up to me afterwards
and said: 'Did we see a tear on the Iron Maiden's cheek?' Cheeky
devils!

The next few minutes, hours, days, were a whirl, and yet I had
to keep my head. I remember a dreadful thirst, although I had
permitted myself a brandy and lemonade whilst watching the race.
My mouth was dry as a bone and I begged my son for a glass of
water. 'You can have anything to drink right now *except* a glass of
water', he replied. The horse was coming back through the crowds,
who were jostling all around him and trying to reach out and touch
him. One man in particular kept tugging on the reins and pulling
Corbiere's mouth about and one of the lads leading Corbiere turned
round and smacked him in the face. You can see him on the video,
that man, rubbing his jaw where my boy had whacked him one!
The lads are like that: they love their horses and they don't like
strangers coming up and touching them. You never know what
people will do!

They all finally made it back to the winner's enclosure and we
were all kissing and hugging while the tears ran down my face.
Tears of real joy, which were saying more than words. The words
would not come – I felt the things I wanted to say sticking in my
throat and tears coming instead!

Ben de Haan was exultant. He couldn't believe the ride that Corbiere had given him and yet, not many weeks before, he had uttered one sentence to me after Corbiere had raced at Sandown: 'Mother, your horse will win the Grand National one day'. Ten words, and they had come true, and now he was facing me, in front of the television cameras, the world in general, talking about the way the horse had won the race. Nothing about the careful way he had prepared him for each fence, nothing about the smooth way he had ridden him. Just about the superb ride the horse had given him.

'Don't forget to weigh in', I had to remind him with a laugh. I wasn't able to go into the weighing room with him – there were too many people yelling at me for interviews and the like – so I was very relieved when I noticed on the television monitors that the BBC had a camera in there, and the monitor showed me that he was weighing in with the same as he weighed out: 11 stone 4 pounds. If he'd lost four pounds, or gained them, during the course of that race, there would have had to be some questions asked. You can explain a pound or two away with weight lost through sweating, but in racing you have to come back off the course with as much weight as you went out with. Thankfully, Ben had not lost anything, nor gained it, and the race was not going to be nightmarishly taken from us on a technicality.

There was an occasion when Richard was weighed out incorrectly, so that when he came back in he was a stone light – and the race which he had won was taken from him. It was one of Ryan Price's horses and after that occasion Richard was never asked to ride for Ryan Price again. So it wasn't just the race he lost, it was the chance of other good rides. I didn't want that happening to my lads!

It was at least a fortnight before I really came to believe that we had actually won the Grand National. I kept thinking that we might be caught out with one of those awful accidents when a substance in the horse's feed gives the horse a positive result on the dope test after the race. But no such awful news came about having the race taken away from me. A month later, finally, I think it sank in: I had won the Grand National. At last.

2
DAYS GONE BY

My first riding hat was 25 years old and I was just 14 months when it was first placed on my eager head. I simply could not wait to start riding the small black pony which my parents had bought in a horse sale the previous day. I had already sat on his back once; the first seed for my future had been sown. My parents George and Mary Harvey had taken me to Melton Mowbray Horse Sale with the specific intention of buying 'a pony for Jenny'. Plenty of other animals had gone under the auctioneer's hammer before a very dark pony, around 12 hands high and only 18 months old, trotted rather prettily into the ring. There was no hesitation in their minds and for £20 Timmy became my first pony. He later grew to around 13 hands, and was dark and glossy in summer, going lighter in winter when his thick protective coat grew in the autumn.

I missed the excitement of the purchase initially because I was sound asleep in my father's arms, my head laid on his shoulder. But my sleep didn't last long. Dad and Mum were determined that I should try out the new pony without further ado and, drowsy as I was, I was nonetheless placed gently upon Timmy's back. My eyes flew open and I was suddenly *very* wide awake. I sat bolt upright and stared in delight and amazement. 'He's all yours, Jenny', said my father proudly. I grabbed hold of my pony's mane and sat for a few moments. I was then removed, much to my displeasure, while arrangements were made to get the pony back to our home, a 60-acre dairy farm which my father leased about a mile and a half from the tiny Leicestershire village of Hoby.

The 25-year-old riding hat, stuffed with newspaper to fit my head, had seen many hours of operation in the hunting field, since it had belonged to the local Master of Foxhounds. It was to accompany Timmy and me on our very earliest rides around the farm together. I began to learn next morning, led by my father as we went around the farm from one job to another. I vividly recall him teaching me to rise to the trot correctly, rather than bump about wildly on Timmy's back: he ran along beside us, leading rein in one hand, encouraging me to 'up down, up down' in time to the beat of the pony's tiny hooves. It was slow progress, but suddenly I began to feel the rhythm and managed a few smart 'up downs' before returning to my previous bumping. Gradually the bumping ceased and Jenny Harvey had learned to rise to the trot. It was a step forward and everyone was very pleased.

The old riding hat was, of course, replaced by something more suitable when it became apparent that my interest in the pony was no transitory phase. My mother added a tiny hacking jacket, boots, jodhpurs, and a smaller cap – thus I was kitted out to ride around the farm on Timmy's safe broad back. Hardly a day went by when I didn't ride Timmy or, as time went on, the other ponies that I grew up with on Dad's farm. It is quite true to say that I grew up either around horses, or on their backs. There were no tractors to work the land then, only the horses which my father bred. Everything which was required, such as shopping from the village, was fetched by pony. When a field needed harrowing, the horse was harnessed and the field harrowed. When the harvest had to be gathered, the mare was hitched up to the flat haycart and the hay loaded. When the field needed ploughing, the plough was fixed to the harness and the land ploughed by the heavy horse. When the sheep which we grazed in summer on keep, or rented land, needed checking, we children were sent off on our ponies to check them. If a ewe had rolled onto her back, it was our job to stand her upright again. A sheep in lamb, heavy with winter wool, wet from lying perhaps all night on her back, cannot get back up again and if left in that condition would die from exposure and exhaustion.

By the time I was four years old, Dad and Mum deemed me fit to ride in some of my first proper shows and they were as pleased as punch when Timmy and I came second in the local Pony Club leading rein event. Dad was mighty proud of his smart little daughter being runner-up from a field of 48 starters, and maintains that I was a much better rider than the winner, in any case.

When I began to outgrow Timmy, who was now more suitable for my younger brothers Richard and David, my father came across another pony. This new acquisition was purchased from a band of gypsies and was brought home and turned out into one of the fields surrounding the farmhouse. Next morning, he had gone. A massive search was mounted since Dad's ultimatum was 'No pony, no fireworks'. It was Bonfire Night and, wherever the pony was, Dad did not want him scared by the rockets. Since most of the village came to our party on Bonfire Night to enjoy Mum's toffee apples and baked potatoes as well as the fireworks, most of the village was engaged in the search with equal determination. The Army could not have conducted a more thorough search! Mum was not at all convinced that the gypsies had not come and removed him in order to sell him to yet another gullible passer-by. But her fears proved unfounded and the pony was discovered, unharmed and quite un-concerned, in a field two miles away. He had simply not liked the field we put him in, and had jumped out of it and taken himself off to a field which better suited his tastes in grazing. It was a relief to have him back. If the fireworks that evening had scared him into fleeing yet again from his surroundings, he might have strayed much further abroad and never been recovered. We decided there-fore to name him Rocket.

Rocket and Timmy were the backbone of our pony population for many years to come. But whereas Timmy was a peaceful and placid soul, Rocket was a strong individual with very firm ideas of his own about life. Timmy was always content, if Mum sent us into the village one and a half miles away, to stand tied up outside the shop whilst we went inside and made our purchases. Being a large family – with Mum and Dad, seven children and a live-in lodger to help Dad on the farm – there were often 14 pounds of potatoes to be carried back to the farm. Fine if it was Timmy: we could load them onto his long-suffering back, clamber aboard ourselves and ride home. But Rocket was not given to being tied up for very long and frequently took it upon himself to rub his head vigorously on the post to which he was attached, in order to remove the bridle from his head. Having disencumbered himself, he was now free to trot happily home again. This he duly did, leaving us to lug the massive bag of potatoes home on foot.

He had clear ideas, too, about how much work a pony should be expected to do. He had a disconcerting habit of packing up the job in hand when least expected, and simply lying down for a rest until he was ready to carry on. He never kicked the habit. Many years later, when he was really quite old, I moved him from Leicester-shire to my home at Hinton Parva in Wiltshire, so that he could teach my own two small sons Mark and Paul the elements of riding a pony. Mark occasionally hunted Rocket as his riding ability became proficient. Many was the time that Rocket sat down for a rest after a couple of hours because he had had quite enough!

Rocket was only 18 months old when my father bought him. He taught a great many young children to ride, including my smallest sister Mandy, and when my own children had outgrown him he went to jockey Graham Thorner to show the young Thorners how it should be done. He was marvellous with youngsters and I recall Paul walking under Rocket's tummy, and throwing his arms around the pony's legs as he grazed. Not many ponies, even at Rocket's age, would tolerate such behaviour. But I knew the boys were safe with this old character, and they were as fond of him as I had been. If the weather was wet, they would run indoors and fetch a blanket from one of the beds and cover Rocket with it. When one of the blankets was missing from indoors at Hinton Parva, I would always have to think back to where Mark and Paul had last been playing around with the old pony and invariably, lying on the ground where the pony had been standing, I would find a damp and often muddy blanket; it never stayed on his back for very long since he had only to shake himself and it would fall off.

I was terribly sad when Rocket eventually died. Having been a part of my life for 28 years, he became rather doddery as he neared the age of 30. He had a minor heart attack, which he survived, but it left him a shaky old man. Since the Thorner children had also outgrown him now, and since it would have been dreadful for Mark or Paul to see him have another, more serious heart attack, I decided that he should be put to sleep painlessly whilst he was still enjoying life, and before crippling old age finally overtook him and removed his dignity. He really was quite a pony. He had given us, as children, some of the greatest fun imaginable.

Amongst the greatest fun, all rather illicit, was pony racing which we indulged in when I was around eight years old, and in which we were encouraged by neighbouring farmer Albert Riley. Albert's brother Stan is now the owner of Burrough Hill Lad, a horse which I train today. In those days, Albert Riley and his great pal Harry Matthews used to love rounding up us children and our ponies, and encouraging us to race our ponies over a mile-long course bordering one of Albert's fields. It was mad, it was fun, and we all took it very seriously! Timmy, whom I sometimes rode, wasn't the fastest pony in Hoby, but my cousin Philip Harvey had a *very* nifty thing called Chicken. Everyone hated Philip and Chicken, mostly because they were the fastest combination in the race, but also because Chicken was extremely intolerant of other ponies and lashed out with both hind feet at anything within 20 yards. Harry and Albert devised a handicap system, whereby Chicken was given more weight than his slower rivals Timmy and Rocket, and they organized a bookmaking system between themselves on the outcome of our races. They thought it a great game, but as youngsters we took our ponies' abilities very solemnly at times and it led to a great deal of rivalry.

This caper would have continued for many months, but for Chicken running smack into a tree when ridden by my other cousin Pauline, incurring a nasty fall for his jockey of the day. It did not best please my parents to discover our racing activities as a result of the accident, and they put a swift end to the sport. It was probably not a bad education for the career which, ultimately, lay ahead. I could not have known that then.

My elder brother Peter, for some reason always nicknamed Joe by our family, was regular party to another equestrian event. As we grew a little older and presumably more responsible, Mum and Dad let us go off to local shows and gymkhanas at weekends. Joe and I had a party turn for the fancy dress events. Joe dressed as Winston Churchill, Prime Minister at the time and a popular hero, whilst I was togged up in Winston's racing colours and led round by Joe upon Rocket, who represented Winston's great horse Colonist II. We swept the board at one show after another and, I dare say, became unpopular with our contemporary rivals. It went on for several years, until the Conservative Party was swept from power by Labour, and Winston's popularity waned with his party's fortunes. Our own popularity waned accordingly. Winston, Colonist and his jockey just weren't fashionable any more.

Ironically, we were better off financially as a direct result of this turn in our fortunes. The few pennies we won for the best fancy dress were replaced by 'tips' from Tory Party supporters who watched us continue to plod round in our outdated mode of attire. The tips were as high as half a crown (12½ pence) and meant we were better off than the winning riders and ponies. It didn't increase our popularity with them, but we were quite delighted to come nowhere and earn more than the rest put together! The act finally bit the dust when my brother became sick whilst smoking the famous Winston Churchill-type cigar and, to add insult to injury, someone shouted 'Bighead' at him from the crowd. Bighead was Winston's rather unfortunate nickname at the time, and it was the end of the line for Joe. He threw a final tantrum and stormed from the arena, dragging me, bewildered, in his wake. No more fancy dress turns took place thereafter!

One of my greatest childhood friends was Geoffrey Dodd, whose parents and mine had been close friends for many years. Geoff and I were of the same age and grew up together; he is now a judo champion and still lives in the Leicester area. We were partners in crime in much childhood mischief and enjoyed many an illicit Park Drive cigarette together, hiding under the milk stand at the top of the drive, upon which churns of milk were placed each day after milking for collection by the main local dairy. Geoff often arrived at our home with a couple of his dad's cigars for my father, and a handful of stolen Park Drives which we then crept away to puff on. Most of my childhood was spent in Geoff's company, to the point where he maintained that we were blood brothers. This notion arose from watching a Wild West film on television – though television did not arrive in our lives until I was about 10 years old. Geoff came up with the rather unnerving idea of cutting our thumbs and rubbing our blood together, thus uniting us as proper brothers. Never mind that I was a girl; I was a complete tomboy throughout my youth. I rather unwillingly consented to become Geoff's blood brother: a ceremony I like to remind him of when we meet today at family parties and reunions. The memory of him cutting my thumb with a knife still makes me shudder today!

Geoff and I had a marvellous game, a sort of lethal imitation of Wells Fargo, which we played regularly as children. The younger Harveys were roped into the act willy-nilly, whether they wished it or not. We would harness Rocket to the governess trap which was usually left lying around the farm, rather than being kept in proper service. Rocket was the faster of our two ponies, and pulling the trap was invariably his role. The trap was then loaded with my brothers Richard and David – little wonder the latter has no love of horses today! – and with Mandy, who was then just a very small child. They were the passengers, Rocket was a team of powerful coach horses, and the trap was the coach. Timmy was then saddled up as the robber's horse. Geoff and I took turns at driving the coach and acting as the robber aboard Timmy. The coach was sent off at a fairly sedate pace to begin with, but lying in wait of course were Timmy and the robber. The robber would proceed to pounce on the coach and its passengers, which combination then set off at one hell of a pace to evade capture. The passengers were bounced mercilessly around as either Geoff or I drove the trap and Rocket as fast as we were able: down rutty tracks, over bumpy fields – anywhere, in fact, it was possible for a trap to be driven, and some places where it was theoretically impossible. Goodness knows what our parents would have said, had they caught us playing this particular game. When I look back it beats me how none of us was killed. The passengers yelled for mercy, the robber caught the coach and horses, and duly robbed the passengers of their gold and diamonds. Somehow we all survived without a trace of a broken bone. Small wonder that David later preferred to take up schoolteaching to a career with horses. Mandy, however, was not put off. Today she is secretary in my racing yard, rides out twice every morning for us, and rides in races wherever possible.

Rocket and Timmy were not always subjected to such treatment, however, and life was often more sedate. When a local garden fete was held in villages surrounding Hoby, we were always asked to take our ponies along to give the other children rides at 3d (less than $1\frac{1}{2}$ pence) a time. After having run up and down with the ponies for most of the afternoon we were pretty exhausted, and to discourage too much business in the late afternoons, we upped the fee to 6d. But we were never given the money; it went always to aid the proceeds of the fete. A glass of orange squash was our usual payment – if we were not forgotten completely, that is.

It was fortunate that my parents *were* familiar with the ways of horses, in view of our love of equestrian activities throughout childhood. My father had been around horses all his life, and my grandfather bred Shire horses. Dad's brothers, Uncle Bob Harvey and Uncle Peter Harvey, often rode their home-bred Shires in specially-organized Shire horse races, with a great deal of success. It was fun and the ground would really tremble as the monsters galloped along in full flight. These races are still held today in some parts of the country. Dad was not a racing man, he never wanted to ride, but Grandad Harvey rode in the occasional point-to-point. Grandad also bred a famous horse called Crispin, who won an individual gold medal in one of the first European Three Day Event Championships, held at Basle in 1954. Ridden by Bertie Hill, who is still a leading horse trials trainer, Crispin was also part of the British team which won a gold at the same event, along with Frank Weldon on Kilbarry, and Major Rook on Starlight. They took the first three individual places, and only the British and German teams managed to complete the course.

My parents met when Mum worked for Grandad Harvey, back in 1937. They were married two years later and, both coming from large families (Dad from a family of nine, Mum from a brood of six), wasted little time in producing Jackie, my eldest sister, in 1940, shortly after they began farming at Hoby. Judy followed, then Peter (or 'Joe'), and I was number four. David, Richard and Mandy completed the clan.

The early years at Hoby were hard. In 1940 there was no gas, no electricity and no running water. There was a war on, and only with grim determination did Dad manage to scrape a living from his herd of 30 cows and his 60 rented acres, as the brood of children swiftly increased. Mum and Dad never quite intended to let the brood grow quite to the size it did; after the first three children arrived, they felt that enough was enough. But then Mum found herself pregnant again, and again three more times. Each time a mouth was added which needed feeding, my father had to work harder and harder to make ends meet and pay the bills, which regularly included a bread order of 22 loaves a week. Water was brought up from an outside pump. Kitchen sinks with taps and running water were unheard of during the early years of my parents' marriage and of our childhood. These things, as well as radio, television and electricity, were each a revelation as they were introduced into our somewhat primitive lives.

One of the ways we could help our father earn a little money was by helping him break in and school the numerous ponies which were sent to us. Dad was frequently asked to take in an animal that was either very young or very unmanageable (or both), which had become too nasty or too difficult for its owner's children. Since I wasn't afraid of anything that ponies would or could do, I was often put on their backs and given the job of making them more manageable for their young riders.

It taught us all a lot about ponies, except for David who shied away from riding these hairy beasts. But it showed us all how to ride difficult ponies, as well as our own two, and what I learned then from those animals has stood me in good stead over the years. The only trouble was that we became too fond of these visitors! Timmy and Rocket were the family pets, but even the ponies which we took in for schooling became our friends, and we always felt sad to see them depart. Dad was usually sent to Coventry for about a week when one left, though we didn't fully realize he wasn't *selling* the ponies, only returning them to their rightful owners. Dad wasn't concerned with 'dealing' in ponies – that is, buying and selling for profit – because his main theory was that learning to ride all these different animals, learning to handle horses around the farm, was all part of our learning about life. It was his opinion that this taught us almost as much as our schoolwork, and the experience gained with the ponies had no price on it. It didn't stop at riding them. It included learning to care for them, as well as getting out to shows and learning to mix with people from all walks of life. 'Getting aired' was Dad's way of expressing it.

And, as I say, since I was the least afraid to climb on these wilful ponies' backs, I was usually given the job. It never occurred to me that there was any danger in it, because my father had not taught us that way. It did, however, occur to Mum! One particular pony we all remember went by the rather dreadful nickname of Sodyer: the name speaks for itself. Since this pony was a particularly nasty specimen, and had an unfortunate habit of standing up on his hind legs for quite long spells, I used to get rather annoyed because he refused to come back down on all fours. Mum frequently heard me shouting 'Sod yer' very rudely at the pony, and this pony probably worried her as much as any horse I rode in later life. Whenever she heard my shouts of 'Sod yer', she would come rushing from the kitchen and say: 'What on earth makes you ride that thing? Why don't you get off it?'

My reply was always the same: 'Why on earth should I get off?'

'You might get hurt', she would say.

'What goes up has to come down again', was my stock remark at that point. It was a philosophy my father always used when discussing rearing horses and it had always been my experience that he was right.

Perhaps because I was not afraid of the ponies, they responded to my quiet reactions to their behaviour. When a pony knows its rider is afraid, it usually takes one of two courses of action. A kind pony, a well-mannered animal, will behave with *greater* kindness if he feels a nervous rider on his back. The other kind of pony will take full advantage of the fear which it feels by instinct in its rider. When this type of pony is ridden by someone who is both fearless and understanding of the ways of naughty ponies, he may play about and misbehave just to test the rider's nerves, but usually, in the end, he succumbs and goes obediently. There is a requirement on the part of the rider, therefore, to be gentle, firm, and fearless. In this way Sodyer and I became firm friends eventually, and the demon in him vanished in due course.

The only other time I can recall my mother being particularly nervous was in my earliest riding days, when I developed a sudden liking for riding Timmy up and down the sides of a steep hollow near the farm. Mother would see me jauntily going off in the direction of this hazard, and deliberately busy herself in the kitchen, banging saucepans about and making as much din as possible. Whether or not this was a warning to be careful, for I could not avoid hearing the racket, or so that if I fell off and started bellowing, she would not have to listen to my screams, I am none too sure! Her version is the latter, but I don't quite believe her.

When I reached school age, I invariably went by pony. We had a tiny village school with a maximum of 28 pupils. With our own brood of seven Harveys and my seven Harvey cousins, our family comprised half the school's population for most of the time! My pony was turned out into my Uncle Percy's nearby field for the day, then tacked up and ridden home again in the evenings. The headmistress of that little school was a remarkable lady, and already past the first bloom of youth when I was small. By the time Corbiere won the Grand National in 1983, she had reached the age of 91, and still was able to attend the party which I gave to celebrate our victory at home afterwards. For all her ability, however, lessons did not hold my attention, even during the six years I attended the little village school and certainly not in my later years with the Sarson Girls' School in Melton Mowbray which I attended between the ages of 11 and 15. I was no scholar; my life was horses. I excelled at sports, not at arithmetic.

But life wasn't all a bed of roses out of school, either. It wasn't all carefree games of Wells Fargo and illicit cigarettes beneath the milk churn stand. We had to work very hard for most of our childhood years. My father, in turn, had worked throughout his childhood for my grandfather, and he saw no reason why we should have an easy time of it, whilst he flogged himself to death on our behalf. Quite rightly, too. Through working hard as children, we learned the most important values in life. We learned that nothing comes without effort. When something needed doing, it was our duty and responsibility, almost as much as our parents', to ensure that it was done. I feel there was little wrong with our upbringing, if anything at all. None of the family has turned into bank robbers or jewel thieves. Each of us has made something of our lives, and never been afraid of hard work.

Early on in childhood we learned to work the farm horses. Dad always had two or three working animals, mostly home-bred for the job. Even the in-foal mares continued to work right up to their foaling date. A big advantage the horse had over the tractor was that it could reproduce its own likeness, and the Harveys had a continual supply of horses to work the land. Very early in life we were taught to drive the horse and cart, including the intricacies of harnessing up the horse. This is a skilled job in itself, since badly fitted harness with straps too tight or too loose can cause the animal pain, even lameness, and we could not afford to have the horses lame and out of work. There was always the safety aspect of harnessing to consider, since a broken item in the harness, or a wrongly connected harness, could cause a serious accident when used for ploughing or harrowing. Dad always showed us the correct way to harness up the horses, and we knew enough about horses by this time to realize the importance of watching him carefully and learning thoroughly.

We drove the cart for Dad for a variety of reasons about the farm. In the early days, the hayfields and the wheat and barley crops were scythed by hand and the corn was piled into 'stooks' at various points about the field. When the stooks were finished, and the hay had dried it was ready to bring into stack for the winter, and I usually drove the cart so that the boys could load the hay on board. It was a very soporific part of the job, since I had merely to drive old Nellie a few yards at a time, and wait in the sunshine whilst the cart was piled up with yet more hay, before driving a few yards to the next stook.

Nellie gave me a fearful turn one very hot afternoon as we lazily went our way gathering hay, when one wheel of the cart rode up the side of a haycock. Nellie and I were both half-asleep at the time, and the sudden movement of the cart startled her. Horses being what they are, and given to running off when they are woken up very suddenly, Nellie and I promptly found ourselves at a flat-out gallop, with the haycart thundering along in our wake. I was quite petrified and suddenly very much awake. Dad, fortunately, was working on the other side of the field where the mare appeared to be running, and he was able to catch hold of her bridle as she sped by, to drag her to a halt. I was about nine years old at the time and I never allowed myself to doze off during haycarting again!

Another of our tasks was the milking. Though Mum says now I always managed to avoid this job when possible, it was only as a result of the unfortunate occasion when a cow kicked me and my three-legged milking stool firmly to the other side of the cowshed. It put me off milking for good. But I was not at all worried by the pigs, and was given the job of carrying the tilley lamp – no such luxury as electrically-lit farmyards then – so that Dad could see where he was going as we checked them last thing at night. I helped him measure their feeds and learned to tell the time on the old scales: three pounds represented three o'clock, four pounds represented four o'clock, and so on. I learned that a quarter to six pounds on the scales looked very much like a quarter to six on the clock, and that six and a half pounds looked very much like half past six. An odd way to learn, but it was effective. I was also very proud to be given my own 'pig stick'. When we entered the pigsty to feed the animals, they tended to come rushing forward in their eagerness for their supper, and as a small girl I was in danger of being knocked flying. My pig stick fended off the animals as they surged forward and kept me safely on my feet in the rush for the trough.

We always worked around the farm during school holidays, at weekends, and when school was finished each day. We learned from a young age that, on a farm, there are no 'nine-to-five' rules. On a farm, then as now, you worked until the job was finished. If we needed to work until 10 pm in summer to get the hay crop into the barns, then we worked until 10 pm without question. And if the milking took until 9.30 or 10 pm, Dad could work on with the tilley lamp; then if the pigs still needed attention there was no question of leaving them to their own devices. This was just part of the way of life.

It had its compensations, of course, and adoring my father in the way that so many small girls adore their father, it was no effort for me to hold the lamp while he finished his work about the farm. I had my rewards. Not the least of these was a bowl of bread, sugar and milk which Father and I consumed upon finishing duties out of doors. We each had our own pudding bowl, Dad's being a two-pounder, mine a smaller version. He cubed the bread, sprinkled on sugar, warmed the milk and poured it over. And we would sit together eating our delicious bowlfuls, after which I would climb onto his lap and fall asleep before he carried me off to the bedroom I shared with my sisters. Some evenings he could not find one of the bowls, and would march round the kitchen, growling in mock anger: 'Where is Baby Bear's bowl?' Being a small child, I loved this particular game.

We were always a close family, but Dad and I had a special relationship. I felt, like so many small girls, that my father was my best friend of all. He would cuddle me sometimes at night, after our bread and milk suppers, and play a game of 'let's pretend'. He would say: 'Shall we clear off and run away together, Jenny? Shall we put old Nellie in the caravan in the field, and take to the roads? Let's just drive off without telling a soul, and we'll go and see the world together. What do you say to that, Jenny?' Loving him as I did, I was ready to take off at the drop of a hat. I was young enough to believe very firmly in his fairy-tale adventures, and always thought that one day Dad and I would drive off with Nellie and the caravan. If he said we would do it, then we would do it. Only as I grew older did I realize that it was a game. As a little girl, I truly imagined it would happen one day.

A task which was not very joyful was taking the cattle to market. The wagon used always to arrive at 6 am to fetch the cattle from the farm, and Dad would send one of us children to accompany them to Leicester where they would be sold. In those days, the cattle were graded. Some, marked with a single letter C, were the better quality animals which were eligible for subsidy. The rest, marked with a double C, were not eligible for subsidy. Most Wednesdays I went off to market with the cattle with the strict instruction that none of our cattle must be given the double C grading, and that I was to ensure they all were marked with a single C and fetched a better price. I used to climb the railings of the cattle pens to watch the man with the marker grading the cattle, though quite what a ten-year-old child could have done to influence the grading system at Leicester cattle market I cannot imagine. Fortunately my influence was never put to the test and Dad's cattle were all graded top quality. But it was a constant worry, that we should be downgraded and then have to face the consequences at home in the evening!

On Saturdays and Sundays and in our holidays, we were also given the task of 'tenting' the cattle. We were supposed to herd them along the sides of the roads so that they could graze the lush green grass of the verges, and during a dry summer or at other times when grass on our own land was short it was an ideal way of accomplishing two things: firstly, the verges did not need cutting by the council as they do today, and secondly, the cattle grazing was supplemented by grass – grass that was unspoiled by the lead from petrol engines, which still hardly existed in our remote area of Leicestershire. We would be gone all morning tenting the cows, and for working between 8 am and lunchtime were paid the princely sum of 6d – about 2½p today. The task was not hard, since we could ride up behind the cattle on our ponies, and it became quite fun when we reached a privet hedge surrounding a neighbouring farmer's garden. For some reason the cattle loved burying their heads in this privet, which may have given them some relief from the heat, but which caused havoc to the hedge. They almost tore the hedge in half when they chose to, and someone was therefore always having to guard the privet from destruction by the wanton cows. It made for a diversion from the run-of-the-mill tenting elsewhere in the lanes round Hoby.

Much else could be undertaken on the backs of our ponies, of course, so that we could combine the pleasures of riding with our work. During the autumn and winter months, for instance, if we had a lot of rain, some of Father's fields became flooded by the river which ran through the farm. This river, when suddenly filled by overnight torrential rain, would completely cut the farm in two, and as it overflowed its banks into the lower-lying fields it gradually put these meadows under water. The cattle and sheep which had been grazing there would find themselves with less and less dry land, eventually ending up huddled together on small islands dotted about the meadows. This did not happen gradually, and was not often a foreseeable event. If it rained suddenly and swiftly, it could occur in a matter of hours. Our job then was to wade through the river on our ponies and rescue the livestock. Sometimes we had to resort to swimming the ponies across the torrent to reach the other side. I wasn't too keen on that, though Geoffrey Dodd was fearless of water and would plunge straight in, whereupon I would feel obliged to follow. The sheep were equally nervous of water and preferred to stay marooned on their islands until the water subsided; the cattle, however, were braver and consented to be driven back to the drier areas of the farm!

Some of our work was, literally, more down to earth, such as hoeing entire fields of kale or mangels. Mangels were a vegetable rather like a swede, which we grew in summer and autumn as a winter cattle feed. Kale too was winter feed for the cattle, and it is still used today: though you will usually see electric fencing stretched across kale fields in winter, permitting the cattle to graze selected areas of the field. As one patch of field becomes bare, the electric fence is moved to allow them access to ungrazed areas. We applied a similar principle to kale in the 1950s, but we used to cut it and feed it fresh to the cattle in the sheds.

The mangels were quite hard, back-breaking work. The mangel seed was sown in spring, and by early summer the mangel tops were showing. They grew too close together, of course, and our job was thinning them out. The smaller mangels had to be hoed up to allow the larger plants room to grow, and we needed to leave two or three inches between each one so that it grew to its maximum size. This was important. Undersized little mangels wouldn't feed many hungry cattle in winter. In the autumn the mangels were pulled up, loaded onto the cart, and stacked in a pyramid shape for the winter. The leafy growth on top of each vegetable was first carefully chopped off and later used as a protection for the mangel stack, preventing rain or frost from ruining this precious crop.

The kale provided excellent opportunities for games of hide-and-seek, since it grew to some five or six feet in height. Another game, less enthralling in retrospect, was to see which of us could chew our way through a stalk of kale the fastest! It didn't seem to taste too bad at the time: something like raw cabbage stalks.

Dad also grew fields of turnips, which it was our job to keep free of weeds, and a raw turnip made a fine meal for a child working on a Leicestershire farm in those days. It was a common sight to see: Dad pulling up a turnip, taking out his pocket knife, peeling away the dirty outside portion, and handing it to one of us by the leafy stalks. No one worried about taking lunch out to the turnip field: lunch was there, growing in the ground. Even now, when I'm peeling turnips, I can't resist eating some raw. It makes me feel very nostalgic.

Mechanization, of course, gradually caught up with our farm as it caught up with the rest of the world. A tractor came along first, to pull the plough that the horses had once pulled. Our first was a John Deare, an old three-wheeler model, which served us well for a few years until we progressed to a Fordson Major. Joe was promoted to driving the tractor when he was old enough and, though he ended up a most proficient tractor driver, there were some mishaps along the way. When ploughing, the tractor driver could employ someone to sit behind him to 'trip' the plough, or pull it out of the earth as the tractor turned round at the end of each furrow. If the blade of the plough was left in the ground when the tractor turned, it would possibly break or even tip the tractor over if it hit a large stone or rock. Joe just wasn't concentrating, or not looking where he was going, on the day he drove the Fordson Major straight into a concrete post and tangled it up in the wire fencing. Sitting on the back tripping the plough, I was somewhat astonished when we came to a sudden grinding halt and managed to get myself into a tangle as well.

Dad, as ever, came to the rescue and straightened out the mess. He was used to doing that when we drove the pony and trap, such as on the occasion when Rocket took it into his head to gallop off one day, just as we were harnessing him up. The cart remained standing still, but Rocket and the harness disappeared over some hedges and came to a standstill in a neighbour's field! We were more careful thereafter and employed someone to stand at Rocket's head, firmly holding his bridle, whilst he was harnessed in safety. Only when the driver was seated, reins in hand and whip at the ready, was Rocket allowed his head once more.

My father always helped us sort out the mess we made as children. He never forced his opinions upon us, always merely offered advice. It was up to us whether we took it or not, and usually, at some stage in our lives, we would recall his words and know he had been right. Even now, things that Dad said to me as a child come back to me: he passed on so much of his knowledge of horseflesh. I never recall him riding horses, only working them, but what he didn't know about them would hardly fill a square inch of paper. Today, when buying a horse, I would not dream of failing to ask my father's advice. A horse can walk up ten yards in front of him for just 30 seconds, and he will have picked out all its faults in that short time. I dread the day when he is not around to turn to, and though I don't run to Dad with every little problem, he has been there, a mainstay of sanity, in the most harrowing moments of my life.

And through the horses, and my father's breeding of them, I learned the facts of life at an early age. So did several other children: brothers, sisters and friends included. The reason for this was quite simply the regular visits to our farm from the stallion man. In those days, mares were not taken off to stud to be mated with a stallion. Premium stallions travelled the county – and often beyond – and visited mares in the region which were thought by their owners to be 'in season'. Although some stallions today do in fact still travel to the mares, in our childhood it was common practice. Perhaps this was because my father would not have just any old stallions serving his mares. He wanted the best.

Cart mares they may have been, but they were still workers. They were expected to be free of leg problems, for their legs had hard work to do. They needed clean windpipes, because they had to strain and lean on the plough and the harrow and weren't expected to run out of breath easily. My father made the same requirements of the stallions which visited the farm, and many was the time I saw him have a stallion run up and down, often for half an hour, so he could ensure the animal was sound in both wind and limb. He always sent for the Premium stallions, which were bred under a special scheme intended to keep hunter and working stallions of a high quality. When our mares came into season, Dad would send word to the stallion owner, who would bring his stallion straight away. A mare is in season for only five days at a time, so there could be no question of delay; it would be a further three weeks before she would be in season again so the stallion man needed to come very quickly after he received word. This may seem haphazard to present-day breeders, but the farmers knew their mares and needed little telling when they were ready for the stallion. The system worked remarkably well and Dad always had a very high tally of mares in foal.

Mum's only problem throughout the proceedings which followed the arrival of the stallion was the children who, quite naturally, expected to watch the big event of the day. Having watched the foals' birth, seen them grow up, and now witnessed the ritual running-up of the stallion for my father's benefit, we were not going to be cheated of watching the actual mating take place. Mother tried her best to find the million and one hiding places about the farm, from which a thousand pairs of young eyes peeped out, unseen to the adult world. Drainpipes, tops of haystacks, barn rooftops, in fact any crevice small enough to take a child's body, contained a silent and somewhat overawed witness to the conception of next year's foals.

But progress was constantly being made in farm machinery and we watched as tractors, and later other machines, took over from horses. Soon the only horses that Dad was breeding were for pleasure. One of these horses was Dan Archer, the point-to-pointer which aroused my early interest in racing. Another he has bred is now in training in my yard at Upper Lambourn. Dad named him All Being Well – an expression he used when we, as children, asked him questions. It is the expression he still uses today, when I ask him to come racing with me: 'Yes, my duck', he will say, 'I'll come racing, all being well'.

The binder made easy the job of tying the straw into bundles. A lorry with a flat back took the place of Nellie and the hay cart. The threshing machine took over the job of separating the corn from the stalks. It was not a job I liked to watch: the bundles frequently contained mice and rats which had crept in to eat the corn. I loathed rats and mice as much then as now. Thus the work became less hard and less time-consuming on our farm and on farms all about us. We as a family were growing up. Things were changing. Only one thing seemed not to change: my love for horses. Mother will tell you today that I was rarely seen in anything other than jeans or jodhpurs, and a pair of wellingtons. There used to be a joke about Jenny Harvey not having any legs! The only times which Mum can remember them being on public display were at weddings. Firstly, at my sister Jackie's, when I was a bridesmaid, and then at my own, to Richard Pitman, when I was a bride. Both these events were a long way off, however, at the time of which I write. I was still a tomboy then, through and through.

3
GROWING ON

There was still a long way for me to go, between leaving childhood behind and becoming an adult. There was a lot of growing on, as they say in the horse world, for me to do. Growing on in my case had very little to do with education of the conventional kind, and I went through school hating every moment. The only subjects in which I could take any interest whatsoever were biology and history, which made a modicum of sense. Biology I understood because I had the advantage of being a farmer's daughter, and there was much about a farm to teach me before I even ventured into the classroom. History interested me more than other subjects such as geography and languages. I could relate to history: on a farm in Leicestershire in the 1950s, I was watching a little of it changing.

School games I excelled at, and sports lessons were a joy. I had been in all my junior school sports teams at Hoby, and when I began life at Sarson Girls' School in Melton Mowbray, the first thing that disgruntled me was not playing for my school. Long before paying attention to lessons, I was concerned with bettering my standing in Sarson's games teams. I made up my mind straight away that I would be playing for the school at the earliest possible moment, and concentrated my energies in that direction between Mondays and Fridays from 9 am until 4 pm. I worked my way through the second and reserve teams, eventually into the first teams, and was delighted to become Games Captain. I had the special job of organizing the school's games programme, arranging matches with rival schools, and taking little notice of the mechanical logic of ordinary lessons which a selection of teachers tried to drum into me. Away from the farm and my horses, I revelled in tennis, netball and hockey. I was a mean hockey player.

There was no way, if I was playing one of the back positions in hockey, that I ever intended to let the ball go past me and into the goal circle. That was for sure, and by hook or by crook I was determined to stop every ball coming my way. Admittedly I inadvertently let the odd one slip the field, the ball or two that was out of my reach, but more often than not I had the ball away and back to the other end, where I felt it belonged. I was never pulled up for fouling, but you could certainly say that I played a very hard game of hockey.

I soon found out that girls didn't like being tackled very much and they soon learned to give Jenny Harvey a wide berth when she came bearing down on them! They preferred to make a wide detour to avoid coming into a clash with me.

Possibly because I had spent so much time with boys, growing up with Geoffrey and many of the other local lads around Hoby, I had very little time for girls and things girlish. I never, ever played with a doll at home. I remember Mum's acute disappointment at my reaction to a beautiful doll she bought me one Christmas. I was disgusted. It had 'real' hair and clothes, it walked, and wailed 'Mama' when you turned it on its tummy. I loathed it. I wished that Mum had given me a new pair of wellies instead. Pretty dresses fell into the same category: I made an awful fuss over being attired for Jackie's wedding in a frilly frock and, of all the most ghastly contraptions, suspenders and nylon stockings. After a lengthy tussle with these unfamiliar garments, I noticed my sisters watching me in fits of laughter. One of them kindly put me out of my misery, pointing out that I had the suspender belt on upside-down! It took Mum hours to persuade me to wear these fancy garments and I didn't stop complaining until we reached home and I got back into my jeans.

Sex was an unheard-of word amongst the kids around Hoby. Sex discrimination was a million miles from their minds, and it didn't matter that I was a girl, I was treated the same as one of the lads. That wasn't a position I reached easily. I had to fight every inch of the way to prove I was as daredevil as they, and I earned my place in the Hoby lads' gang just as every other member. And as long as I could hold my own, they were content to treat me as one of the team.

My first mission, in order to reach the lower ranks of acceptance in the gang, was scrumping apples from the orchard of a particularly difficult and grumpy old lady. She was also very watchful of her precious apple crop and constantly aware of our designs on the fruit! It was some two miles from our farm, but I set off quite determined that I would steal my quota of apples from her garden and return, triumphant with my loot, within an acceptable time. I was not to know, of course, just how watchful the lady was, and was dismayed to find her sitting firmly planted in the garden like a watchful lioness keeping an eye on her cubs. They were *her* apples and she wasn't going to have them scrumped easily. There was, on the other hand, no way I dared return to the gang minus the apples. I should probably have lost my honour forever in their eyes, reduced myself to just another mere female, incapable of the most simple apple orchard raid. All I could do was sit and wait. And I

25

waited and waited; it seemed she would remain forever guarding her orchard. I was close to giving up when, finally, she hobbled off indoors. I flew over the fence, gathered up apples and stuffed them into my pockets until I bulged, and hot-footed it back to the crowd of young lads whose respect I so badly needed. I got it – but only after lengthy inquisition as to why I had taken so *long*. My late return was almost considered reason enough to refuse acceptance!

Having now gained the status of gang member, I was then, of course, expected to run with the pack and never turn a hair. We were not, looking back, exactly a danger to society, since apple-scrumping was probably our most dastardly occupation. But at that time, whilst things had moved on from the days when stealing a loaf of bread was a hanging offence, nonetheless discipline was decidedly strict and the local bobby was able to cuff an offender's ear without a national newspaper outcry about police brutality!

One poor old lady, who lived close by the school, was prey to probably the worst of our tricks. At the time, we felt she was fair game, since she refused to return our balls. Ball games were quite naturally a regular part of the school curriculum and, games being what they are, our balls sometimes went off course and landed in her apple orchard. Poor lady, she probably got very tired of constantly having to search her garden for a stray tennis ball from the school, but we didn't see it that way then. We just regarded her as a rather short-tempered old woman, whose obstinate refusal to return our property made her, in our opinion, a game target.

When she caught us climbing over the wall to retrieve the balls we had accidentally lost, she committed the unforgivable crime of taking us to see our headmistress. That was her Waterloo. She was Target Number One from then on. We waited until after dark, when we knew the trick up our sleeve would be all the more scary to the poor old lady. Having waited, we crept into her orchard and gathered every single windfall we could find – we weren't planning to rob the trees themselves on this occasion. We did not want the apples to eat.

Opposite the lady's front door was the local church and, loaded with windfalls, we clambered over the churchyard wall into the graveyard. It did not occur to us to be afraid of the ghosts; we were bent on revenge. My next missive was to take a handful of windfalls and place them very carefully in a row on her front doorstep. This accomplished, I joined my friends behind the wall and we very carefully began aiming apples at the old lady's front door, ducking down swiftly behind the wall and out of sight as each apple hit the target. Revenge was sweet and very funny. The poor old dear never did discover who it was that had apparently been knocking loudly at intervals on her front door, let alone who had left a row of apples there, when there was apparently no one about and it was long after dark. It must have scared the wits out of her. Later, satisfied that honour had been done, we crept home quietly, not wishing to meet the village policeman who was quite likely to appear at any moment upon his bike. We ran home across the fields, hiding in the hedgerows, and we did not get caught. Dad did ask us about the event a few days later, when the old lady had told all and sundry about her ghostly experience, but of course we strenuously denied all knowledge of such happenings.

Brooksby Hall, a nearby farm institute, grew some of the best apples and pears in England, let alone in Leicestershire, and their orchards were a regular late-night scrumping ground. It was our custom to meet Geoffrey Dodd off a train which arrived at the nearest station to Brooksby Hall at around 10.30 pm. We then, since it was long after dark, had a good night's scrumping ahead and came away well loaded with delicious fruit. It was unfortunate that on the only night we should be caught red-handed, my sister Judy made her first foray in our dubious company. Half a dozen students from the institute were lying in wait for the Hoby visitors that night, and since Judy had come along merely out of interest, it was very unfair that she wasn't quick enough away, was caught, and clipped round the ear by the students. Luckily for me, Dad wasn't angry. He regarded our pranks as part of growing up, and scrumping apples hardly compares with the kind of 'pranks' which some youths indulge in today.

This is a sad fact of life, and I believe children growing up today miss out on a great many of the things which made our growing up fun. The games which we played as youngsters went out of fashion years ago: games like fox and hounds, where one of the gang was given a set length of time to hide, before the 'hounds' gave chase. Or tin-alerky, a game which once earned me some fearful but well-deserved verbal abuse from my mother. The game involved one of its players picking up a tin can and throwing it as far away as possible. One day, when it was my turn to throw the tin, I was running in full flight at the same time and the tin went, to my horror, straight through my mother's bedroom window and smashed the pane into a hundred tinkling sharp-edged pieces. Mother wasn't amused.

Although she told us off on occasions such as this, on the other hand neither she nor Dad regularly gave us a hiding. But when Dad did decide to dish out a dose of medicine, he meant business and we didn't forget it. But we never defied our parents in the way I hear children defy their parents today; there was no allowance made for 'teenage emotions' or 'growing pains'. If there was any insolence, you were given a hiding and you refrained from being insolent on the next occasion. When we sat with our elbows on the table as children, it was not for long. Dad had a bone-handled carving knife, and used the bone handle to rap our elbows so that they were too sore to put on the table again. I look back on the way my parents brought us up and hope that, somewhere along the line, enough of their teaching rubbed off on me to make an impression on the way that I, in turn, have brought up Mark and Paul. There was one essential difference between my childhood and that of my own children. The Harveys were a happy united family, whereas Mark and Paul had to grow up watching their parents' marriage disintegrate and eventually end in divorce. Mark was, I feel, old enough to cope by the time Richard Pitman and I parted. Paul was more devastated by his father's leaving and, quite naturally, I made certain allowances for this heartbreak in his childhood years. Only time will tell if making such allowances was a mistake or not.

Possibly the most momentous event of my childhood years was falling from a pony at a gymkhana and fracturing my skull. It had a profound effect on me and in my childhood years drove me, at moments, very close to despair. I was, I suppose, nine or ten years old when the pony I was jumping at a local show stopped in front of a fence. I did *not* stop and went straight over the pony's head, which probably made amusing viewing for the crowd round the ringside. But, as was so often the case when I wore a hunting cap for show jumping, the cap flew off and, as I landed, a jump pole cracked me smartly on the head. I was not, I hasten to add, wearing the 25-year-old former Master's hat brought back into work because I had now grown into it. It was a specially-purchased cap that I always wore when hunting, which was considered safe at the time. Such caps are now outdated, and modern safety riding helmets include a special chin strap and harness which prevents them falling off in the event of a sudden accident. I did not feel unduly hurt by the jump pole, and since neither the pony nor I appeared the worse for the fall, I simply got back on board and finished my round. I felt slightly dazed, as one might expect after any fall, but outwardly nothing appeared damaged. I went home after the show feeling fine and, to all intents and purposes, looking my usual self.

Later I went off to bed. I shared a double bed at the time with my sister Judy, and as I began to drop off to sleep, I heard her telling me, very firmly, to shut up. She repeated this a couple of times, before I suddenly heard her scream. A strange sensation crept over my entire body, and I felt very removed from it. I could hear what was going on about me, but was unable to take any part in the proceedings. The next words I can remember were my mother's:

'Send for the doctor, quickly'. I lay there, wondering who on earth could need the doctor at this time of night. I did not realize it was me, that I was in fact having a convulsion, and that everyone around me was worried that I might die. It was later, when I recovered, that events frightened me. The realization that I could have a convulsion, and not know that it was happening to me, scared the wits out of me, and I spent a great deal of time worrying about having another. As it happened, the convulsions returned several times over the next few weeks and events of the following months did little to help me think I might soon return to normal.

Several doctors were prevailed upon to look at me, to try and assess my condition. I was taken to Leicester Royal Infirmary for further investigations, though I admit that I failed to produce a specimen upon demand for the simple reason that there was a *boy* in the cubicle next to mine. I quite literally dried up and found myself unable to spend a penny under the required conditions. 'You'll have to do one later and come back with it', they told me severely. Various tests were performed, nevertheless, at Leicester, the net result of which was one of the worst blows of my life. No one could actually pinpoint the cause of my convulsions, but one thing they were unanimous about was that there was to be no more riding horses. It needs little imagination to understand my feelings. Horses were my life's blood. The only possible reason that anyone could give for the stricture was that riding – or rather falling – had caused the accident. Prevention being better than cure, if I gave up riding, it ought not to happen again. It was a terrible blow and I left the hospital feeling as though life would no longer be worth living.

However, being a tomboy, I listened to this advice for the space of precisely one night. Next day, I knew I could never give up riding. I saddled up my pony and, though the rigours of trotting made my head feel as if it would burst, I was nonetheless able to enjoy a sedate walk out with Rocket. Still, officially, no one knew that my skull was fractured. Concussion was the nearest any doctor had yet come to diagnosing my condition.

A few weeks went by, during which I continued my clandestine gentle rides, telling no one of this guilty secret. I did not enjoy the deception, but I could not help myself. Life without riding was not worth living. A visit to Nottingham Infirmary followed, when I underwent further tests. On this occasion I became very frightened, as the detection techniques included having various wires and suction pads attached to parts of my head. No one thought to tell a young girl why she was apparently being prepared for electrocution! Mum was made to wait outside. Inside, I felt lonely and afraid. It was an unpleasant experience which remains clear and lasting in my memory. Lights, very bright, flashed on and off. It was not long before I had the most awful headache and I badly wanted to cry. My tomboy training stood me in good stead, however, and I continued to appear as brave as possible. The answer, when it came, was not as a result of any of these hair-raising tests at all. All became clear when a specialist began to feel all over my head, very carefully, one section at a time. He came across a very small ridge and, after thinking for a moment, asked me: 'Why didn't you mention this bump before?' The answer was painfully straightforward: 'No one asked me about it'. The specialist turned to my mother and smiled. 'Your daughter has fractured her skull, Mrs Harvey.'

What was the most blissful relief to me, after the weeks of worry, was that the specialist reversed the orders not to ride. His words were: 'Ride as much as you like. You could just as easily fracture your skull falling downstairs. Life is short enough. Do what you want to do, and enjoy it.' Unfortunately, that was not the end of the story, and I was prescribed a course of phenobarbitone tablets to take three times each day. The morning and the evening tablets presented no problem, since I could take them in the privacy of my own home; but the lunchtime tablet caused me continual embarrassment in school. I hated the ritual question from the teacher in front of my entire class: 'Jenny Harvey, have you taken your tablet yet?'

The hated tablet therefore had to be explained to my schoolfriends, and it distressed me intensely to explain that I had suffered convulsions, and that this was the reason for the tablet every day. It made me shudder just to think that these fits might return, let alone have to talk about them to classroom companions. An idea crept into my mind, born of this embarrassment and distress. I would cease taking the lunchtime tablets as soon as my teacher stopped asking me publicly whether I had remembered them. Inevitably, in the course of time, she forgot to mention it, and I deliberately forgot to take the tablet. To my surprise I was none the worse for having just two tablets each day, rather than three. I then, perhaps somewhat stupidly, made a human guinea pig of myself. Without a word to my parents – who obviously knew nothing of my cutting out the midday pill – I simply started giving the nightly tablet a miss. Once again there seemed to be no ill effects, and before many more weeks had elapsed, the morning tablet also was disappearing down the loo. Still, happily for me, the convulsions did not return. I felt perfectly well. Had I been a few years older, I probably would not have taken such a chance. But being young, and some might say rather unwise, I took the risk. The missing tablets were not discovered until a medical examination prior to leaving school when I was 15. The nurse told Mum, who was annoyed to say the least.

But since I hadn't taken the pills for several years, there seemed little point in returning to the thrice-daily routine!

The fractured skull had one remarkably good effect on my life. My sister Jackie was several years older than me, and we had never been particularly close. I had been the tomboy Jenny, busy with the lads, anxious to join as many orchard-raiding missions as possible, between riding ponies and working on the farm. Having a fractured skull reduced me, for a while at least, to the indignity of spending long hours lying in bed. It was Jackie who got me through this unhappy spell. She spent hours with me: she sat on my bed reading to me, talking to me, helping keep up my spirits at a low point of my life. Because of that association in my childhood with my eldest sister, Jackie and I remained very, very close. Years later, when Richard Pitman and I parted for the last time and I needed an emergency appendicitis operation two days afterwards, Jackie simply packed her family into her car and brought them all down to live with me for a few weeks until I recovered. It was Christmas Eve when she arrived, but you would never have thought it an inconvenience, from the way she sailed through. Presents and Christmas trees were packed into the car alongside her husband and children; she just came to my home and coped with everything. History was, in a sense, repeating itself.

The two associations we enjoyed at times when I was in deep trouble have drawn us so close together that there is nothing I cannot now tell Jackie about my life, and I like to think she can be as frank with me. Such relationships between sisters may be common enough in families, but it was a new experience to me when, at the age of ten or eleven, I found a deep and close friendship with Jackie.

The fractured skull was probably the most memorable injury of my life, though it probably seems minor in comparison with injuries experienced by others. Jockeys receive terrible afflictions from racing falls, and I know show jumpers and event riders have received worse injuries. It was the emotional effects of a fractured skull which affected me the most; the thought often recurred that I might once again endure convulsions, and, far worse, that I might have to stop riding.

The only other injury I clearly recall was inflicted by my brother Joe, who threw a lump of wood at my pony because I would not let him ride it. He scored a direct hit on the pony's bottom. Rocket reared straight up in fright, whereupon I fell out the back door and landed heavily on the ground. But immediately we conspired to conceal the injury fron our parents who, fortunately, were due to go out for the evening. I was hidden by my brothers in the cowshed until the coast was clear, when they took me indoors and cleaned me up, good as new. Mum and Dad were never told and never noticed the cut on my lip!

My pony days were, however, gradually coming to a close. By the time I was 13 or 14 I was hunting regularly on Dan Archer with the Quorn under the Mastership of Colonel Murray Smith. Since I was regularly stealing off from school on Mondays and Fridays to hunt, lessons suffered even more noticeably! Colonel Murray Smith was this schoolgirl's hero. He constantly encouraged the younger riders who followed the Quorn, and though in hunting etiquette it is preferable to ride well behind the Master – and certainly never to get in front of him – the Colonel was always concerned that we should get as good a run as possible and enjoy our hunting. He was also kind enough to provide us with steaming mugs of hot tea at the end of the day, to warm us for the long hack home. Perhaps *that* is where I first became so addicted to tea!

Dan Archer was a wonderful hunter, whom my father had bred out of a Thoroughbred mare from one of the visiting Premium stallions. We raised him from a foal, gradually breaking him in and introducing him to hounds, and I soon realized that, if I qualified him, he would be eligible for point-to-point races. To become a point-to-pointer, a horse needs to have hunted for a specified number of days in the preceding winter. The Master of Foxhounds with whom he has been hunting then issues a certificate, which makes him eligible for entry into the series of point-to-point races held throughout England between February and May. These races are a unique opportunity for farming and hunting families to race their home-bred progeny with a view to National Hunt racing in the future.

Point-to-pointing to the outsider may seem comparatively easy, but it is indeed a strenuous test in its own way. The best-class horses may choose to race in National Hunt races under Jockey Club rules for the bigger prize money – the current average prize for the winner of a point-to-point is merely £100. The effect of keeping the prize money low is to ensure the sport is kept for the amateur competitor. For all that, I do not feel it should be approached in a sloppy or unprofessional way, since to do so courts disaster for horses and jockeys alike. Most point-to-point races are three miles or more in length, and the jumps are usually proper steeplechase-sized fences. There are no hurdle races, where the jumps are lower, less substantial, and where the obstacles flick over when hit at speed by a racehorse. Point-to-point jumps are every bit as unforgiving as proper steeplechase fences: demanding, and requiring care and due attention to the job in hand.

When we began hunting Dan Archer with a view to point-to-pointing him, it was my mother who chose his proper racing name. Not satisfied with naming the horse after her favourite radio character, she decided to write to the actor who played the part of Dan Archer to ask his permission to run the horse in the fictional character's name. The actor duly replied that he would be delighted. Furthermore, would my mother like to race the horse in the colours of his favourite London club? She most certainly would, and she did: Dan Archer was raced in blue, with black crossbelts and a gold and blue quartered cap. Now all he required was a jockey. I was just 14 years old and, at that time, still permitted to ride in point-to-points. The age limit has since been raised in the interests of safety. No one thought I had it in me to undertake the role of Dan Archer's jockey; feeling slighted, I mentally decided that I would ride him at least once in a point-to-point.

Dan Archer's training continued under my father's instructions, with me as work rider. We kept him at Albert Riley's farm, and each morning I would rise before 7, walk up to the Riley farm, and muck out his stable and feed him before school. It was the first time I worked seriously in an area of horse racing that would in due course ensnare my interest for life. After school, I went back on the school bus to the Riley farm, changed into jeans and rode out Dan Archer for exercise. Dad's orders were usually very simple: a given number of circuits of a particular field, not necessarily our own. I wasn't always as strict with Dan as I should have been. If, after a couple of circuits, the horse began to blow a bit, I would slow down the pace and let him have a breather, and possibly even allow him to walk the rest of the circuit. Had Dad known of my soft-heartedness, he would have been rather cross, I think.

Dan Archer's first run in public took place in May, at the tail end of the season, six weeks before my fifteenth birthday. My uncle, Percy Harvey, refused to believe I would go through with my undertaking to ride in the race – it was almost unheard of at that time for a girl to ride in races. The jumping game was considered far too dangerous, let alone unladylike. Uncle Percy and I had a private wager of £1 (a vast sum then) that I would not compete, which made me more determined than ever.

I was just becoming aware, for the first time, of my appearance. I was no longer quite the one-hundred-per-cent tomboy. I couldn't have been, because I recall parading in the paddock prior to the start of the race, when for some reason I took it upon myself to pretty up my appearance. It was perhaps not the ideal time to make adjustments, but I removed my skull cap and pulled some of my hair down so that it hung, rather fetchingly I thought, around my face. I replaced the cap when I was satisfied with the effect and immediately regretted even that modicum of vanity. The voice came over the loudspeaker for all to hear: 'Would the young lady who has just removed her cap in order to show us her new hairstyle please make sure she has fastened it back on correctly before we commence racing'. We did not win our race, but I won my £1 from Uncle Percy; my first, my one-and-only ever professional riding fee!

I was always sentimental where our animals were concerned, but when Dan Archer ate some leaves from a willow tree and died, I was quite distraught. The vet tried to save him, but it was no use, and the night he was put down I was greatly distressed. I was not particularly impressed by the joke told on television that evening by a comedian, since it concerned three naval ratings and several dead cab horses. It was most indelicate and my mother felt obliged to turn the television off whilst I recovered from a fresh bout of crying for my lost hero.

But I could be naughty, too, in spite of the sentimental side of my nature. Many years before we lost Dan Archer, we had lost a cat. A lorry driver had been forced to make the choice between killing one of us children, or the little cat which followed us everywhere. Mother was pleased in one sense that he chose to kill the cat, though we children were all extremely tearful at the time. It was unfortunate that Mum chose that evening to serve rabbit stew. The moment she placed the dish on the table she realized her mistake. I pointed serenely at the dish and said: 'Pussy'. That was enough. The entire family downed tools and refused to take a single mouthful. Nothing Mother said could persuade us that the meat in the dish was not the cat. Put it down to extreme youth: I made the comment on the meal from my highchair!

My sense of humour let me down on just one serious occasion as I was growing up. It was a vivid experience which took place one evening in winter, when my mother was helping to organize a village hall dance in Hoby. She had left the raffle tickets at home, and telephoned through to the farm to ask someone to take them to her. No one seemed willing to make the mile and a half trip, though for some reason I was eventually persuaded. It seemed too much effort and too late to tack up a pony, so I set out for Hoby on foot.

By the time I had delivered the raffle tickets to my mother and set out for home again, it was dark. It might seem imprudent in this day and age to have considered walking about alone after dark, but short of riding – an action fraught with danger in darkness – there was no other form of transport. We had no car. There were no buses. Walking alone seemed perfectly natural and normal at that time. I had noticed a motorcyclist on the way into the village, but thought very little more about him as I went on my way. By the time I set off for home he had gone. And yet, somehow, I felt apprehensive, which was unusual. In those times there was still very little regular traffic around Hoby and a girl could feel safe at night walking alone in the dark. Why, then, did I have this feeling of apprehension that night? A moment or two after leaving the village hall I heard the motorcyclist coming up behind me. He slowed right down and stared at me very hard as he passed, then went on his way. I fled into the churchyard – the same one that had hidden us when we threw apples at the old lady's door – where I hid amongst the graves for a while. I wasn't sure what to do. In retrospect, I would have been wiser to turn back for the village hall and wait for Mum to come home with me. As it was, when the bike could no longer be heard, I continued making my way home.

My heart began pounding very loudly as I heard the motorcyclist coming back towards me. Before I knew it, I was running like a hunted fox. He went down the road once again, and I darted into the hedgerows and hid. I was close to one of the few street lights around Hoby, and when the motorcyclist returned yet again, as I had expected he would, I took a careful look at him from my hiding place. I had secretly hoped that my pursuer would, in fact, turn out to be a friend having a practical joke at my expense. It was not. I heard the engine die away as the motorcyclist continued down the road once more, and I began walking yet again. And then for the umpteenth time I heard him heading back towards me. A lone car approached, giving me some temporary safety, but it did not stop as I frantically flagged it to slow down. Mercifully it gave me enough time to seek refuge in a driveway leading to a house owned by Miss James, from whom my father rented our farm. By the time I had run helter-skelter down the driveway, I was beside myself with terror and began banging on her door in a most hysterical fashion. My heart almost burst through my ribcage, and it was some time before I calmed down enough to tell Miss James my story. My father walked to Miss James' house and collected me, and we heard no more of the motorcycle that night. I was not hysterical for nothing, however. The motorcyclist was later arrested for molesting another woman in a village not far from Hoby.

Before Dan Archer's premature departure from our lives, he did me one very special favour. He introduced me, in a roundabout way, to racing proper. Whilst exercising Dan on a regular circular route, I first became aware that there was a professional racing stables close to our home. I had enjoyed a taste of racing with my effort in the point-to-point, and thereafter took a greater interest in the string which I noticed being exercised regularly. Although I was riding a Thoroughbred, and he was now being raced in point-to-points by my brother-in-law, I could see immediately that there were some noticeable differences between Dan Archer and the horses being ridden out from Tom Venn's yard. They looked very different in appearance, to begin with. Whereas in winter Dan Archer tended to have a long shaggy coat which was often difficult to groom, these horses had professionally clipped coats which always shone. They had an elegance about them which was difficult for me to match. The lads riding these horses occasionally spoke to me, usually to say: 'What's *that* you're riding?' I would proudly reply that this was my point-to-pointer. From there our conversations progressed and I soon found myself working at Tom Venn's yard on Saturdays and Sundays. From that moment on, I knew what I wanted to do with my life. I wanted to ride racehorses. I found I really enjoyed the work, and loved the horses. Dan Archer died in the meantime, and I found working in a professional racing yard a satisfying and rewarding replacement for my old horse.

Tom Venn's horses were trained by Chris Taylor, and since I was so convinced that this was now what I wanted to do as a career, I went, on Chris' advice, to ask Tom for a job. Tom duly interviewed me and closed the conversation with the words: 'These aren't like your dad's hunters, you know. These horses are different.' And so they were. Worlds away from the ponies and hunters upon which I had learned to ride, they were full of life and fire. They felt as though they had muscles in different places to the usual type of horses. They were so *fast*. Dan Archer was that obliging type of horse which always went at the speed asked by the rider. These racehorses had other ideas. They always wanted to go flat out, and needed just the faintest pressure on the accelerator to surge forward. I revelled in their pace, their streamlined action. I was in my element and on the day after I left Sarson Girls' School at the age of 15, I gave up the job of part-time stable lad and went to work for Chris Taylor full time at the Brooksby Grange yard.

The job never ceased to fascinate me. At first I was slow with mucking out two horses, and was frequently late in for breakfast, since everyone had finished before me. But I slowly learned to catch up and was as quick and thorough about the stable duties as the other lads. Perhaps a girl working amongst stable lads might have seemed out of place, but I had grown up with boys and knew how to keep on level terms with the opposite sex. I knew how imperative it was for my self-respect that I learned to do everything about the stableyard that a boy could do. I learned to control the pace of my horses, though I found it difficult, sometimes, to find out how the braking system worked. I had to learn that there is a knack to holding a racehorse, and that it is not all brute force and sheer strength. Horses may sometimes need a strong rider, usually because they have been badly broken and had their mouths ruined by rough handling – but I found, within a year of riding for Chris Taylor, that technique, and not strength, was required.

However, I can recall Chris Taylor advising me that, if a horse were ever to bolt with me on the gallops, I could always resort to reaching down his neck and head for the bit-rings. This seemed to make a certain amount of sense, though not much; it made even less when I saw Chris himself trying to practise what he preached! I watched with some amazement, mixed with curiosity, when Chris, whom we called 'Toes' because of his habit of riding with toes balanced on the stirrup irons, rather than the balls of his feet, disappeared from the string at an uncontrollable gallop. My horse, obviously thinking to itself 'what fun', took off in hot pursuit and we scooted along for some way at full racing pace, before Chris' horse took it into his head to change direction and take off across some stubble. I managed to dissuade my own horse from following, but in doing so found I was heading, still at racing pace, towards some schooling hurdles. The wrong way – the backs of the hurdles were facing us and I sent up a small prayer of thanks as my horse thought better of jumping them, but shot sideways instead. I was still on board, but not for much longer. The horse, galloping by now downhill, finally swerved violently as he reached a bend on the gallops and, like most other riders in the same situation, I disappeared through what is called 'the side door' in racing terms. I hit the ground resoundingly hard.

Someone rather brilliantly had the idea, as I struggled to my feet in considerable pain, of asking me to swing my arms about to make sure they weren't broken. They weren't, but my collar bone was. Someone else thoughtfully chased after my runaway horse, and I slowly walked back to the stables, in agony with my collar bone, and gasping for a reviving cup of tea. Chris' wife Sarah, who worked alongside us in the yard, very kindly drove me to the Leicester Royal Infirmary. No one was more surprised than me to find my brother Joe had arrived there before me, but not because of *my* accident. He had had a mock fight with my mother whilst she was cooking eggs in the kitchen at home. She had gone to whack him with the egg slicer, but the joke had misfired and my brother had a nasty cut on his arm.

I was eventually strapped up in a dreadful figure-of-eight contraption, which it was thought at the time would help my collar bone to heal. In fact it made life quite unbearable for six awful weeks, and I was relieved to see the back of it. It took me a further six weeks to get back enough strength in my arms to hold a galloping racehorse. Jockeys who break collar bones today are not subjected to strapping up, and less barbaric methods are available of helping them make a quick recovery! I never did hear how 'Toes' Taylor stopped his own runaway, but the bit-ring theory was never mentioned again! The memory of him leaning sideways, desperately struggling to reach his bit-rings, for which his arms were simply not long enough, remains. I would *not* recommend it as a sensible way of trying to stop a runaway horse.

Chris Taylor left Tom Venn's yard after I had been working with him at Brooksby Grange for about a year. He and Sarah bought their own yard, and began training at Bishop's Cleeve, near Cheltenham. They departed for their new premises, and I soon became unhappy working with the new trainer. Sadly we could see eye to eye about very little – I once ventured the opinion that he should buy himself a pet dog, and take his irritations out on that, instead of on me. I decided to follow Chris and Sarah Taylor to Bishop's Cleeve as soon as possible. There was the problem of my mother to overcome, but Chris and Sarah rose to the occasion and invited her and Dad down to Bishop's Cleeve to see my new surroundings. They could see I would be leading a perfectly normal respectable life. What else did I know? When my father said: 'Don't get yourself into any trouble', I genuinely thought he was referring to apple-scrumping. The facts of life as I knew them still applied to horses, not to people! I had such a lot still to learn about people.

4
MARRIAGE

I was sad to say goodbye to my horses at Tom Venn's yard, as well as the stable lads who had been so good to me: particularly Pete Brightwell, the head lad, and another lad named Victor with whom I had been out on quite a few occasions. I missed the fun we had, since I always enjoyed mixing with boys, from the earliest days of my youth, through my tomboy years.

Chris and Sarah Taylor had already been at Bishop's Cleeve for six weeks when I arrived. In order to get me there, Dad drove me to the coach station at Leicester and put me on one of the Black and White coaches which run round Leicester and the outlying districts. I felt nervous, but excited, about the adventure lying ahead. When Dad kissed me goodbye I tried not to cry, and went to sit at the back of the coach with my suitcase. It was a long way from the days when I had sat at the back of our old school coach on its daily journey to and from Sarson School at Melton Mowbray. In those days, the back section or the back seat was a privileged position and, in view of the enormity of the Harvey clan using that coach, we tended to have most of the say about who sat where! If you were not a Harvey, it was wiser not to argue: you weren't taking on just one Harvey, but 14 of them! But as the coach pulled out of Leicester and headed towards Gloucestershire, and I waved farewell to my father, I felt very much alone. My loneliness was temporarily relieved by the conductor of the coach, who must have thought I was running away from home, sitting there as I was with my few belongings. He came and sat by me for a while, questioning me about my destination, and looked very relieved when, as we reached my stop, I was met by Josie Hooley. Thankful they were not harbouring a runaway, the driver and his assistant roared away in the Black and White coach.

Josie Hooley was Chris Taylor's head girl at Bishop's Cleeve. She and I became close friends, and shared a room together at one end of Chris and Sarah's house, approached via an outside staircase. There was one other lad, and the three of us, with Chris and Sarah who always took their turn at mucking out and riding, comprised a yard of five people and about a dozen or so racehorses. Chris was a fairly successful trainer. He had sent out a decent number of winners from the Brooksby Grange premises and continued to saddle good horses from Bishop's Cleeve. Josie and I were often asked in for meals with Chris and Sarah, frequently when there were visiting trainers from other local yards, and we managed to overhear most of the local racing gossip. It was during one of these dinner conversations that the wife of 'Frenchie' Nicholson mentioned to the Taylors that they knew of a very good young jockey, still claiming his 7-pound allowance, who would be willing and able to ride races for them. He worked at the yard of trainer John Roberts. His name, said Mrs Nicholson, was Richard Pitman. It was the first time I had ever heard him mentioned.

Only a couple of weeks later I was to hear the name again. This time I met the owner of the name as well. I was riding a mare called Clouded Lamp at the time. She was a very difficult customer, a tricky mare to handle, and she was very nervous about traffic – including bicycles. When passing even a silent parked car or van, she would start playing up and shying away from it. Her rider had to be very careful that she didn't shy into the path of traffic approaching in the opposite direction, as well as watching for traffic coming up behind. So I was not exactly best pleased when a certain young man, riding a bicycle, came hurtling from around a bend on the wrong side of the road and almost collided with Clouded Lamp and me. He instantly received a stream of verbal abuse from Clouded Lamp's rider, who thought he was an ignorant idiot to travel about the roads in such an irresponsible manner. In spite of the rude words I hurled in his direction, the young man came cycling back in a leisurely fashion, as though nothing had happened, and began riding, to my annoyance, alongside our string of horses.

I tossed my head somewhat haughtily and concentrated on my horse. I just let him chatter away to the other riders. I decided I didn't like him one bit and preferred to ignore him. He asked Josie and Harry, the other stable lad, where we came from, what our horses were like, and a dozen other questions. In spite of his careless bike riding, they were unperturbed and chattered back to him like the greatest of friends. I was, in a word, furious. It had taken me some time to build up a confident relationship with Clouded Lamp. She had not always been my ride; when I arrived at Bishop's Cleeve, Harry was her regular lad. He tended to become a bit annoyed with her during her moments of naughtiness or nerves. He felt it was the former; but I felt that it was nerves, and that she was genuinely frightened.

A lot of horses have an inborn fear of traffic, stationary or otherwise. Others never turn a hair when a 20-ton juggernaut rumbles right past their hindquarters. Once the fear is there, however, it is extremely difficult to overcome. Clouded Lamp, I was certain, was not playing up. She was truly afraid of traffic. In my opinion, a little gentle talk from the rider, a positive forward-going attitude of mind, and a reassuring pat would be more effective than physical punishment. Beating a horse when it is afraid serves only to make it more afraid, not less so. A horse which, on the other hand, is given some steadying words and a stroke or pat on the neck, learns gradually that there is nothing to be afraid of. Horses take their confidence from their riders, and that is the reason it is said that 'fear travels down the reins'. A nervous rider and a nervous horse, put together, form a gruesome combination, since the nervous rider transmits his fear, the horse's fear thereby increases, and together they can easily come to harm. Put the nervous rider on a wise, safe, older horse and the older horse will teach his rider not to be afraid. Likewise, put the nervous horse in the hands of an efficient and good rider, and the horse learns not to be afraid. It is more true of Thoroughbred racehorses than almost any other type of horse, since by their very nature Thoroughbreds are highly strung.

A bad stable lad can ruin a good racehorse for this very reason. A horse which is unhappy at home cannot possibly hope to win races. If a lad aggravates a horse, either in his treatment of it in the stable, or by his riding of it – constantly hitting it, jagging on the reins and pulling on its mouth – then he can turn the horse sour. My own stable lads don't carry on like that. They'd last precisely one minute working for me if I were to catch them upsetting a horse, and I wouldn't have them within a mile of Weathercock House again. My head lad John Ricketts knows this, as do all the lads who work for me. None of them would permit this sort of bad behaviour with my horses, and would instantly report to me a new stable lad who might act in a way which is detrimental to the yard.

Of course, if a horse is *genuinely* difficult, it is another matter. That sort of horse has to be sorted out, otherwise he becomes a danger to all and sundry. If a horse is scared, I'll make a fuss of it and coax it to behave. If, on the other hand, it is pretending to be scared, using this imaginary fear as a means of 'taking the mickey' out of its handlers, as a way of disposing of its rider, that requires another kind of treatment altogether. Not brutality, of course, but some strong words and firm handling. A horse we had in the yard last summer, which began playing up, was a prime example of the genuinely naughty sort. He 'dropped' two lads on the gallops, and thought that this was a fine old game. He developed a trick of whipping round suddenly and dropping his shoulder, depositing his rider heavily on the floor. He never ran off, though he could quite easily have galloped home alone, encountering goodness knows what dangers such as barbed wire, potholes, traffic and other things. A loose racehorse can quite easily run into a sharp object and cause itself a lasting, if not fatal, injury. Willow Red wasn't just tipping his lads off gently: he was throwing them down hard. They could have been hurt, too, and this little habit needed putting right before things got out of hand. John Ricketts, who is very experienced, rode him for a few mornings and, when the skylarking around began, he delivered a couple of well-placed smacks on Willow's rear end. When the horse tried to repeat the performance, John repeated the punishment. It did not take long for the message to sink in and Willow Red has behaved pretty well ever since! A horse misbehaving and acting like a lunatic on the gallops is, of course, a problem in that it makes everyone else's horses very nervous, not to mention their jockeys! A loose horse flying wildly about on its own on the gallops tends to make everyone tighten their grip on the reins. Everyone is wondering if they'll be the next one to be dropped off sideways, no matter how sedate their horse might have been prior to seeing the loose horse come galloping along.

When Clouded Lamp and I began working regularly, we developed a relationship that was almost telepathic. It reached the point where I knew what she was thinking almost before she thought it herself. I knew what she would do, and how far she would go with me. When riding her, I could always feel the tension in her muscles as she began to 'wind herself up' like clockwork. When you ride horses, or a particular horse, regularly, you develop a sixth sense about its habits. You can normally read the warning signs. If it is about to behave in an extraordinary manner, you can feel the tension. Very few horses, unless frightened very suddenly, perhaps by a dog barking at them from behind a fence, will misbehave without a signal. It is up to the rider to learn to read the signals and act accordingly. Sometimes the muscles tense up; sometimes the horse's ears will prick very sharply, almost to the point where they meet. Another warning sign is the head going up very suddenly as something 'spooky' catches the eye. Plastic dustbin bags are always a good excuse for a horse to mess about when it is fit and corned up. During an autumn when there hasn't been a lot of rain and the ground is hard, the horses are crying out for a sharp canter to work off their pent-up energy. If they are kept to walking and trotting for several weeks, being fed a lot of corn at the same time, they become virtually suicidal and even a butterfly coming too close is an excuse for bolting off, or jumping 20 feet into the air!

When a horse is relaxed, he goes forward at a nice regular pace, his stride even and balanced, his head rocking gently in rhythm with the rest of his body. When he stiffens up underneath you, shortens his stride and brings his head up sharply, then you know he is seeing dragons or fairies where there are none, and needs riding forward strongly and with determination.

I was riding Clouded Lamp in just such a determined manner when Richard Pitman almost ran into us. Although I ignored him, he seemed to get along particularly well with Harry. I had very little time for Harry; he was frequently asking me to go out with him, and, furthermore, Josie and I frequently found ourselves doing little tasks in the stableyard which we felt he should have done. Under the impression that we were doing more than our share, we did not have a lot in common with him. The fact that he and Richard were in conversation annoyed me in the extreme. Eventually, however, we continued our morning ride in peace after Richard cycled off in another direction – though not before he had asked Harry my name.

Harry no longer asked me out, but it was some days before I knew the reason why: Richard Pitman had asked Harry to persuade me to go to the pictures with him instead. I refused, point blank. I did not like Richard and thought him a boastful young man. This impression was strongly confirmed at our next meeting. One evening, after Josie and I had been to see a film together, we were waiting at the stop for the bus to take us home to Bishop's Cleeve. Who should come sauntering rather cockily up to the bus stop but Richard Pitman? I kept silent and let him chat with Josie, whereupon they embarked on a conversation about the merits of sheepskin coats. Richard's opinion was that sheepskin coats should be made only of *real* sheepskin, not of the rather cheaper nylon imitation material, which he said looked shoddy and down-market. Josie agreed. They went on to discuss their education, and Richard bragged about the vast quantity of 'O'-level passes he had obtained at school. Not only a big head, I recall thinking, but a clever one. I learned much later on that he did not, in fact, have any 'O'-level passes at all! The coat I was wearing at the time was my pride and joy. It was the first proper coat I had ever bought, and of course it was made of nylon imitation sheepskin. Furthermore, I had no 'O'-levels and very little in the way of conventional education. I positively hated Richard Pitman at that moment.

Hate, it is said, is close to love; the emotions go side by side. Indifference is more insulting than hatred. So it was to prove, in the years ahead. But for the present it was hate . . . which, as one might expect, was to turn into the biggest love of my life. Richard was big-headed, in my opinion, but he was also very, very charming, and I became as much a victim of his charm as the next girl. Several weeks went by, during which I saw Richard more and more.

Eventually, against my better judgement, I agreed to accompany him to see a film called *Tom Thumb*. It was an awful evening, and I was very bored by the movie. But Richard's charm still won through and I began going out with him more regularly. Sometimes we would go out in a gang, with friends. But I found myself wanting to be alone with Richard. My feelings for him were deepening. I was very much involved. I had fallen in love.

There was never any doubt in my mind as to my reply when Richard asked me to move to Lambourn with him. Yes, I said, instantly. The whys and wherefores could follow. If Richard was leaving Bishop's Cleeve for Lambourn, I would go with him. The reasons behind Richard's move were quite simple. Fred Winter, the great champion jump jockey, winner of hundreds of top-class races including two Grand Nationals – on Sundew in 1957, and Kilmore in 1962 – had decided to hang up his boots and take up training in Lambourn. Richard wanted to work for Fred, so he wrote to ask for a job and was given it. It only remained for Richard to find me a suitable job in Lambourn, so that we could live close to each other.

He introduced me, one Sunday morning in the village of Upper Lambourn, to Major Geoffrey Champneys, who was to become my employer for the next couple of years. Today, Weathercock House, where I train Corbiere and my other horses, is directly adjoining Major Champneys' land. Then, duly employed by the Major, I took up residence alone in a small caravan in a field which I can see from my landing window today. Not alone entirely, however, for I had a small black and white mongrel dog which accompanied me everywhere. I had bought him from a dogs' home, when Josie Hooley had left Chris Taylor's yard to work elsewhere and I had been left alone in the room we had once shared. Rip became my constant companion for many years, until one day he bit Mark on the face when he was a small baby. We could not risk the dog biting the children and sadly he had to be destroyed.

I liked Major Champneys immediately. He is still a great friend today, and I have a great deal of respect for him. He was a hard taskmaster, but he was fair. Sad at leaving Chris though I was, I knew that Lambourn was the place to be if my career was to revolve around racehorses. The potential for riding horses and working with them in Lambourn was enormous. There were many racing yards; practically every large house with land is a training establishment. The move from Bishop's Cleeve to Lambourn was as natural a progression in my life as leaving home had been. It was a move forward. Again, I looked ahead to starting a new job, in new surroundings, with pleasure and a certain relish not altogether unconnected with the fact that the man I loved would be living a few hundred yards away at Uplands, where Fred Winter was training. Richard was just as keen that we should live close to one another and spend as much time together as possible. Marriage had not, however, been mentioned at this stage. Being together and working with horses were our prime considerations for the moment.

I would have loved, during those days, to become a jockey. Girls were not, however, allowed to ride professionally and certainly not in jump racing. They were allowed to ride on the flat as amateurs, but since I was a paid stable girl, and had been from the day I began working for Chris Taylor, I was banned from riding either in amateur flat races or point-to-points which were also open only to amateur riders. Had it not been for these factors, I wonder if I might have ended up as the first woman to *ride* a National winner, instead of train one. However, someone else will one day have that pleasure and privilege. I am more than content to have become the first woman trainer of a Grand National winner and therein lies any further ambition; I'd like to train another, preferably for my son Mark to ride, before I retire.

Any frustrations I might have felt at not being able to ride in races were compensated for firstly by my sister Mandy and later by my son Mark. When Mandy grew up and began riding, I was very tough when teaching her to ride. I was determined that *she* should do the things that I had missed. It gave me great pleasure to teach her and to take her off every weekend to shows with her pony Johnny Boy. We would drive together practically anywhere for a show and I was always delighted when she won. I was even more delighted when she began riding racehorses, especially the ones I was by that time training. Her first ride in a race was an even bigger thrill, since she was doing something that I had badly wanted to do myself. You could almost say I was riding the race through her, and because I had taught her in the first place, the pleasure was twofold. She is as good a rider as any I know. More lately, any frustrated ambition I may suffer through not riding in races is channelled through my son Mark. Just as I drove anywhere to watch Mandy ride in a race (and still like to do so), I now drive miles to watch Mark. As with Mandy, I want Mark to be the best. Just as I had Mandy on a pony's back the moment she could hold her head up, so it was with Mark. In Mandy's case I would scoop her up from her pram, sit her up in front of me as I rode Rocket, and we would canter around together in this manner all over the place. Mother, needless to say, was speechless with horror! Mandy, however, thoroughly enjoyed herself and can still remember our antics today.

On the other hand, I was always happy just working and being with horses. Much as I would have liked to race, I did enjoy the benefit, when working for Major Champneys, of being allowed to school, as opposed to merely ride work. Schooling racehorses is a skilled job and one which is normally left to jockeys rather than entrusted to stable lads. I felt pleased and proud that Major Champneys thought me a good enough rider to teach the young horses to jump their hurdles and fences at home, rather than just ride them on the roads or work them on the gallops. There was a world of difference in this new job, and I found myself riding and schooling alongside some of the magical names of racing, some of the top jockeys of the day. Terry Biddlecombe was one of these jockeys.

One morning, during a schooling session, Terry was riding a horse called Riversdale whilst I was riding Domaru. The Major instructed me to go ahead with Terry, riding upsides of his horse. I was very chuffed. Terry was champion jockey, no less, and I thought it an honour indeed as I set off with him, quite determined not to let myself or the Major down. It was an important moment in my career. As Terry and I rode down the line of schooling hurdles, it occurred to me that we were going rather fast. But I kicked on, determined not to fall behind the champion and Riversdale. Whatever Terry did, I copied. The faster he went, the faster I went. It is a sin in racing, whether at home or on a racecourse, not to follow instructions. The Major had told me to stay with Terry, and to do as he did. I was obeying instructions. Stride for stride we went, faster and faster, until I began to realize that everything wasn't quite right. We were approaching the end of the gallop and Terry was still going absolutely flat out. I felt Domaru tiring and decided to take the consequences of my decision, and I duly pulled my horse up. Then the truth dawned: Terry didn't, and couldn't, stop. He hadn't intended going at that speed at all; his horse had run away with him! Afterwards came the Major's comment: 'I think that horse got the better of you there for a moment, Terry, don't you?'

Fred Winter, also watching the debacle, addressed his remarks to me: 'Jenny', he said with a faint smile, 'we have a runner in the lads' race at Wincanton next week and I think you ought to ride it for us'. As it happened, Fred's own stable lad Richard Pitman took the ride, his first ever for Fred Winter. I did wonder, afterwards, whether the horse would have won had I ridden it instead! One Seven Seven unseated his young rider at the first fence – a rather ignominious start for Richard. However, it taught him something about riding in public, if not actually winning.

Richard was, as 'Frenchie' Nicholson had predicted, a good 7-pound claiming jockey, and though it took him several seasons of very hard slog to lose his claiming allowance and ride at proper weights, once he was with Fred Winter and riding good horses, he began to excel. Good horses, as he once remarked, make good jockeys!

The 7-pound claiming allowance can be compared to a golfer's handicap. The allowance is made for beginners to racing, and when they have won a specified number of races claiming 7 pounds, the allowance is reduced, and later removed altogether and that rider becomes a fully-fledged jockey. Some trainers will, in certain cases, employ a jockey with a 7-pound claim to ride a horse that is heavily handicapped, since the 7 pounds may make a difference to the horse's performance, and can be the borderline between winning and losing a race. But the claimer must be a good rider, otherwise his 7-pound claiming allowance is worthless – it can even act as a distinct disadvantage if he does not ride properly. It has the same effect as 7 pounds overweight in such cases.

Whilst my career was developing on the gallops, so was my personal life developing in the little caravan where Richard and I spent most evenings. He taught me to drive his old Mini, and helped me to buy my first own car: an ancient 'sit-up-and-beg' beige Ford Popular with real leather seats and three gears plus reverse, which we bought for just £22. Richard nobly offered to drive it home from the car auction – I say nobly because it had no tax, lights or insurance – and I drove home in the comparative safety of his Mini. But it was my car and I loved it. Its eventual demise was very sad, though it found another lease of life as a somewhat unconventional henhouse in the garden of my friend Chris Leason. As far as I know, he still has it!

I had worked for Major Champneys for a year, living in the caravan behind the house, while Richard lived in a caravan at Uplands. We continued our steady relationship, and I never, in fact, went out with anyone else at all from the moment I met Richard until our marriage foundered. I had no desire to do so; I was head over heels in love with him and had no wish to spend time with other boys or men. No one else mattered. I was just 18 years old. Possibly, had I given myself a few more years, allowed myself to take my time, look around at the world outside Lambourn, I might have taken stock of my relationship with Richard and thought more carefully about the way I was inevitably heading for marriage. But at 18, who thinks to look 10 or 20 years ahead? At 18, you think you will always be young, in love, and unfettered by mortgages or children. Perhaps I was unwise and headstrong to marry the first man I fell deeply in love with, but I don't think I was the first girl to act in this way, nor the last. Today, if anyone of 18 told me that they were getting married, I would strongly advise them to wait. But I wouldn't expect them to take any notice!

Ironically, it was guilt which actually pushed Richard and me towards the marital state. We had been, for a certain length of time, quite happy with the normal kissing and petting involved in a relationship. But once we moved to Lambourn, there was a none-too-subtle change. Richard, as most men, wanted to sleep with the woman he loved. Kissing and cuddling was no longer enough. He wanted more. So, as a matter of fact, did I; I was no virginal angel at this time. I had consented a couple of times to let things run to their natural and ultimate conclusion, but the guilt was pressing and horrible and took away any pleasure that sleeping with Richard should have given me.

Talking of sex and guilt in the same breath may, today, seem peculiarly old-fashioned. But then, when I was 18, permissiveness was unheard of, the pill a rarity issued to married ladies only, and sex quite unmentionable in public. It was still something that young people sniggered about and indulged in illicitly. I cannot quite decide whether our attitudes today are for the better or for the worse, but at that time, I knew that my parents, if they found out Richard and I had slept together on one or two occasions, would have reeled back in horror and possibly even demanded that I return home. *This*, I realized, was what Dad had meant about keeping out of trouble. Apples had nothing to do with it!

Major Champneys, funnily enough, was the catalyst which finally set us off on the march to the altar. Richard stayed a night in my caravan. Major Champneys, an early riser, watched with interest as the young man stole across the field, trying to keep out of sight, soon after dawn the following morning. I knew nothing of his having seen Richard and was somewhat taken aback when I went into the Major's house for tea at 6.30 am before riding the horses and he asked: 'Jenny, when are you and Pip getting married? You might just as well, after what I saw this morning.' Shocked, I told Richard later what the Major had said. I was in any event unhappy about our illicit pleasures, and although I wanted to be with Richard more than I wanted anything else in the world, I felt dreadful about our stolen moments. I was in love and I wanted him, but it just wasn't on to sleep together outside marriage. So Richard bought me a pretty engagement ring with three lovely diamonds, and we became officially engaged. He telephoned my father on his way over to my caravan with the ring in his pocket, to ask officially for Dad's approval – which was granted with delight – and produced the ring as a complete surprise to me. It was very romantic and sweet, but it did nothing to dispel the acute guilt feelings harboured in my heart.

There was another problem, too. This was a far more serious matter, for it concerned religion. Richard was a Roman Catholic and I had always been brought up in the Church of England faith, attending Sunday School or church, sometimes both, nearly every Sunday throughout childhood. It was a problem because the Roman Catholic church frowns upon intermarriage. It does not like a Catholic marrying a Protestant, and I pondered long and hard on the pros and cons of converting to Catholicism. I went, as always with the major problems in life, to my father. Dad, as ever, could be relied upon to give unbiased and sound advice and he said, very simply: 'One thing is for certain, Jenny, my duck. If there ever was a God, there certainly wasn't a God solely for the Church of England.'

The way I saw my marriage to Richard was, in effect, as simple as my father's philosophy about God. Marriage was for ever. Richard and I would live the rest of our lives together. We would have children and bring them up together. Eventually, we would die and be buried side by side in the same grave. That was how I saw the future from the age of 18. The simple faith I held in my heart was, in retrospect, appallingly sad. Living in a fool's paradise, one might say. However, I knew that unless I took up Richard's faith, whilst I might overcome the problem of marriage itself, I could never overcome the problem of not being buried beside him, in the same churchyard. That thought positively tore me in two, and the idea of being buried in a grave far away from Richard disturbed me deeply. It may seem odd, in the light of subsequent events; at that time, it consumed me. I would have to become a Catholic. I decided there was no other way to marry the man I loved.

I began visiting the priest in Lambourn for instruction in the Catholic faith, and we had lengthy and deep discussions together. I was unable to accept the Catholic teaching without question. I had strong opinions of my own and, whilst he could see my opinions were logical, nonetheless his indoctrination would not permit other views to be acceptable. A main source of our argument was the matter of birth control. Surely it is better, I argued, that if I'm doing wrong by practising birth control, then only I should be punished. If I had had any more than two children, the number we planned and were prepared for, and I had found myself unable to cope, then the children would suffer. I was hardly prepared, as it turned out, for the two children which I did have in only 14 months, and afterwards took my doctor's advice not to have another. But I liked the priest, for all that he could not see my point of view.

Whilst I was grappling to come to terms with the intricacies and unusual balance of views in the Catholic church, however, I don't feel that Richard ever regarded it as a problem. He was pleased that I was taking the trouble to learn his faith and become a Catholic in order to marry him; any inner conflict I may have felt did not seem to communicate itself to him.

We also had to resolve the problem of finding somewhere to live. Our first married home was a cottage belonging to Fulke Walwyn, since there was nowhere else and we had little money to permit us to be choosy. The loo was sited at the very end of the garden. There was a sitting room, a kitchen, and a bedroom upstairs. Not much, but it was home and I was very happy there. I was still working for Major Champneys who had given us a most generous wedding gift. The wedding itself, however, had not been quite the happy event I'd imagined!

I went home for a few days prior to the big day, and Richard arrived in Leicestershire the night before the nuptials took place, accompanied by Brian Delaney, his best man, and two other lads, Steve Midgeley and Derek King. We were to marry at the Catholic church in Leicester. Richard and his friends were despatched to spend the pre-wedding night with our family friends, Florrie and Walter Dodd. I discovered later that they stayed up most of the night drinking and playing cards. It was the only time Richard won money at cards: he was too drunk to play his own hand, and with due assistance came out in front. I, on the other hand, spent my last night as Jenny Harvey more sensibly. I was not nervous at the thought of marriage; on the contrary, I was looking forward to being free of the guilt which I felt at having slept with Richard out of wedlock!

There was, however, one very nice touch to my wedding day which was a lovely surprise and a mark of just how much some owners do appreciate the efforts made by jockeys to win races with their horses. It was a white Rolls Royce. Richard had asked Bill Shand Kydd, for whom he rode several good winners, if he could borrow the car to transport me from my parents' home to the church. It was fabulous!

The day was to prove full of surprises, not the least of which was our honeymoon venue. Between the arrival of the white Rolls Royce and the first night of married life, there was a minor incident which remains to hand when I'm looking for something to smile about. It concerns my younger sister Mandy. I recalled Jackie's wedding as we dressed Mandy as my bridesmaid, and remembered how I had rebelled at wearing stockings and suspenders! Mandy looked a picture when we had finished with her. It was a big day for her as well as for me. But we did not wish her to spoil her lovely outfit running about the garden getting dirty; she was told to sit quietly on a chair and not to move until we said so. She duly obeyed . . . and we all completely forgot her. Forgot her, in fact, to the point of dressing up ourselves and departing for church in the white Rolls Royce. As we were about to enter the church, someone remembered Mandy. No one had seen her since she had received her orders to sit down and be quiet. There was a minor panic and my father belted back home to find her. He came upon her before he reached the house. She was running along the street in her finery, tears streaming down her face, headed towards Leicester Catholic church. It was all the more galling for Mandy that Carol, the niece who was my other bridesmaid, had *not* been left accidentally at home! Mandy had always wanted to be someone's bridesmaid, and had first come close to her dream when my elder sister Judy was married. However, she managed to contract measles a few days before the big event and the nearest she managed was being allowed to dress up in her bridesmaid's outfit on the wedding day and sit at home while we all went off to the wedding. It had upset her enormously, and almost being forgotten at my wedding was the last straw!

There were various heated discussions over the matter of dress at our wedding . . . should Richard wear top hat and tails, or an ordinary suit? Not being an ostentatious family, I did not want my father looking, as I thought at the time, a proper fool dressed in topper and tails. Richard and I managed to reach a compromise, with the men wearing ordinary suits. Margaret, Richard's elder sister, refused to attend her brother's wedding on the basis that if he wasn't going to dress properly, it wasn't worth her while going. Richard's other sister Pamela, with whom I struck up a fair friendship, was pleased to come, as was his father. His mother I was never very sure of; I always felt she believed her Richard had married beneath his status. This may not be remotely true. It was just the way she made me feel. Pop and I were always friends and, in the years ahead, after the separations between Richard and I occurred, Pop was always anxious to put me at my ease when we met. He was a lovely man, and many years later, after I won the Grand National, I thought about Grandad Pitman. He, I knew, would have been delighted at Corbiere's victory. He would have smiled broadly at the triumph! Since his death, his grandsons Mark and Paul have put a wreath on a plaque commemorating him every single Christmas. We have never seen another wreath there; Pop died before Richard and I divorced. He, of all people, made me feel at home when I visited the Pitman family. Right from the early days of our marriage, he always seemed genuinely to care.

In those early days, we cared, Richard and I, for each other.

Living in our small cold cottage throughout our first winter – we married on 2 October 1965 – we were content enough with the living conditions, even the electric cooker which gave out an electric shock if anything containing water was placed on one of its very solid, old-fashioned hotplates.

We had been married for just six weeks when I became pregnant with Mark. I had been forced to wait rather longer than expected for a normal marital relationship to take a regular pattern, since Richard had contracted yellow jaundice shortly before the wedding and had been sick as a dog throughout the honeymoon, which wasn't helpful. The journey to Yorkshire, where our honeymoon took place, was not made any more pleasant when I learned that Steve Midgeley would be accompanying us! There had been some discussion in the previous days about a honeymoon 'in a hotel in Yorkshire'. Little did I realize it was to take place in a pub belonging to friends, still less think that Steve would be lurking in the background all the time. Not only Steve, either. His parents, who owned the very nice little pub (which I had been led to believe was Yorkshire's answer to The Dorchester), insisted upon accompanying Richard and me wherever we went! They acted as our official tour guides throughout the entire honeymoon. But they were very kindly people, and Mrs Midgeley's Yorkshire puddings helped make it all worthwhile. Richard's yellow jaundice was the final straw. So when we returned home and began life together, finally alone, free of illness *and* Steve Midgeley, I was more than happy.

When I began feeling ill two months later, we naturally assumed that Richard's yellow jaundice had finally caught up with me. On the other hand, I knew we had been taking risks. Contraception was out of the question, and the moment Mark was conceived, even as we made love, I knew the risks involved. However, lust took over and, newlyweds that we were, we threw all caution to the wind.

I found pregnancy a horrible experience! I was sick every day, and when I felt most ill I would dash behind the stables at the Major's yard and throw up out of sight of prying eyes. The Major's son-in-law, however, caught me as I heaved my heart out one morning; and when I needed a day off to recover and Richard called in at Major Champneys' establishment to say he was sure I'd caught jaundice, the Major's reply was predictable. 'Richard, it isn't jaundice that your Jenny is suffering from. What she's got will take nine months to get over.' The Major's son-in-law, though I had sworn him to secrecy, had apparently told the Major of his discovery.

In a cold, damp cottage in the middle of winter, I became more and more miserable as my pregnancy progressed. I tried very hard to continue working, but left the Major's employment shortly before Christmas. Even though he had already given us a generous wedding present, he arrived on Christmas morning bearing a card which contained £2. Then, in our slightly poverty-stricken condition, it was a week's housekeeping for the Pitman family. My salary for a whole week was only about £9, Richard's was £14.50. It was a seven-days-a-week job, involving early mornings and long hard days, and it was dangerous for a pregnant woman to ride racehorses in any event. I needed to work for as long as possible so that I would qualify for my maternity benefit, and the Major was kind enough to let me stay on, not riding at all. Instead I was given the job of leading out horses which had raced the previous day to let them pick at grass, and I could continue mucking out, cleaning tack, and helping in other ways about the yard, for the time being at least.

Baby clothes were a problem. Then, as now, all new items for babies, including prams, cots and pushchairs, were impossibly expensive for a young couple to buy. My sisters rallied round and produced lots of their own babies' clothes, whilst I scoured the local newspapers in search of a second-hand pram, carrycot and playpen. Mark had nothing new as a baby. We simply could not afford it. I was, however, particularly pleased with the bargain pram I found. After looking at several tatty ones which had seen better days, and deciding that no baby of *mine* was going to be pushed about in anything so scruffy, I came across a middle-aged woman who'd had a late baby and had consequently purchased a rather handsome new pram. Used for just one child, it became mine for a mere £5. The kind lady also gave her pram's new owner some very smart baby clothes indeed. I considered myself a very clever bargain hunter. I took the pram straight home and filled it with teddy bears, to await the baby's arrival.

The cottage remained damp and cold and, as Mark's arrival grew closer, Richard and I shared the view that it was no place for a young baby. We had to start looking around for somewhere new to live. The primitive surroundings, such as a car seat with a floral cover which we took turns to sit in, and the solitary coal fire which heated the entire house, just would not do. Fine for two healthy people like Richard and me on our own, in love and oblivious to much of the discomfort, but hell for a baby of only a few weeks. Love conquers cold and damp. Babies can die from them.

A new development of small bungalows was being erected in Lambourn and, though we agreed that judging from the foundations there wouldn't be room to swing a cat, nonetheless they had central heating, would be dry and warm, and would make an ideal first 'own home'. Such a bungalow would make an ideal starting point from which to move to bigger things. All we required now was £2,950 to buy it. I was apprehensive at the idea of a mortgage. It seemed an horrendous debt and I hated owing money in any shape or form – though I have since learned you sometimes have to borrow to get on in life. But Richard was unconcerned and confidently went off to the Ramsbury Building Society in Newbury, where the branch manager Alan Barter advised us that racing people, and jockeys in particular, were poor risks for building societies. However, when he heard that Richard's job was with a top racing stable such as Fred Winter's, he agreed to make the advance and 29 Tubbs Farm Close, Lambourn, became ours. It was the first property that either Richard or I had ever owned and we were as pleased as punch. It was our kingdom and, to begin with, I felt the luckiest person alive. Only later, when the four walls of 29 Tubbs Farm Close began to envelop me like a fog, did I grow to hate the confinement.

Richard began to do very well with his riding, though we were still stretched to the limits by our mortgage. We never dared go to the supermarket without a shopping list with the price of every item clearly marked so that we did not end up at the checkout, an event I dreaded, without enough money to pay! Things looked up when Major Verly Bewicke offered Richard the job of first jockey. Verly Bewicke then trained horses for Lord Cadogan, who was to play such an important role in my own early career as a trainer. He was also to lend us the money to buy our later home at Hinton Parva. Richard's life became very, very busy. He was still working for Fred Winter, doing his two each morning and riding them out, before rushing off to school some of Major Bewicke's runners. Then he would go racing for the afternoons, returning home late, tired and sometimes very battered. I went racing to watch him ride whenever possible but, with Mark a small baby, and only five months later with Paul on the way, it was not easy. More often than not I was tied to the house, weighed down with babies and household chores, confined within four walls and with just the dog to talk to. I had not enjoyed the birth of my first child and anticipated the birth of my second with a certain dread.

Mark had been born in the very early hours of a Monday morning. I'd been watching the World Cup all Saturday afternoon and, not wishing to smoke cigarettes to relieve the tension of watching the English team fight it out with West Germany, I had eaten apple after apple instead. I woke in the early hours of Sunday with pains in the gut, which I immediately put down to the apples. But they became worse and I woke Richard up to tell him. He agreed it was the apples and promptly went back to sleep; but I was beginning to realize . . . this was the first early stage of labour. I couldn't lie in agony for another moment, so I got up before it was even light and began the housework. It's strange the things women do at such moments in their lives. My thought was: if I'm in labour, I'll be away for several days, so I'd better clean the house before I'm taken into hospital. It was extraordinary and Richard thought I was mad upon discovering me at 6 am, labour pains developing, scrubbing away at my kitchen tiles! He ran up the road and rang the hospital from our local callbox, and a few minutes later, we were on our way.

To say I hated the next few hours is an understatement. It was an experience I could well have lived without, and after an epidural anaesthetic and a lot of pain in between, Mark arrived. Paul's imminent arrival, therefore, was not a welcome prospect. It was ironic that, after the trouble I endured giving birth to my first son, Richard said: 'You'll never have to go through this again'. Five months later Paul was conceived!

I find it hard now to describe the way I felt about my lifestyle at that time. I was living in the confined space of a bungalow, with no horses in sight except the racehorses we saw on occasions in the village, and if I say it was like being a sparrow in a budgie's cage, it might create the right impression. I was a wild New Forest pony shut up in a stable. I was a free child, trapped and ensnared. I endured terrible depression and, though the doctor might have felt that a handful of tranquillizers would relieve me of these feelings, I knew they could not. It was unlikely I would be able to endure such a life for very long. Something had to be done and, fortunately for me, something was done: we moved to the Parva Stud in the Wiltshire village of Hinton Parva, some eight or nine miles from Lambourn. It was manna from heaven. I think, without it, I should have gone completely mad.

5
EARLY TRAINING DAYS

It was snowing hard on the morning that Richard and I lay in bed, having a rare break from our usual early morning rush. Normally, he would have been up and gone from the house before 7 am, to ride out with the first string for Fred Winter. There would be the usual stampede for the bathroom, cooking breakfast for him and the kids, as well as getting myself dressed. This day, however, was a quiet one. With thick snow there would be no racing and no chance of getting the horses up to the gallops to work. So it was a leisurely pace instead of the usual dash. From my point of view, of course, once Richard had gone to work and left me alone with Mark and Paul, life was a dull round of washing and ironing, cooking and cleaning, shopping and gardening. I hated all those things, so it was a rare pleasure to lie in bed for an extra hour or so reading *The Sporting Life*.

Richard began reading aloud an advertisement from the property pages. The following had caught his eye: 'Six acres of land for sale, with stables and indoor school. Caravan on site, planning consent obtained for agricultural bungalow.' I instantly pricked up my ears, since we had been mulling over the idea of buying just such a place. We had even been to see a couple of properties and had come close to buying them. The first one we had investigated we had liked very much, but were 'gazumped' by another bidder. Then there had been a pretty cottage for sale with some land attached. We had been very keen on that, too, until we found out from the local planning office that the new M4 motorway (which was not then built) would run practically through the kitchen door and out the other end of the house! Whilst being close to a motorway is useful in some respects, especially with the amount of travelling involved for racing people, we felt we did not really want the sound of juggernauts echoing across the breakfast table, and the thunder of passing traffic sending the ornaments flying off the shelves. We abandoned the idea immediately, and continued our search elsewhere.

Richard continued reading the 'for sale' advertisement aloud to me. It sounded an ideal property and I listened excitedly – until he came to the pay-off line, the price. It was advertised at around £12,000 and with our own bungalow still worth only about £4,000, the property, in my mind at least, was well beyond our reach. I had not banked on Richard's determination. Confident as ever that we could beg, borrow or steal the £8,000 difference in price from one source or other, he suggested we get dressed, have a bit of breakfast, and set out through the snow-driven roads to take a look. It was only eight miles away and, since I was intensely sick of the four walls of 29 Tubbs Farm Close, I agreed. It would, if nothing else, get the children and me out of the house for a few hours.

A couple of hours later, Richard and I found ourselves driving along the lane slowly, for two reasons. Firstly, the snowy roads didn't invite one to spin along too quickly; and secondly we were searching as we drove for the stableyard we had seen advertised that morning. Suddenly, I spotted it, situated on the right hand side of the lane. I took in everything I wanted to see about the property in one short glance. It was perfect. A man appeared at the gated entrance to the yard and waved the car to a halt. Were we looking for his stables? he enquired. Had he not been there, we might not have stopped the car. My instinct, in any event, was that in view of our shortage of ready cash, it would have been wiser to drive straight by. When he invited us to come and look around, I was about to say 'No thank you very much' when I heard Richard's voice reply, very firmly: 'Yes, please. We'd love to.' Somewhat aghast, I followed him through to the stableyard for a proper look.

It was, as I have said, perfect. The yard was beautiful, and absolutely immaculate. There was a saddle room with rows of spotlessly clean tack hanging neatly on pegs and racks. There was not a wisp of straw or hay out of place. The paintwork on every box was fresh and clean, with not a chip or a scratch anywhere. I could visualize already the boxes filled with *my* horses. I could hear the sound of their hooves on the tarmac, see the heads looking keenly out from over the stable doors. I was hooked.

Our idea, in buying a small yard, was to offer a livery service with a difference. Most livery yards take in hunters and hacks; their service usually includes bedding, feed, grooming, veterinary care when necessary, maintaining the horse's shoes, and exercising if required. We had a service in mind that differed slightly. We planned to take in racehorses that had perhaps broken down or had suffered other injuries, and needed nursing back to health. I would bring them slowly back, after a rest period, to early roadwork and return them to their trainers ready to go back to proper training. There was no other yard in the Lambourn area offering this service at the time, and we felt it would catch on quickly. A trainer with a 'lame duck' needs somewhere to send it for the purposes of recovery, since this can take up to a year. Today, of course, there are plenty of yards providing just such a service to racing trainers, but then, when Richard and I first came up with the idea, it was unique. It would give us a business in which I could be involved whilst he continued his riding, and would release me from the depressing routine into which I had slipped at the bungalow. This yard, I realized straight away, was the ideal place.

Whether or not the racing yards undertaking this service today have the same dedication that I intended to make my trademark is another matter. At that time, I knew I had a lifetime of knowledge about horses behind me. I knew I understood about helping horses recover from operations, and I cared deeply enough about horses to make sure the job was done thoroughly and properly. When the idea became reality in the ensuing months, I was able to put my knowledge to the test, and was proved right. I also learned a great deal from these horses and was able to use that knowledge in the later days, when I began to train professionally. But that was still a long way off.

I was still worried about the finances. Richard, however, was undeterred by the lack of money and seemed not to regard it as a problem. He bore in mind the words of Bill Shand Kydd, who had lent him the white Rolls Royce on our wedding day: 'Richard, never be afraid to ask anyone for anything. The worst they can say is "no".'

So Richard went to see Lord Cadogan, one of Verly Bewicke's owners, whose horses he rode. Would Lord Cadogan consider lending us the money which we required in order to purchase the stableyard and land? When Lord Cadogan did agree, it was like pennies from heaven. I would now be able to escape from my Tubbs Farm Close prison. The tranquillizers that the doctor had prescribed for me could now be thrown cheerfully out the window; they hadn't helped at all and had, in fact, only created problems. Even though I took the pills only on those occasions when I was feeling particularly low and unable to cope, they were not the answer. I knew that I needed this change of environment more than anything, and Lord Cadogan's generosity was the answer to my prayers. We could now go back to Peter Tozer, whose stables and land we wanted to buy, with the benefit of knowing we had the loan in our pockets. It put us in a far better bargaining position, since purchasing the land and stables was only the beginning of our expenditure. I was acutely aware that there was no house in which to live, only the small caravan, and in addition to the cash needed to buy the little stud farm, further cash would be required to erect a habitable dwelling – the agricultural bungalow for which planning permission already existed.

Richard telephoned Peter and said that our absolute top limit for the stables, land and indoor school was £10,000. We had calculated that, provided Peter accepted the offer, if we borrowed £10,000, we had paid for the stud. Whatever profit was made from the sale of our bungalow in Lambourn would pay for a new bungalow to be erected. The price we offered Peter really was the absolute maximum and, if he refused it, we would have to start looking around all over again. I wouldn't have liked to do that; the stud, which we had already named the Parva Stud in our own minds, would be hard to match. The reason we chose the name was simple. The stud was situated in the heart of the village of Hinton Parva, and we felt Parva as a name kept the association with the village. It helped give us an identity.

We sat and awaited Peter Tozer's reply. It was somewhat nerve-racking, because we wanted the place so badly, and though there was no house, at least there was a caravan that we could move into straight after we had sold 29 Tubbs Farm Close. We simply couldn't afford to raise our price. Peter would have to agree, or we did not have the property. Fortunately, after deliberating about the price for a further week, Peter telephoned and said he agreed to accept our offer. At last things seemed to be really going our way. It now remained for the bungalow to be sold.

This proved easier than either Richard or I could have anticipated. Next morning, as he prepared to leave for work, Richard told me to put our home up for sale with the local agents. He then went off racing for the day, and left me to it. An hour or two later as I stood in the garden, pegging some nappies out on the line, my neighbour Mrs Harris came and stood talking with me, and I told her excitedly about the way our plans were working out. 'All I want now', I said to her, 'is to sell this place'. Her reply was almost un-believable: 'I'll buy it. My mother is getting very old and I was thinking of moving her closer to us. Your bungalow would suit her very well.' 'Sold', I answered confidently. When Richard came home that evening he was more than surprised to discover his wife's hidden talent as a saleswoman! We did not even have to involve the estate agents and that, of course, saved us paying commission.

I sometimes think that, in life, things are either meant to work out, or they aren't: if something is right and the time is right, all the cogs slot neatly into place and the wheels start turning. If something is wrong and the timing incorrect, then nothing seems to work out and there is little one can do except sit back and wait until the right time does arrive. It's true of life in general, and it's true of horses. When a horse isn't right and not ready to race at his best, you cannot hurry the process or change the horse's condition. You just have to wait until he does come right, when all things fit together properly, and the horse romps away with a race. Life, as much as racing, is a glorious uncertainty and things might just as easily have gone the other way for Richard and me at that time. As it happens, the winds blew in our favour for a change.

Time seemed to move very slowly from the moment of selling the bungalow to the April day when we took over our new home . . . if the caravan could be called a home! I moved most of the furniture – we had not acquired very much, in fact, since the bungalow had lots of built-in units – in my small pick-up van, making one journey after another, and leaving only the heavy items to any male help which became available. It took an age, heaving the boxes packed with our possessions. On the other hand, it saved removal fees and that was precious cash saved. Just because it was April, however, did not mean that we were suddenly blessed with mild and clement weather. The snow remained with us throughout most of the winter and lasted into the spring. As we trooped over to Hinton Parva and left behind the warmth of the Lambourn bungalow for the last time, a little nagging doubt began to worry me. Two adults, two small children, one terrier dog and a huge financial undertaking were all to survive under one tiny roof in freezing conditions – for how long, I wondered? It really was freezing hard and snowing yet again as we went to bed for the first time in the caravan. I wrapped the children in extra woollies and coats, whilst Richard and I slept in our overcoats. My mind drifted nostalgically back to my warm bungalow for a few seconds before we finally dropped off, in spite of the cold. My thoughts as I lay there were obvious: we must be bloody mad.

Richard went off to work as usual next morning, leaving me to give the children their breakfast. I'm a firm believer in the Great British Breakfast and we never start the day without a proper meal. Today we all sit around the table in my kitchen at Weathercock House to tuck into egg and bacon – it's like Piccadilly Circus, with jockeys and family taking it in turns to sit and eat. In the cold and tiny caravan, I felt that with a full stomach, my children would at least be warm from the inside! After tidying up – no hoovering and little housework with a small caravan – I put on the children's coats, dressed up warmly myself, and went down to the stables which we now owned.

As I opened the stableyard gate and walked through it, any doubts I might have had vanished into thin air for all time. An overwhelming sense of relief flooded through me as I realized that, no matter what I might have to face in terms of living conditions in a small caravan for the next six months, this was where I needed to be. Nothing else mattered at that moment. We had not made a mistake. Someone had opened the door of my cage and finally set me free . . . it was a blissful feeling. Once again I visualized my horses, their heads watching for me eagerly for their morning feeds. I allowed myself to daydream about the racehorses which would fill the empty boxes just as soon as I could organize it.

It was Richard Pitman's Guv'nor, Fred Winter, who sent us our first injured horse for repair. We had been living at Hinton Parva for less than a month when a big dark gelding arrived, which needed some rest before I could give it some careful work to prepare it for the next jump racing season. I had him for the entire summer, and gradually, by word of mouth, several other horses followed. We never had to advertise our services in the conventional sense, because Richard was constantly moving in racing circles, talking with trainers, and when one trainer was satisfied with the job I'd done on his horse, he would soon spread the word. Quite soon after we began, there was a total of eight horses living in the yard. The dream of filling my stables with racehorses in need of care and attention was slowly becoming a reality.

They weren't all sick horses, however. Realizing that I had endless and enormous patience with horses, some trainers asked me if I would take in their 'rogues' for a few weeks of re-education. Rogue horses, politely known to some as 'characters', are those which have, for one reason or another, gone sour. They have ceased to enjoy racing and need a change of scene and some patient retraining. The hunting field is an ideal place for such retraining, since it is a real day out at the fair for any horse. We also took in young horses to break for other trainers, prior to them starting their racing careers.

Meanwhile, the bungalow which Baker Brothers and Wood & Highnet were building for us was gradually rising out of its foundations, brick by brick. The door and window frames went in, the rafters went up and, lo and behold, a roof was put on. Plasterers busied themselves inside, whilst I continued to try and manage in the caravan. It was not, as you can imagine, an easy undertaking!

The caravan sink had a plug-hole no larger than a little finger, which meant that when the sink was filled to do the washing up, it took an intensely irritating half-hour for the water to drain away! Whilst the sink was emptying I could, of course, clean the caravan inside out and from top to bottom, which was a saving grace from my point of view, since I hate housework in any shape or form. Cooking and preparing food I don't mind quite so much, and I'm a great one for big roast dinners and tasty casseroles, as well as my breakfasts. The fridge and the washing machine had no place in the caravan, since there wasn't an inch of empty space to accommodate them. The fridge was placed outside in the horses' feedroom, with the twin-tub washing machine alongsides. The daily wash, with all the nappies necessary for two young babies, involved my running backwards and forwards between the tiny caravan sink with its somewhat slow and reluctant water supply, a filled bucket of water in each hand, until the machine contained enough water to do the washing. Fortunately, when the April snows vanished, the weather warmed up and the caravan became a healthier place to inhabit and the nappies dried quickly on the line in the June sunshine. However, as summer went by, whilst the nappies dried in about five seconds in the heat, the caravan became a positive bakehouse. Just as it had been an icebox in April, so it became a sweatbox by August. I watched the bungalow's progress with a very keen eye!

At the point where we had eight horses, it became a little difficult to manage both the horses and children on my own. I had all eight living in, which therefore involved me in mucking them out every day, feeding, grooming, keeping their feet picked out, clean and oiled, and all the while attempting to do this with two small babies around. I managed to organize everything by putting Paul's play-pen in the saddle room and letting Mark, then aged about three years, toddle around the yard 'helping' me with various small jobs. It was history repeating itself. At the same age I had toddled about the farm at home with my father, helping him with odds and ends, holding his tilley lamp. Mark, just as I had done, loved helping to measure up the horses' feeds, and even at that age he was a useful addition to the staff of one. He seemed to fit into this new way of life like a hand into a glove.

Richard, meanwhile, was beginning to enjoy considerable success. Between 1970 and his retirement in 1975, he enjoyed his best riding years. He was winning some really big races, on horses which have since become racing legends: Bula, Lanzarote, Killiney, and the mighty Pendil. Killiney was a particularly handsome animal, with a very promising career, and Richard was extremely upset when the horse was killed at Ascot while he was riding it. Most of those horses are gone now . . . Lanzarote broke a leg in the Gold Cup, Bula broke a shoulder, and Pendil suffered from a leg problem, was eventually retired, and now hunts with Bob Champion. But in that five-year period, they were the superstars of National Hunt racing and Richard shared their success with them. As a result, other trainers were clamouring for his services and, as well as his arrangement on a retainer basis for Major Bewicke, he was eventually made Fred Winter's number one stable jockey.

My own days consisted, after Richard had left in the mornings, of feeding the children early, before mucking out, feeding and grooming my stable of eight charges. If they needed a little exercise

I could turn them loose in the big indoor school, where they would be unlikely to injure themselves. It frequently took me the entire morning to muck out the eight boxes, let alone put the beds back down, fill the haynets, make up feeds, and attend to any domestic matters such as shopping and washing. The household tasks were finally relegated to their proper place in my life, and I usually began these tasks at around 7 pm. The horses and my children came first now, and boring matters such as cleaning the oven could conveniently be ignored if I was busy in the stableyard!

By August, just five months after we took over the stud at Hinton Parva, we decided that, with Richard now making good money, and with eight horses in the yard, I could afford to employ my first full-time stable help. For some while I'd had extra assistance during out-of-school hours and in school holidays from two boys, Paul Price and Paul Bentley. It began when I caught them peeping at me from behind the stables – I was younger then, and much slimmer and attractive in my tight jeans and summer T-shirts! The best way to keep them out of mischief, I decided, was to give them a job to do. Firstly I sent them down to the fields, to cut down the unwanted weeds such as thistles, nettles and docks which always flourish on horse grazing, since horses simply will not eat them – though they are quite partial to the soft thistle tops. The boys also cut back the overgrowth around the edges of the fields; both were jobs I had once done for my father, years ago.

In time, the boys progressed to jobs in the stableyard itself, such as filling the water buckets and haynets. When I first gave Paul Bentley a haynet to fill, he was in the hay store for absolutely ages and I thought he must have fallen asleep or had an accident. When I went to investigate, I discovered him trying very diligently to push small handfuls of hay through the sides of the haynet. He had not realized you could untie the long string which runs through the top of a haynet, thus opening it right up. After half an hour, using his method, there was enough hay in the net to feed one rabbit! In return for their labours the lads were allowed to ride the children's ponies, old Rocket and Mandy's show pony Johnny Boy. They loved their rides and worked hard to earn them.

The first full-time stable lad we employed was Melvyn Saddler, who was to stay with us for several years. There was another reason why we could now employ him full time. The bungalow, which we had waited for so patiently throughout the summer, was finally completed and, as we thankfully left the caravan behind for good, Melvyn took up residence there. It was an enormous relief. No more running out to the feedroom for bacon in the mornings. Butter no longer running and melting everywhere, no racing across the yard for a pint of milk late at night. The bungalow was warm in winter, cool in summer. In fact, it was a paradise and our life slotted into a happy routine at last. The only drawback was, of course, that our new home demanded more of my attention than the caravan had done. I was quite determined, however, that under no circumstances would I become a slave to the hoover and the mop once again. The horses were my business, and as such needed to take priority. If I neglected them, the livery side of our business would fail and I'd be back to square one. So I was more than happy to take on Paul Price's mother Joan in the capacity of 'treasure', and as I became busier and busier, she took over more and more of the domestic load. There were three bedrooms, a living room, bathroom and kitchen to cope with, as well as the two boys when they were young, and Joan became indispensable. She was invaluable to me, and it is no exaggeration to say I could never repay her in monetary terms for the way she looked after Mark and Paul when they were small. They loved her in return and, when they were a little older and had begun at Rose Thorn's playschool, they were quite happy if they could go to Joan's house for a few hours after school until I had finished with the horses. In fact, sometimes when I drove up to collect them, they were having such a good time that they hid from me when it was time to go home!

By the August and September of our first year at Hinton Parva, the horses which had arrived in the spring were beginning to recover from their operations, and needed something more each day than a fling in the indoor school. They began to need some proper work and required riding out each day. The 'rogues' I could hunt, taking them out with the Old Berkshire Hounds; I suppose the thought vaguely entered my head that, as well as hunting some of these horses, I could point-to-point them if I wished. Christopher Stevenson and Chris Tregonning brought me two horses: Sheer Courage and Marciano. Christopher Stevenson did not intend me to race the latter, but brought him for me to school for the forthcoming hurdle season, after which he would go into Nick Vigors' yard to race under National Hunt rules. I was delighted when Chris Tregonning suggested that we might, however, point-to-point Sheer Courage. He put into words something which had previously been only a vague idea floating around in my head. I was intrigued by the suggestion, since it would be the first horse since old Dan Archer that I was asked to train for racing. The training career upon which I was then embarking happened, therefore, rather more by accident than by design.

I needed no special licence. Since one can train point-to-pointers from a livery yard, all we had to do was qualify the horses by hunting them with the Old Berkshire Hunt. I started their preparations. Both horses took to their hunting, after some slow roadwork prior to cantering, like ducks to water. I was beginning to get an idea of the thrills involved in being a National Hunt trainer. As a stable lad in my days with Chris Taylor and with Major Champneys, I was unable to ride in point-to-points, but now I was free to train horses for that sport. Point-to-pointing was also, of course, a natural way to bring my previously-ailing horses back into racing slowly and gently, without all the hustle and bustle of a noisy National Hunt meeting.

I was given, at around this time, an ex-racehorse with leg problems called High Tide, swiftly followed by a request, to my delight, to take in a horse for Lord Cadogan. It was a 'character' named Road Race, who had lost all interest in racing. Richard thought, and had suggested to Lord Cadogan, that Road Race might benefit from a spell of hunting, which might work its usual miraculous cure on a sour horse . . . and so it did with Road Race. He became one of my most loyal servants, the foundation stone upon which my professional training career was built. Road Race put me on the long and winding road which led, eventually, to Aintree in 1983. He was everything I would *not* want in a racehorse: long, spindly legs, a club foot, a lanky great body, and the ugliest old face you ever set eyes on. But he had masses of character and, though he was never going to turn into a superstar under National Hunt rules, he was to be a world-beater in the point-to-point field. He was defeated only once in his first season with me, and that was due to inexperience on the part of both his jockey and his trainer.

Having Road Race as well as Sheer Courage and High Tide meant that we could all – Melvyn, Richard and myself – hunt regularly. It was in the hunting field that I first noticed the difference between Richard's attitude to horses and my own. My view of hunting was that the horses benefited from it directly, since it was, for them, a carefree day out with plenty of excitement to refresh them. Their riders, at the same time, could enjoy the day. Richard seemed to think it was the other way around. We, in his book, were out to have a good day and, if the horses gained some benefit, all well and good. His main concern appeared to me to be for his own pleasure, rather than that of the horses. He would, I remember, gallop over grass, jump a hedge, and then gallop over ploughed land. I was not in agreement with this practice; my policy was to gallop over grass, jump the hedge, then pull up and *walk* through the plough. I would never trot or canter a horse through ploughed land, particularly in the wet when the earth became sticky and clinging; 'holding' the horse's legs, it could cause tendon damage. It seemed unwise to risk injuring a horse that had been sent to me for recuperation. Fortunately, it never happened and my worries were to prove groundless. But worry I did, and I made my views clear to Richard.

Meanwhile, I noticed that our reputation with sour and injured racehorses was beginning to grow, and very swiftly I found myself with more horses than stables in which to house them. We put up a further block of four stables at the Parva Stud, which meant two things: firstly, I could now take in an extra four horses, and secondly, I would need to employ more full-time help. Paul Price had left school by this time, and was working alongside Melvyn and me. The yard had grown from eight to 10 in our second year, and now numbered 14. We put an advertisement in *Horse and Hound* for a lad, and that was the start of Bryan Smart, 16-year-old son of a miner from Barnsley in Yorkshire, becoming a National Hunt jockey of some repute.

Bryan arrived one Sunday morning, accompanied by his father, for a trial ride. Such a trial is important, for whilst a lad might work his heart out in the yard at home and keep his horses groomed to perfection, he must be able to ride reasonably well, too. Knowing the lad hadn't been on a racehorse before in his life, I decided against trying him out on one of ours which might have given him a bit of a hard time; so I put him up on Mandy's pony Johnny Boy, to see how he fared. It was like watching a clod-booted farmer trying to join the Royal Ballet. He was, in a word, 'green': an expression we use for a person who sits on a horse like a sack of potatoes. It amused me no end, but there was something about his determination, some element in his trial ride, that made me say 'yes'. I had the feeling that, with the rough edges knocked off, Bryan could become a smooth and talented rider. He had the raw material which I could mould into a jockey.

So now we were four: Melvyn, Paul, Bryan and myself. Whilst I was part-owner of the yard in conjunction with Richard, and to all intents and purposes 'the boss' or 'the Missus', I could never afford to sit back and let the lads do the work alone. It was always a case of all hands on deck. Fourteen horses and four people is still a slightly unbalanced ratio in any case: my lads nowadays have three to do each, which is a handful in itself and requires some effort. We had, if you like, 3.5 horses each to do. Every day was a busy day. The yard was full, winter and summer, and I must say that, during June and July, the months when National Hunt racing does not take place, I rather resented the fact that Richard was not prepared to come and 'muck in' with the rest of us. I sometimes felt that, with time on his hands, he could have knuckled down and helped us with some of the real donkey work. It made me rather cross to come home from the yard after a hard day, to find him sitting in an armchair watching television or reading *The Sporting Life*, when he could quite easily have chopped up some steak for a casserole, or peeled a few potatoes and vegetables and popped a joint of meat in the oven for supper. As it was, I attended to dinner myself.

One night towards the end of the hunting season the telephone rang. We had been riding Road Race, Sheer Courage and High Tide to hounds. Road Race had now, we felt, recovered from his 'ungenerous' moods and was ready to go back into training. The caller was Jimmy James, Road Race's official National Hunt trainer. Richard spoke to him. Jimmy said that he had talked over the horse's future with Lord Cadogan, the owner, and between them they had come to the conclusion that Road Race would not be suitable for steeplechasing any longer. They had agreed to offer me the horse to go point-to-pointing next season. Richard's immediate reaction to the suggestion was a vehement 'no', but I felt differently. The horse might look like a daddy-long-legs, but I wanted him. When he left the yard I'd be left with just two possible racehorses, High Tide and Sheer Courage. This was fine but, as any trainer will tell you, a third horse in a string is invaluable. If one horse should go sick, or suffer an injury and be unable to work, the trainer is still left with two horses. Two horses work together on the gallops better. They are less 'spooky' in each other's company than if alone. A racehorse will work more keenly with the competitive spirit provided by another horse upsides. Two horses bring out a spirit of rivalry in each other and will stretch themselves and work better. With only two point-to-pointers in the yard, I would be pounds worse off if one were sick – since the other would not gallop to his best advantage alone and would therefore be less fit for racing. The third horse could make the world of difference. My argument won the day, and Richard agreed that Road Race should stay with us as a point-to-pointer.

Around this time we were also joined by a mare called Red Biddy. An acquaintance owned the mare originally, and showed her regularly in hunter classes. But the mare always behaved appallingly badly and, on the occasion when Richard drove the mare to a show for the owner, Red Biddy went over the top. It was all the show judge could do to stay on her back, and the mare was put up for sale. Richard, for all the mare's manners, liked her pedigree and her conformation. He offered the owner £750, for which sum we became her owners instead. It meant that, as well as my 'invalids' in convalescence, my 'rogues' in for refresher courses, and my youngsters for breaking, I had several horses who were potential point-to-pointers: Road Race, Sheer Courage, High Tide and Red Biddy.

In the spring of the year following our move to Hinton Parva, I had my first point-to-point runner as a trainer. I entered Road Race for the first division of the open race at Tweseldown on 9 February 1974. It was a momentous day for me. It was the first step forward in a whole new career – though I was not to realize at the time just how important the step would be. On the day, it caused me some concern. Richard was due to ride Pendil at Newbury, the important National Hunt meeting of the day. Normally, whenever possible, I went racing when Richard was riding. It was not just the fear of injury that drove me to accompany him; I cared for him, and loved to watch him win big races on those magical horses of Fred Winter's. Admittedly, injury was always in my mind, and on the occasions when he did fall and hurt himself, I loved him so deeply that I would look at him and wish from the bottom of my heart that I could lie there in his place. That was the depth of my feeling for him. I did not mind how far we had to travel to race or how late we might return at night, I just liked watching him ride, as I now like to watch Mark ride. When Richard was hurt, I was hurt, and wished deeply to take the pain from him and would have gladly suffered to help him.

So I felt all the more deeply wounded when, on the morning of Pendil's Newbury race and the morning of Road Race's first run, Richard rebuked me rather sharply when I ventured to ask what he thought my tactics for the race should be. I felt as if he had slapped me in the face, since I had only asked him the question because he had ridden the horse. I felt like a dog that had been kicked. Looking back, of course, I can see the reasons for Richard's shortness with me. I didn't realize at the time the pressures that riding top class 'chasers was putting on him. Why indeed should he be worrying his head about his wife's runner in a dotty point-to-point when the country's top steeplechaser was due to race and he was its jockey? Somewhat chastened, I loaded Road Race into the lorry we had recently bought. For all that I was hurt, I felt a great sense of achievement to be running my first horse as a trainer. I had already decided that Bryan Smart would have the ride, since his riding had improved out of all recognition in his time at Hinton Parva. We had even sent him show jumping to improve his seat, and he was now deemed a good enough jockey to take the ride on Road Race. Bryan and I set off for Tweseldown with rather mixed feelings.

Every lorry we met on the road seemed to be loaded with horses headed for Newbury. As the name 'Richard Pitman' was emblazoned across the front of our horsebox, everyone driving towards Newbury looked somewhat astonished to see 'Richard Pitman' driving in the opposite direction. It was pouring with rain, too, and turning back and following everyone else to Newbury *did* cross my mind. I said to Bryan: 'We must be completely mad, driving this old horse down to Tweseldown for a race he probably won't win, when we could be in a dry grandstand at Newbury, watching Pendil run'. I wondered, at the time, if Richard was annoyed with me for going off to race elsewhere when he had such an important race. I had covered that possibility the previous day, sending Pendil a telegram which read: 'GOOD LUCK PENDIL. THE MISSUS WOULD HAVE LIKED TO BE THERE, ONLY SHE THOUGHT I WAS MORE IMPORTANT. SIGNED ROAD RACE.' That morning saw one of the first major signs that an element of discord was creeping into our marriage. The feeling was to be heightened later in the day.

Bryan and I didn't turn back, but drove on and arrived at Tweseldown in the heavy rain which continued to fall. I took Bryan to walk the course, giving him the best advice I could on the way to ride Road Race, showing him the drier ground which, if he could find it, would give him the advantage. The rest of the course was a flounder of mud. We saddled the horse and paraded him in the paddock and, for the first time, my nerves began to take a grip on me. They tweaked at my stomach muscles and turned my tummy upside down. It dawned on me, as the horses went to the start and lined up for the race, just what every trainer, of every racehorse, every day, all over the country, has to go through before every race. I discovered just how exciting racing really could be when you had a runner. This was my first and I had trained him and his young jockey. My heart was pounding under my ribs, and I was so keyed up I could almost have galloped round with them. I felt a brief moment of disappointment that Lord Cadogan had been unable to watch his horse run. He had thought I would have enough pressure with my first runner, without an anxious owner peering over my shoulder.

Then, as the flag went up and the horses surged forward to race, I have to admit that Richard, Pendil, Newbury and everything else slipped into the background and vanished from my mind. Road Race went lobbing along with the field and, to my joy, jumped round with every bit of the new zest he had acquired from hunting. There was a red-hot favourite, Sir Kay, whom no one believed would get beaten that day. I was happy enough if the old horse of mine went clear and came home in one piece. To my astonishment, I watched Bryan Smart sitting very still, his hands full of keen horse. The old boy was motoring quietly along like a Rolls Royce, and I realized that Bryan, whose second ride this was in public, was only biding his time.

There is a hill in the centre of Tweseldown racecourse and, in order to watch the entire race, you have to run round the top of it to keep track of the horses. I flew round it at a fantastic pace, watching with growing disbelief. As they turned for home, Sir Kay was leading Road Race by four lengths. As they cleared the second last, Road Race made up two of those lengths and sat menacingly behind the leader. At the last he reduced Sir Kay's lead to half a length. By the time the post arrived, he had caught the leader and had beaten him half a length. My first runner was a winner. It was a golden moment.

In the dying strides of the race, I noticed a man haring along the rails on the opposite side of the track. He was shouting and screaming for my horse and I could only think he must have had a decent wager on Road Race. When the horse won, the man took off his hat and threw it high into the air. It was Richard. Racing had been abandoned at Newbury and he had driven to Tweseldown, arriving just in time to see Road Race win his race. I thought it was a loving and romantic thing for a husband to do . . . but the smile was soon wiped off my face as the Press crowded round us in the winner's enclosure.

I had trained the horse and the jockey, entered them for the race, saddled them for the race and I felt, in some small way, that a little of the credit was my due. However, the Press asked all its questions of Richard, not of me. Nobody seemed to notice my existence. After the incident at breakfast, here was my second disappointment. Richard duly took all the praise. I could have been the stable girl, for all the notice anyone took of me. I thought it would have been nice if Richard had, just once, turned to me and said: 'Here's the trainer, not me'. My disappointment was slightly alleviated when Michael Williams wrote an agreeable piece on the race for *The Sporting Life*, under the heading 'Pendil? My Road Race Comes First, says Jenny'. Someone realized my need for a little pat on the back!

It was the first real evidence that Richard's life and mine were taking slightly different directions. My yard and my horses kept me very satisfied and busy, and possibly I became less deeply involved in Richard's work. But it had to be this way, since I could not immerse myself totally in his life and revolve every second of my day around him. I needed some identity of my own, and if this was causing faint echoes of discontent, it simply could not be helped. I was at last leading the life I truly loved and needed. I knew I could never return to the kitchen sink existence. At the time, I wondered if Richard really understood my needs. In retrospect, of course, I understand that all the good horses he had to ride for Fred Winter, which were always expected to win, must have made him feel

very harassed and probably somewhat overworked. I simply did
not realize it then. I felt sulky about his apparent lack of interest
in my career. I suppose it was a little arrogant of me to think that
the rider of big race winners would have time to spend thinking
about his wife's broken-down or rogue racehorses winning point-
to-points. And yet, I thought then, why shouldn't he, just occasionally, appear to be a little more concerned?

Our marriage was so very different by this time. When I had
married Richard in 1965, he had been my only real boyfriend and
my world revolved around his every move. But that situation could
not realistically be expected to last. Nor, funnily enough, do I think
it would have helped our marriage if I had remained moonstruck.
I would have been unbearable to live with, a clinging vine, and it
would not have saved our marriage. I don't feel that anyone should
submerge their personality and turn their back on things they need
in life. I needed Richard, that was certain, but I also needed something in which to immerse myself, something which was independent of him. I had to be true to myself, and since I had grown up
around horses, they were as much part of my life as breathing,
eating and sleeping. They were all-important in Richard's life too,
but in a different way. I think Richard loved racehorses because they
were sleek, good-looking and fast, like E-type Jaguars. He could
become very interested in some of the old racehorses we had, like
Into View and Larbawn, which had been important steeplechasers
in their day. But he showed very little interest in the veterans like
Road Race – and several other animals which I, who love horses for
their personalities as much as for anything else, had in training over
the next few years.

I felt, in the days before Hinton Parva, that in my relationship
with Richard I had become very much the underdog, and had lost
my personality in the process. I firmly believe that marriage is an
equal partnership in which the wife, even though she may not be
the breadwinner, plays an equally important part as unpaid adminis-
trator of a thousand household tasks, from washing nappies up-
wards. With the endless rotation of thankless tasks, her life could be
compared to the car worker's, who may have an endless stream of
car seat belts to fit from 8 am to 5 pm: the difference being that the
car plant worker can leave the factory at 5 pm, collect his pay packet,
and go home to relax in a fresh environment at the end of the day.
The housewife, on the other hand, may have no wage packet except
her housekeeping, and cannot down tools at 5 pm to disappear into
the pub for an hour of idle chatter with her friends – if she did, there
would be no evening meal prepared, and babies would be screaming
their heads off. The average housewife has no real earnings and no

relief from her routine, and there was no way I could consider subjecting myself to that existence again. Though at this time the question of my giving up horses did not arise, it was to be asked of me at a later date. Quite what Richard expected of me in the Hinton Parva days I'm not sure, since we never really discussed the matter; if there was ever any problem, we tended to gloss over it.

Another aspect, of course, was the financial one, and having a livery business and training horses meant that I had an income of my own and could be independent of Richard's finances. I had always hated my previous lack of personal cash, and loathed having to ask Richard for money every time I needed a pair of shoes for Mark, or some clothes of my own. I was never a big spender, needing fox furs and diamonds, nor have I changed over the years. The money I got from my share of Corbiere's Grand National winnings, for instance, was ploughed back into the business. We had a party or two, drank a few bottles of bubbly, and I treated myself to a necklace and a pair of earrings. The rest went into improvements at home. I saw no reason, in my marriage, for not being an equal partner. And once the Parva Stud became successful and began to pay its way, I was able to make a contribution towards paying off the debts we had incurred. We had borrowed a great deal to buy the stud, and I felt the need to help repay the money to Lord Cadogan.

The Rabbi was an older horse, sent to me after it had been running for several years under rules without success. It had even been tried out in a three-mile selling hurdle race and made little impression. He had never, as they say, been mapped under rules; or, in other words, the horse had never even finished in the first 10, and was therefore not eligible for serious discussion in *The Sporting Life*'s daily results pages. *The Sporting Life* is, of course, the racing world's answer to the *Financial Times*. There were two daily racing papers at one time, but the old *Sporting Chronicle* closed down in 1983, leaving its rival with a clear field. We believe that *The Sporting Life* has most of the answers, and owners, trainers, jockeys, bookies and punters alike scour its pages daily, avidly searching for information. The paper publishes lists of horses declared to run four days hence, and aspiring jockeys can telephone trainers to offer their services. We find detailed form guides for every horse due to run on the day of publication, and there are columns of horses for sale, job vacancies, racing properties, stallions at stud, and much else. It is, above all, a hopeful newspaper. The gloom and despair of the outside world is forgotten as you pick up the paper with its famous green-flagged heading: 'Flying Star Will Get There' it emblazons across the top of the front page. Lower down you might find: 'Green Lord is the Banker Bet', or 'Lambourn Lady Will Be Hard to Beat'. It's littered with hopeful headlines, in contrast with any other daily newspaper you may pick up, although the losses may be forgotten next day when a host of fresh and equally optimistic headlines will cover the front page. The Rabbi had, in the past, failed to make any headway in *The Sporting Life* pages; as little headway as he had made on the racecourse, in fact.

When he arrived, Richard took a rather scathing look at him and remembered instantly that this was the horse with no form. His appearance matched his record. Richard told me, quite categorically, that I was mad to take the horse on and that I would never win a race with That Thing. If you do, he added, I'll eat my hat. The words were, to me, a challenge.

I qualified The Rabbi in the hunting field, so that he could at least run in point-to-points. He was leased to two Welsh gentlemen, both of whom I later discovered to be great gambling men. I entered him for a race at Kingston Blount, and booked Bryan Smart for the ride; whereupon the two Welsh owners produced £500 in cash from their wallets and announced their intention of placing it all on The Rabbi's inelegant old back. I was horrified. 'There's no way the horse can win', I advised them firmly. 'Tell you what, you put £100 on him and give me the other £400, which I'll keep safely in my handbag until the day is over. That way, you won't lose so much.' The horse was hardly worth £500 in the sale ring, let alone as a banker bet!

The two Welshmen placed the first £20 with one bookie, when the horse was still a rank outsider. His form had arrived there ahead of him! By the time they reached the end of the line of bookmakers, placing £20 with each, the horse was favourite. Eventually the runners lined up and the race began. After an entire circuit, Bryan Smart was clear of the field, way out in front. I decided he must have had a brainstorm at making so much use of the horse's energy in its first race with us and, sure enough, at the second last, the field appeared to swamp him and take him over. The Rabbi appeared to be struggling and the race, from our point of view, was over. The Welshmen had not, in retrospect, had a bad run for their £100: the horse had been in front for most of the three miles. I was pleased they had not parted with £500.

It was, therefore, with mixed feelings that I watched, incredulous, as The Rabbi managed, somehow, to hold his own. He looked, in fact, like winning. The Welshmen might not be very pleased! On the other hand, Richard had made that remark about eating his hat, and the vanity in me wanted very much to prove him wrong. However, I had little control over the result and watched with a certain degree of fascination as The Rabbi, who would not be denied his first-ever chance of winning a race, stretched out his neck, put down his head, and battled for the line. He won. I did not know how I would face his owners. However, when I handed them back the £400, with a muttered apology, I was relieved, delighted in fact, to hear their reply: 'Jenny', they said, 'don't worry about the money. We've never had a winning racehorse before in our lives and there's no money could compare with the pleasure you have given us today.' They took off with their £400 unspent betting loot, plus their winnings, and a very big heavy silver cup, all with a great deal of pride and happiness. Without such sporting owners, what would National Hunt racing be?

We drove from Kingston Blount to Hinton Parva laughing our heads off, happy as sandboys that the old horse had finally won a race. I could hardly wait to get out of that horsebox as it pulled into the yard and I ran, flat out, to the bungalow to tell Richard that the no-good Rabbi had broken his duck. As I burst through the door, Richard held up his hand: 'OK', he said, 'you don't need to say anything! You wouldn't come running in here like that to tell me he'd been beaten, would you?' I never did hold him to eating his hat.

There were some owners, from time to time, who tried to persuade me to bring off a betting coup. One day we took a horse to Larkhill, near Salisbury, but the moment I arrived at the course I knew the ground was too hard to jump him, and immediately withdrew him from the race. I didn't want to risk his already-dodgy legs on ground that resembled an iron road. I left him loaded up in the box, and brought out the portable television set which I always carried with me when Richard was riding at a meeting elsewhere. I had the best of both worlds – runners of my own, and watching Richard on television!

The horse's owners were a bit peeved with me for withdrawing their runner. Rather jokingly, they suggested I let him run and just jump the first couple of fences, before pulling up. They would, as bookmakers, take a lot of money on him through their gambling connections, for he was out-and-out favourite and looked unbeatable. They could hardly fail. If I did as they asked, and pulled the horse up, it wouldn't matter a jot to them which horse won, since they'd still have a satchel full of money. I laughed it off, but I was never quite sure if they were entirely serious about the idea. In any event, I was not prepared to comply with their wishes and become involved in such skulduggery. Upon subsequent occasions, when they half-jokingly suggested similar malpractices, I managed to laugh it off every time. Fortunately, they never appeared intent on putting me under real pressure to 'pull' a horse for the wrong reasons, though no doubt they would have been delighted if I'd agreed! They would have cleaned up, and no doubt I'd have been given some sort of financial reward in excess of my prize money – but I would not have been able to live with myself afterwards. Once a trainer succumbs to such pressure, it is very hard for him to turn back. It is understandable, when a yard has gone for weeks without a winner and needs money badly, that a trainer can be persuaded to start 'fiddling' his horses. My horses, however, are trained to *win* races and then, as now, there was no question of starting to try and deliberately lose them.

6
CHANGING TIMES

Whatever Richard thought of my success with the horses in our yard I'm not quite certain, but one thing was for sure: in my first season as a point-to-point trainer, I sent out 14 runners, won nine races, was second twice, and ran unplaced on only three occasions. Road Race was the yard's mainstay and, from that first season right up to the time he ran and won his final race in October 1976, he remained a source of dependability. It was in that final race, at Fontwell Park in the three-mile 'chase, that his funny old legs eventually decided to give out – he had a boxy front foot, a conformation fault, which was always a weakness. Old Peg Leg, our dear daddy-long-legs, was finally put down. He had won us a lot of races, and I loved him dearly. So did the boys. They naturally asked me what had happened to the old fellow. I explained that he had gone to 'Horses' Heaven', which they readily accepted.

I used always to wish that Richard took a greater interest behind the scenes at Hinton Parva. I can see now, looking back, that all his energies were drained by his role as number one stable jockey for the country's top jump racing trainer, but at the time I felt resentful that he appeared to take little interest in the everyday running of the stable. As stable jockey at the Winter yard, he was no longer required to perform duties such as having two horses to do, and quite rightly so, for the jockey may ride perhaps five or six races during an afternoon and hardly needs the added strain of two horses to gallop and muck out in the morning. He would go to the gallops most mornings to school horses that were due for a run, but that was nothing like the hard work of being a stable lad. When I was working very hard myself, I felt annoyed that he would not join in our endeavours. He would be quite happy to ride out occasionally, but would expect the horse to be tacked up, ready and waiting for him to mount, in the same way as his horses at Fred Winter's stables would be ready for him to school.

The following summer served, if anything, to increase the aggravation. After any schooling or other work he might do in the morning, he enjoyed coming home and sitting with his feet up for the afternoon. Since I was working a 12-hour day with the horses, once again I found myself becoming very irritable, resenting

Richard's apparently easy life. I was always the one who made the supper, and usually prepared meals at around lunchtime so there would be less to do in the evenings. Again, in retrospect, I can see that, having worked hard throughout the season, Richard *deserved* a break from horses. These summer afternoons were the only rest he could take all year. I could, perhaps, have shown a more understanding attitude. At the time, however, I was just boiling with resentment and, being me, I never hesitated to let my annoyance show.

On the other hand, I never found it difficult to combine the role of trainer with that of mother and wife. It didn't bother me to get up at 6.30 am, help with the mucking out, and be exercising the first lot by 7.30. Joan Price started coming in to cook breakfast, leaving me free to work in the yard. I hated housework so much that, when I knew there was a job indoors awaiting me, I would stay out in the yard, keeping busy with the horses as long as possible to stave off the evil moment! There always seemed to be enough hours in the day, and with willing help from Joan and my stable lads, I coped very cheerfully with the endless routine that horses demand. They cannot be left to their own devices when you feel ill, since they are shut up in a stable and unable to fend for themselves. You have to get up and go about your duties, sick or otherwise, and only when the horses are fed and comfortable can you afford to relax. But it was a way of life that I truly loved.

The change from livery yard owner to professional trainer began when a young man named Tony Stratton-Smith asked me to take in a horse called Biretta. Tony was a very keen owner, with several horses in training. He was managing director of a company called Charisma Records, and he sponsored a race at Kempton each October, the Charisma Records Chase. It is a race I've often tried to win. Tony knew Richard very well, since they often met at race meetings and on social occasions. Biretta suffered from joint problems, and whilst he had not actually broken down, he required a spell of hunting to help freshen his mind. I duly qualified him for point-to-pointing, but I realized that he was a good horse and would probably win a hunter 'chase. Hunter 'chases are the step between point-to-points and National Hunt races. They are run at National Hunt meetings and under National Hunt rules. They form a natural progression for horses making their way into jump racing proper, and I was certain Biretta was a cut above the average point-to-pointer. I found a suitable race, and, undeterred by the fact that it was at Fakenham, I entered him.

Fakenham racecourse is somewhere off the end of the earth, but I rose to the challenge and drove Biretta to the Norfolk course – I always drove the horsebox in the early days. We left in the small hours of the morning, Bryan Smart and I, in order to be there for the first race, both to give Biretta a rest and so I could watch the other horses run, in order to see how the ground was racing so Bryan would have the best chance. I saddled Biretta, Bryan mounted up, and off they went. Biretta ran a very good race and finished second to a horse ridden by a young man called Joey Newton. Coming over the last fence, however, Joey's horse jumped right across Biretta's path, causing some interference to Biretta's running. At the line, the distance between them was a length and a half. Joey turned to Bryan and apologized for the interference, but in any event I had already decided to lodge an objection to the winner for 'taking our ground'. After an enquiry, the stewards awarded Biretta the race and I received a lovely decanter on behalf of Biretta's absent owner.

Since it was my first runner, let alone winner, at Fakenham, the stewards very graciously invited me to their office afterwards for a celebration drink. Worried about the very long drive home and not really wanting to drink, I would have preferred to decline but felt it discourteous not to accept. I was soon wishing that I had not bothered to be so polite, and gone straight home instead. As a racecourse official handed me a drink and began to offer congratulations, he caught sight of Joey Newton's mother standing behind me. His words of congratulation suddenly stuck in his throat. Mrs Newton was a regular at Fakenham, my horse had taken the race by default, and the official was spluttering with embarrassment. In his confusion he all but withdrew his congratulations and made apologies to Mrs Newton. Disgusted, I put down my drink and left the course for home. It made me feel very cynical. I just wished the man could have had the courage of his convictions, and spoken his words of congratulation with some sincerity. As it turned out, they were hollow and meaningless. I have not willingly taken a horse to Fakenham racecourse since.

I had still, at this stage, not taken out a training licence. I was able to train point-to-pointers from my livery yard without needing a permit from the Jockey Club, the only requirement being that the horse was qualified in the hunting field and could produce a certificate each season. I was still also able to train horses for hunter 'chases, held at most racecourses such as Stratford and Warwick, which gave me a little taste of greater things. Biretta, though by default, was thus my first runner and winner under National Hunt rules, even though I was still not, as yet, a professional. After Biretta's success, however, Tony Stratton-Smith threw down the gauntlet by asking me to take on his horses and train them professionally. This would be, I knew, a major turning point in my career and a move which could affect my marriage, and it therefore required a great deal of thought. There were points for it, and points against it.

Firstly, as a successful point-to-point trainer, I had become a 'big fish' in a small pond, with an excellent first season behind me. Moving into National Hunt racing would suddenly make me a small fish in a very big pond indeed. I would be struggling for survival, as one game is for amateurs, the other for professionals. Whilst I prided myself on turning out my point-to-pointers in a professional manner – for which I was occasionally criticized, incidentally! – I might easily become unhappy in the professional racing world.

On the other hand, would I be happy training point-to-pointers for ever and a day? It seemed I could quite competently take on old has-been racehorses and, with a mixture of patience and knowledge, convert them into winners. I had helped them all to a new lease of life on the racecourse. They weren't aware of the difference between winning at Larkhill and winning at Ascot. Knowing I could win with old rogues, I guessed I could become fairly successful if I started racing good horses. If I refused to take up Tony's challenge now, wouldn't I always regret it? Would I not always be wondering if I might have been capable of better things?

Our personal life was another factor to be taken into consideration. Richard had given me something of a shock one evening when he came home and sat down in the armchair and announced, quite baldly, that he was giving up riding. I was, I recall, doing some ironing at the time. His words hung in the air for a few seconds before they sank into my head. 'Retire?' I asked, 'when you are doing so well?' 'Yes', he replied briefly, 'retire'. Apart from a few minor arguments which I put before him, that was the end of the matter, and in 1975 Richard stopped riding and began life as a BBC television commentator and racing journalist. He had not confided in me his dissatisfaction with life as a jockey but of course the continual strain was taking its toll and stripping the veneer of glamour from his work. Riding endless races, always being expected to win, driving miles between racecourses, schooling horses for Fred Winter on bitterly cold, wet, windy mornings: all had played their part in helping him decide to retire. When he knew that the BBC would accept him as a member of their racing commentary team, it made his decision final.

My training point-to-pointers had been a bone of some contention between us, and it occurred to me that, if I became a professional trainer when he retired, it would cause an even greater rift between us. Instead of training from just February to May (the point-to-point season), I would be busy from early August until late May each and every year. On the other hand, an inner voice said, if the rift is there already, turning down Tony's offer could really do very little to alter things. I hoped that Richard might, with more free time on his hands, play a greater part in training the horses, which might serve to bring us closer together.

Tony Stratton-Smith telephoned me again and gave me a final ultimatum: you have two weeks to decide, Jenny, and come up with a definite answer. I dithered for just a few more days, wondering whether or not to accept the challenge. I'd had a taste of winning. The horses would be working for 10 months each year, instead of just four, and my stable lads would enjoy the life far more. I was bored in the summer sometimes, following my first point-to-point season, when the season ran out and I no longer had runners to train. I missed the stimulation and the special 'high' of training a winner. After just a little further reflection, I made my decision. I would meet this challenge head on. Consequently, Tony brought me Gylippus, another very good horse, in addition to Biretta. And for £300, Richard and I bought a horse called Bonidon which we had seen at the Ascot Sales, where it had failed to make its reserve price.

In order to take out a licence to train these and other horses, I was obliged to travel to the Jockey Club headquarters in Portman Square, London, for an interview. Richard accompanied me as far as the door of the interview room. I was determined that I should undergo the interview alone and obtain a licence on my own merits, not because of my husband's fame as a jockey. I felt it imperative that the venture into training should be mine, and mine alone. Call it foresight if you wish, but I had no desire for anyone other than *me* to become the trainer at the Parva Stud. I remembered my humiliation by the Press at Tweseldown with Road Race, and I did not want any repeat of that in my professional life. This would be Jenny Pitman's training licence, not Richard's.

There was a very long table facing me as I entered the interview room at Portman Square. A thousand would-be trainers had faced this table, I thought, in circumstances similar to my own. I should not be intimidated by either the length of the table, or the officials of the Jockey Club who dealt with trainers' licences. They invited me to sit at one end of the table, at the other end of which sat Piers Ben Gough and other stewards, who began to ask me various questions related to my application to train. Did I, they enquired, have adequate facilities in respect of gallops, stables, accommodation for stable lads? Which horses would I be training? Did I have enough horses to comprise a reasonable racing string? And, most

amusingly, if Richard died, would he leave everything at the Stud
to me in his will? Somewhat taken aback by the last question, I
could only reply as honestly as I knew how: yes, as far as I knew; the
last time Richard had shown me a will, I was his beneficiary. I also
added that he might have changed his mind by now!

The stewards scribbled small notes which they passed to each
other as they sat in judgement of my abilities. I longed to know the
contents of the notes, and wondered what was so private about them
that I should be denied such knowledge. I had always been brought
up to believe that it was impolite to whisper in public, and I felt
that the passing of little notes in front of me was tantamount to
whispering! I thought it slightly unrefined. I was then asked to wait
outside the interview room while the stewards discussed me aloud
and in detail, and I wondered why the little notes had been so
necessary when they could talk all they wished once I was out of
the door. They soon called me back inside: 'Mrs Pitman', they
pronounced grandly, 'it has been agreed unanimously that you
should be granted a licence to train racehorses under Jockey Club
rules, both on the Flat and in National Hunt. We wish you the
very best of luck.' That was the end of the interview and I was dismissed. I had gone into that room feeling 20 inches high. I came
out of it feeling 20 feet tall. I was, officially, a trainer.

There had, in fact, been little doubt in my mind as to the outcome. My season 'between the flags' (as point-to-pointing is sometimes known) had been convincingly successful. Training old Road
Race for Lord Cadogan naturally went in my favour, since the Earl
is a member of the Jockey Club, and a host of friends had sent me
in with good references, including Fred Winter, top trainer of the
day. My only doubt, albeit a faint one, was that few women trainers
had been granted licences at that time, though it would have been
spurious if they had withheld mine on such grounds. Florence
Nagle, who had been training racehorses for years in the names of
her head lads, including her own horse Sandsprite which came
second in the 1937 Derby, had taken the Jockey Club to court. She
won her case, and Lord Denning's verdict was that women should
be allowed to train horses in their own name. Several women trainers
had since taken out licences, including Florence herself, Norah
Willmott, and Auriol Sinclair. They had proved themselves just as
successful as men in the business of training winners.

This, then, was the beginning of my new career. So much had
happened in the few years since that snowy morning when Richard
had read out the advertisement declaring the Parva Stud for sale.
The future looked full of challenges, and as I left the Jockey Club
with that precious piece of paper in my hands, I knew it was another

turning point of my life. There would be lots of ups and downs around the corner, I felt sure, but I was confident I could take pretty well anything that came my way. I was not to know just quite how much trouble and unhappiness I was later to encounter in my personal life, but it would not have deterred me or spoiled that day for me.

I knew about disappointments. I had become used to nursing injured racehorses back to health and patiently coaxing stubbornly puffy tendons down to their normal size, only to discover them swollen up like fat balloons again next morning. Life with race-horses, especially jumpers, is like that. Always, at moments when things seem to be going well, there is a fresh blow waiting to knock you sideways. But what would life be without these highs and lows? I had friends whose most exciting moment each day was painting their toenails red; friends who had only the job of cleaning the oven to divert their boredom. I might not make a million pounds a year, I might never drive a Rolls Royce, but I was so happy. I was a trainer. It was enough.

Bonidon, whom Richard and I had bought for £300, was the first horse to run for me as a licensed trainer under National Hunt rules – at Worcester on 9 August 1975. He was a seven-year-old, a bay gelding by Tacitus, and he was what we call a 'box walker'. He stalked round and round his box for most of the night, and by the time morning came his straw bedding was totally wrecked, chewed to shreds by his constant pacing of a triangular pathway for hours on end. Having read somewhere that a sheep or a goat is a good cure for box walkers, I went out and, for £5, acquired a black and white goat named Nicky whom we put into Bonidon's box. Nicky is, incidentally, still alive and well and living at Weathercock House! I tested the theory carefully, of course. We didn't just toss poor Nicky in with Bonidon and hope for the best. I warned the lads to watch Bonidon's reactions most carefully. But there was no need to worry that he would tear his new companion apart: he loved Nicky, and they soon became inseparable. When my children put Nicky on his lead next morning to take him for a walk and a pick at some greenery, Bonidon went berserk and threatened to jump out after them! He had not walked his box at all. The bedding was almost as good as new. From that moment, everywhere Nicky went, Bonidon wanted to follow.

We quite naturally took the goat to Worcester for Bonny's first run, since we did not want the horse to become upset by his friend's absence. We did not realize that the goat was small enough to squeeze out through the lower half of the stable door. He was very young then, and nimble, and as he made his way towards the racecourse, he evaded all attempts at recapture. He nipped past the security men and tagged onto the tail of the first brown horse he laid eyes on – any brown horse would do, as he didn't know if it was Bonidon or not! He duly toddled along behind the horse and followed it out onto the course, and the first we knew of any of this was the loudspeaker announcement: 'Would Mrs Jenny Pitman please remove her black and white dog from the racecourse since it is in danger of going down to the start with the runners?' Startled, I ran to the weighing room to explain that it was a goat, not a dog, and to apologize for its behaviour. But that wasn't the end of the story. As I flew down to rescue Nicky, I saw that a large, heftily-built gentleman had beaten me to it, and was holding the goat in his arms. The goat, afraid of the stranger, began to scream blue murder at the top of its voice. Goats let out the most blood-curdling noises when in distress, and Nicky was no exception. It was an amusing incident in one sense, though I wanted very badly, since this was my first-ever professional runner, to appear a professional trainer. The goat wasn't exactly helpful in achieving the image I was seeking!

A week or so later, Bonidon became my first winner as a professional licensed trainer. It was also his first winning run, and the occasion of our double celebration was a selling race at Southwell. In a selling race, the winner is put up for auction afterwards to the public at large and some of the proceeds go to the racecourse. We felt Bonidon was worth buying back in for £600. When he won again in September, however, we didn't feel it was worth paying around £800 to buy him back a second time, and we let him go to the highest bidder. Though he was a good horse, he still had his problems, not the least of which were his very bad feet and the foot infections he suffered. I had read somewhere that cow dung was an excellent cure – indeed, I know of people who have used the cure with great success. One or two lads were duly despatched to collect some dung from our fields, where we let our neighbour graze his cows. The dung was mixed with a clay powdery substance and applied, rather like a woman applies a facepack, to the bottom of the horse's feet. My memory frequently returns to an occasion when Bryan Smart and Paul Price disappeared into the night with shovels and buckets to collect the magical cow dung. I was creased up with almost uncontrollable laughter as I listened to their voices in the darkness . . . 'Hang on, Paul, there's a beauty here' . . . 'Watch you don't tread on that one, Bryan' . . . 'Look at this whopper' . . . 'I've found a beauty' . . . 'No, not that one, Paul, that's horse's!'

One of my early horses was owned by a charming gentleman from Swindon called Ken Dale. Ken asked me to look out for a good racehorse, and Richard suggested we buy Stan's Boy, who was being sent from Fred Winter's yard to the Ascot Sales. The horse had suffered an injury, and Richard felt I was just the right person to train him. He was a very well made chestnut, a stayer, a horse who acted on all going, and he became one of my favourites. 'Stan' was a professional racehorse. Once he had recovered from his injury, you could race him every day of the week and he wouldn't turn a hair. He was sensible, reliable, and ran his best race over fences when beating Polly Wall by half a length at Cheltenham. A month later, Stan's Boy pulled up lame in a race at Ascot. He had dislocated a fetlock. I deluded myself that rest would put the problem right, but it didn't. A few days later he was destroyed. I was dreadfully upset, as I always am when losing a horse – it's like losing a friend when one goes from the yard. I couldn't speak about the horse for days, until one of my lads said: 'Never mind, Missus. Old Stan is happy now. He's probably gone hunting.' He nodded his head towards the sky as he spoke. For some reason, the remark seemed logical and I began to get over Stan's loss from that moment. It's odd how an occasional remark can make great sense and help a person get over a crisis.

Biretta, the handsome grey horse which had been instrumental in my becoming a professional trainer in the first place, was another horse for whom I felt great affection, of course. He was bred to *fly*, never mind race. His sire, St Paddy, won the Derby in 1960 ridden by Lester Piggott, and his dam won the Oaks in 1954. He was a horse who liked the top of the ground best, and he won his first race for us, excluding his Fakenham victory 'by default', at Wincanton. I remember him more, in fact, for his range of circus-like tricks than his ability on a racecourse. He drew crowds of admirers, particularly when I had taken him to Fakenham, where the security for the hunter 'chasers was not so tight as for the other horses. When fed a sweet, for example, Biretta would agreeably shake hands with the donor on the premise, I assume, that it would produce another such gift. It usually did, and he was often to be found very gently shaking hands with a bevy of youngsters, who were only too happy to part with sweets in exchange for the chance to shake a real racehorse by the hand!

Gylippus, Tony Stratton-Smith's other horse, was, of course, my first-ever real Grand National hope. I was convinced that this horse had the talent to win the great race. I had grown up with the Grand National, listening to it on the radio in my childhood, and later watching it on television as 'progress' caught up with our household. As I grew older, it dawned on me that this was the ultimate race for anyone to win, whether they were a jockey or a trainer. As the years went by, and I began riding racehorses myself, and

Jenny Harvey, aged seven.

My father, George Harvey.

With my first pony, Timmy.

Grandad Pitman.

Below: Josie Hooley (right) and me at Bishop's Cleeve.

Below right: With Clouded Lamp – who played an important role in my first meeting with Richard Pitman!   *Berrow's Newspapers*

Our wedding day, 2 October 1965.

Below: Road Race (right), the first
point–to–point winner I trained.

Frank H. Meads

Left: Paul with Rocket.

Below: My sons Paul (front) and Mark.
Gerry Cranham

Opposite above: Training in the indoor school at Hinton Parva. *Gerry Cranham*

Opposite below: With Nicky the goat at Weathercock House. *Daily Mail*

Top: Roll of Drums (right) in action at Worcester, when he won the last leg of my first treble in 1981. *Selwyn Photos*

Above: My son Mark (centre), aged 16, on Artistic Prince at Cheltenham during his first-ever race at that course. *Kris Photography*

Left: Making a wish in the eye of the White Horse at Uffington before the 1982 Grand National . . . though I had to wait a year for my wish to come true. *Daily Mail*

Top: My three 1983 National hopes (left to right): Corbiere, Monty Python and Artistic Prince. *B.Thomas*

Above: Corbiere jumps Becher's, Grand National 1983. *Kenneth Bright*

Right: Corbiere clears the last. *Kenneth Bright*

Corky comes home, with (left to right): Paul, David and Mark. *Gerry Cranham*

Celebrating Corbiere's victory (left to right): Mark, Mandy, Dad, Mum and Paul.
Gerry Cranham

eventually training them, the idea took hold that I should make every effort to win this race one day. By the time I received my professional training licence, the idea had become a burning ambition, and Gylippus was, in no small way, responsible for bringing me a step closer to achieving that aim.

He was seven years old when Tony Stratton-Smith brought him, a chestnut by Spartan General, to my yard. Out of an aptly named mare called Rainbow Battle, he was a very useful animal indeed. He won at Sandown, Worcester, and at Leicester, where he beat a horse called Hinterland by no less than 25 lengths! He was nicely-made, and a good racehorse; and he helped make my first season as a fully-fledged trainer a successful one. He came very close, towards the latter part of that first season, to winning the Welsh National at Chepstow in February 1976. He looked all over the winner approaching the last fence, only to take a nose dive as he landed. I hardly need mention the feelings we all had at that moment: a mixture of disappointment, horror, disbelief, and hope that no one was hurt.

Gylippus was unplaced only twice in 11 outings, winning three races, coming second three times, and third on other occasions. He was a really good servant and helped my training career get off the ground in no uncertain terms. He was a cracking good stamp of a 'chaser, tough and genuine, who went on any going and stayed for ever and beyond. His character and his racing ability were not unlike those of Corbiere, in fact, both horses being tough cookies. Gylippus had the same habit as Corbiere of coming out of his stable every morning at about a hundred miles an hour!

He became very cute at whipping round unexpectedly in the mornings on the gallops, and dropping his lads swiftly out the side door. Since we fine anyone who falls off on the gallops a traditional sum of £1, which goes into a Christmas spending pool for the lads, Gylippus' antics were hardly desirable. But the lads grew wise to the trick, and learned to land on their feet instead of falling off head first. Many a time did Paul Price, Gylippus' regular lad, fall off, land feet first, and nip back on board again before anyone saw him, so that he escaped paying his £1 forfeit!

Another of Gylippus' tricks at home included a Houdini act from his stable. He learned to play with the bolts on his stable doors until they worked loose, whereupon he swiftly let himself out. One particular night, shortly after we had moved to Upper Lambourn, he was not content with merely escaping from the stable. He dug up the rosebeds as well. They were pretty roses, actually, which I had bought at considerable expense from a local garden centre, and planted in alternate colours – one red rose, one blue rose, to match

85

my racing colours. They made an attractive border to the flowerbeds in the yard and I was pleased with my artistic handiwork. The roses were not in bloom when I planted them, but this made no odds to Gylippus.

He escaped at the dead of night from his box and had a wonderful leisurely game, ripping the plants up and scattering them like a well-trained vandal from one end of the yard to the other. Bryan Smart and Paul Price were speechless when they awoke next morning and saw the evidence of his wanton destruction. The horse was running about loose and the rosebeds were in ruins. What on earth, they said to each other, would the Missus say to this new act of villainy? Together they decided to try and patch up the rosebeds as best they could, and hope it would go unnoticed. It did, in fact, although it took them a long time to do the replanting, and I bawled them out for being so slow at pulling out in the morning. I like the first string on its way by 7.30 am, and this particular morning it was 7.45 before they got going, and as a result they had their heads chewed off by the trainer.

I had no clue as to what had happened, since the yard looked perfectly normal. It was some months later, in the early summer when the roses began to bloom, that I noticed my colour scheme had not worked out as planned. Instead of red roses alternating with blue roses, it was a mish-mash of red and blue, bearing no resemblance to my original design. I took a careful look round the entire flowerbed before exploding with fury. I aimed my remarks initially at the garden centre which had sold me the roses before Bryan and Paul, sniggering a little and shuffling their feet in an embarrassed manner, told me the truth.

Although Gylippus had met with some problems during his second season at Hinton Parva, he returned admirably to form as a 10-year-old, winning handicap steeplechases at Warwick, where he beat Majestic Touch, and at Stratford, where he beat Game Gentleman very decisively.

Dorothy Squires, the extrovert singer, had three racehorses in training with me in the early days. There was Esban, Norwegian Flag, and an old rogue called Walberswick, otherwise known as a 'character'.

Esban was a very nice old grey and had always been forced to make the running in races prior to joining my yard. He was 12 years old, a sound type of jumper, and he would run a good race on any type of ground. We ran him in the Crudwell Cup at Warwick in March 1976, and his jockey and I discussed the race on the way to the meeting. Aly Branford was riding the horse, and I instructed him to keep Esban settled in *behind* the field, and to take no notice of any instructions he might receive from Dot. For some reason she liked him in front, but I was certain he was best 'covered up' and then brought with a late run. Aly duly did as I had asked. Esban tucked up in the field, and went on when asked to win from Clonmellon by eight lengths! It was a three and a half mile handicap 'chase, a good race to have won: among the horses behind Esban that day was Rubstic, who went on to win a Grand National. Dot was absolutely delighted and ran down to greet her horse with arms outstretched, heaping praise on all concerned. It was the first time I had witnessed the lady in full flight! She was demonstrative, to say the least, whether she was very pleased about something, or very cross.

We did not have the same success with Norwegian Flag, a tremendously brave old horse which met a most unhappy ending at Sandown where he broke his back and had to be destroyed – one of the few times I have lost a horse in a race. It really was dreadfully sad, and his poor jockey, Bryan Smart, took a terrible fall and smashed his nose almost flat against his face. As well as the dreadful business of seeing Flag killed, and having him destroyed and removed from the course, there was the matter of getting Bryan's face repaired as soon as possible.

We took him to the local hospital first where, after a lengthy wait, they referred us to Oxford Hospital. It was dark by that time, I'd only one headlight working on my car, and I certainly didn't relish the long drive with a quite badly injured jockey on board. But there was no choice. Paul Price, Norwegian Flag's lad, was with me, fortunately, to help. We drove flat out for Oxford and, of course, were stopped by the police for driving with one headlight. We were detained only briefly, however; when they saw Bryan's face covered in blood and his nose almost flat, they let us go with a caution. After more waiting at Oxford Hospital, Bryan was told by the doctors that, since he was a jockey, the nose was best left to heal itself. The chances were that it would probably be smashed up again in future falls, and they suggested he waited until the end of the season before having it put right. Since by that time it was very late we collected a Chinese meal on our way back to Lambourn, but the sight of Bryan's face and the memory of Norwegian Flag's death was enough. We couldn't eat a mouthful.

Norwegian Flag's demise was a particularly sad loss for the yard, since he had had problems when he arrived in my yard. I had spent a long time getting him sound enough to race, and Sandown was his first reappearance on a course. The accident wasn't even his fault. Castle Gay fell directly in front of him and brought him down, which in itself would not have been too serious, but the horse jumping behind landed on his back and broke it.

When Flag was killed, and Esban retired – his legs were showing signs of very great strain – Dot was left with just Walberswick. He was amazing. He was such a total rogue that he would run practically anywhere on the racecourse provided he did not actually have to pass the winning post in front of another horse. He put even my patience to the test, but I did not take his attitude to racing personally – he had already been with David Nicholson, and Pat Butler and Marshalla Salaman were two other trainers who tried to persuade him to win a race between 1975 and 1979. He eventually won for me at Cheltenham, though more by accident than by design on his part. He would certainly have taken evasive action had he known he was going to win, and would have carted his jockey off elsewhere to avoid it. He was a very strong gelding, and a difficult ride for any jockey.

Against this backdrop of triumph, however, a human tragedy was about to be staged. In the summer of 1976, Richard and I decided upon a trial separation. During May of that year, we were getting along very badly. Richard was not riding, nor did he seem very happy. He packed a few of his belongings and left Hinton Parva to live for three months with his mother. I did not want him to leave, and I could not understand how we had reached this stage in our marriage. I still loved him, but I was beginning to wish that I didn't.

7
ANOTHER TRY

After Richard's departure, I was left to carry on alone at Hinton
Parva. I was very unhappy with the situation between Richard and
me, but I could do little about it. Since retiring from racing, he
seemed to prefer to spend his newly-acquired free time out with
friends in the evenings, or playing squash in the afternoons. It hurt
me that he seemed to prefer the company of others to that of his
wife and children. If I hadn't loved him so much, of course, it
would not have bothered me.

By this time Mark and Paul were day boys at a school called Pinewood. It was fortunate that they had not yet started boarding, for I
should have felt very lonely without them around. As it was, once
they were in bed for the night, the evenings stretching ahead of me
seemed long and empty. The boys were naturally deeply upset
when their father left home, but I don't think that they were particularly surprised. We had been quarrelling constantly over all
manner of things. Since he left, at least it had been peaceful . . . I
could hardly quarrel alone! I used to wonder, as I lay in bed alone
at night, where I had gone wrong with Richard and what, if anything, I could possibly do about it.

A common cause of our arguments had been money, as is so
often the case in marriage. I had never been used to a lot of money
and had an in-built sense of caution when it came to spending.
When Richard and I were younger and newly married, we had been
forced to be extremely careful about what we spent, since we had
borrowed so much and earned so little. When he began to make a
lot of money from riding, he naturally became more lax about his
spending – which was fine, since it was his money and there was
plenty of it. But when he retired from racing and ceased to earn the
big fees and prize money, he didn't seem to realize and carried on
spending as before. It worried me and I nagged him constantly to be
careful. It was a natural cause of combustion between us and the
balloon always went up when I broached the subject.

From that point of view, it was better we were apart. For the boys
to witness these rows was not pleasant. It was not advisable for them
to watch their parents' marriage falling apart before their eyes, and
I thought the separation might help. It would give us both time to

think things over, and we might be able to meet halfway and solve the problems. Though I missed Richard desperately, and hated my long lonely evenings, I knew it was for the best. When you row with a person long enough and often enough, there comes a point when you dread that person walking through the door. You wonder how many minutes will pass before another row starts. Our marriage was at boiling point and needed a few months cooling-down time.

We were still communicating and Richard telephoned regularly to see how we were. I was able to telephone and speak to him when *I* had a problem, usually with the boys. And when I suggested that we put the Parva Stud up for sale, in order that if we were ever reunited we could start somewhere afresh, Richard agreed. So the Stud went on the market for £40,000 and it was bought almost immediately by Paul Cook the jockey. Richard and I continued talking but could not, however hard we tried, manage to find any sort of compromise. After we had spent a few weeks apart, I began to adjust to my new situation. Richard presumably was adjusting, too, and we decided to make our separation a permanent one. The proceeds of the sale of the Parva Stud, we agreed, would be split equally between us. This meant that I had £20,000 with which to face the future on my own, and I began to seek a new home for the boys and myself, where I could carry on training.

One of our main problems at Hinton Parva, as our yard grew larger, was the distance between ourselves and the gallops at Baydon which we needed to use almost every day. When I had eight horses, it was fine to box them up to the gallops in our lorry, four at a time, in two lots. When the stables grew to 14 horses, however, it was a hair-raising problem. Even before Richard and I had separated, we had in any event been talking in terms of moving closer to Lambourn. The care of the horses still, quite naturally, fell to me, since although Richard and I owned the Parva Stud business jointly, in essence it was mine; I held the licence and trained the horses. However, though he was no longer living with us, he was still a partner in business.

I searched the area around Lambourn for several weeks, finally settling for a pleasant but somewhat dilapidated old white building called Weathercock House, which had once been a pub, in the tiny community of Upper Lambourn, a mile or so from the main village of Lambourn. When I say dilapidated, I mean it. The floors needed pulling up, whatever plaster was left on the walls needed stripping, and in fact the house had once been twice its present size. One half had fallen down some 300 years before, and the rest looked like following suit! There was a general consensus of opinion among my friends that I could have gone for something a little sounder had I looked further. But I liked Weathercock House, with its old beamed walls; and the stableyard, though overgrown and run down, had potential. It would have been even better if I'd been able to buy some land, too, but properties with adjoining land in the area were well beyond my pocket. As it was, I would have to wheel and deal a bit to find the money for Weathercock House.

The house was on the market at around £30,000. I knew that if I went back yet again to our faithful old Ramsbury Building Society and borrowed £10,000 from them, and added my own £20,000, I could buy the house and stables and nothing more. There would be no money left for renovation work, or to improve the yard. My first move was, therefore, to get a loan agreed. The £10,000 was duly granted and I returned to Simon Morant, owner of Weathercock House, with an over-optimistic offer of £18,000 for the property. When I telephoned the agents the following day to see if Simon had accepted the offer, they laughingly announced that he had been rushed off to Swindon Hospital and was now in intensive care, so shocked was he at my low offer for his house! Simon later accepted a more realistic offer of £25,000. I could not have gone a penny higher.

I moved, alone, into Weathercock House in September 1976. Though Richard continued to telephone, and even came to take me out to lunch occasionally, we still could not reach a compromise. But I was unhappy living alone; I wanted him home, make no mistake. It was his practice, every third Sunday, to take Mark and Paul out for the day. When the children went and I was left totally alone with my Sunday lunch, I felt most dreadfully depressed. I didn't try and stop them going, which would have been grossly unfair: Richard was their father and, whatever was wrong between the two of us, they still needed him. He was still their Dad. I found, however, that for two or three days after they had been out with him, they were unsettled at home. They would then return to normal, but it showed me just how much they still needed him and cared for him. It was sad. They missed him deeply, and so did I.

Today, looking back over the years at what happened to the marriage I cared for so deeply, I cannot but feel a sense of betrayal by the Catholic church. Throughout the early part of my marriage, before things had begun to go wrong between us, we had been regular churchgoers, attending every Sunday without fail. I felt the church would assist me to become a better person. I thought it would help me to be nicer to other people, and thereby improve myself. I devoted myself to the faith, confessed my various sins, such as they were, and generally felt myself a good Catholic. Thus, I felt dreadfully deluded about the fact that, when Richard and I first began to drift apart and ceased going to church together, no one from the Catholic church approached us to see if we had any problems. I feel someone should have noticed our absence and made an effort to ascertain the reasons behind it. I felt they had let me down.

Even when Richard and I actually separated, still no one from the Catholic church came to help us. Part of my instruction from the priest before my marriage had included the belief held by the church that marriage is totally inviolate; that, unless special dispensation were granted by the Pope in Rome – as in the case of Prince and Princess Michael of Kent in 1983 – then my marriage to Richard was for all time. Divorce did not exist, I had been told. Without this special dispensation, for all that Richard and I might have legal documents to declare the end of our marriage, and might even marry different partners, the Catholic church still regarded us as married to each other.

I was all the more shocked when Richard, having left me, began taking a new girlfriend to Catholic church social functions. The church knew he was still married to me; yet they not only accepted him into their social affairs, but went a step further and asked him to act as chairman for some of the quiz games they held. I wonder to this day how Richard could have thus been acceptable to the church when he was still my husband. I found such double standards inexplicable and, when a church as unbending and strict as the Catholic one did not practise its own preaching, it made me dreadfully sad. I no longer attend the Catholic church, since they have let me down. Yet I cannot go to the Church of England, because I rejected their beliefs in order to marry Richard Pitman. It is a problem which, privately, I find difficult to resolve and leaves me with a dilemma to which I have yet to find the answer. Where shall I lie when I'm dead? I can no longer be buried as a Catholic, as I no longer practise my faith. I am no longer Church of England. What is left? Cremation? It's a solution, though one of which I am not at all fond. One day, somehow, perhaps an answer might be provided.

On the other hand, religious matters have occasionally caused me certain amusement. Mark was frequently letting us down in church as a little boy and caused a great deal of giggling in the vicinity of the Pitman family on the day the priest faced the congregation and blessed wine in the chalice containing the Holy wine. Mark's young voice piped up, loud and clear for the entire congregation to hear: 'Mum, that's champagne, isn't it? You always drink champagne from a cup like that at home, don't you?'

There are aspects of the church which I miss, not the least of these being the confessional. I found it a help to be able to go to God and apologize for such sins as I committed. Perhaps my worst sin is being unfair on people. Today, I usually find that an apology to the person concerned is almost as cleansing for my soul. I try and adopt my father's philosophy: God is in the life you lead and all about you. I still believe in God, and on occasions in my life have had evidence that some power from outside exists. Once, as a child, the plough fell on my father. I was only very small at the time, and Dad, in pain and unable to move, begged me to go and fetch Mother. Tiny though I was, I bent forward and lifted the plough off my father as if it were a Dinky toy. God, quite literally, is alone in knowing where my strength came from. I could not lift a plough single-handed today, since it would have weighed about 15 hundred-weight. Then, it was as though it were made of plastic and not steel and iron; it weighed nothing at that moment. Dad's arm may have been saved; certainly injury was minimal.

I do recall Richard, however, putting things very much in perspective a long time before our separation, at a time when I would not have believed divorce possible. His words remain in my head to this very day: 'Jenny, you think that when we die we are all going to Heaven to spend Eternity together all holding hands. I've news for you. It's not like that.' I was shattered and puzzled by his words. Today, I know he was right.

The world at large came to know of our problems shortly after Richard had taken me to a retirement dinner in honour of Bill Shoe-mark in Marlborough, when one of the national newspapers published the story: the Pitmans were separated. There was still no word from my own church although, strangely enough, a Church of England vicar, who had read of our separation in the Press, wrote to me and suggested himself as 'middle man'. He offered to try and bring us back together. Richard agreed to meet him, and as I sat and listened to the conversation, I became more and more bothered. It was still Jenny, not Richard, who would have to make all the adjustments if the marriage was to succeed, it seemed. There was no mention of Richard making any adjustments. For one thing, he wanted me to give up training the horses!

I had not actually made the move to Weathercock House at the time, though contracts had been exchanged, and I was still living at Hinton Parva. There were many reasons why I was not able to give up training, not the least of which were the financial considerations. The yard was paying for itself, and giving us a living. Richard's writing commissions were not adequate to keep a family of four, and he was not getting a lot of regular work from the BBC since it was still summer, and his role was commentating on jump racing, the winter sport. The other reason for my reluctance to give up training went far deeper. If I stopped, I would have burned all my boats. If I sold the horses, gave up my way of life, I would be back where I started. I would become, once again, totally dependent upon Richard for everything, including money. I had no wish ever to depend on one person again for as long as I lived. I had grown up; I was no longer the lovesick stable girl. I did love Richard, very deeply, but I knew enough to realize that if I gave up training and our marriage *still* didn't work, I'd be left high and dry with nothing in my life at all. During our separation, the horses had given me something to hang on to. They had provided a purpose in daily life. They and the children were something to live for, and once the children had gone off to school, the horses kept me occupied; they had been my salvation.

I suppose when I first married I still tended to believe in the romantic old notions one reads in books. I thought if you loved someone enough, it overcame all your problems. The disillusionment I was facing now, therefore, was pretty terrible. I realized love does not conquer all, and began to see how many different kinds of love there are. The love you have for your parents, or the love for your children, is different to the love for your husband and, for me, that love was both passionate and painful. Very painful.

I was particularly vulnerable to verbal outbursts from Richard. I always felt that if he had knocked me black and blue, I could at least have fought back! But words I had no real answer to, and the words we exchanged in our most serious rows remained with me for days, longer than bruises. I didn't harbour a grudge, or throw those words back at him days later, but the pain they caused would lie just beneath the surface and, at moments when I was alone, they would rise up and come back at me. The painful things that were said had a lasting effect and I'm only thankful that the boys were still too young to understand. I believe that in the case of most marriages which end unhappily, it is the words that linger and hurt most in later years.

The love I have for David, all these years later, is so totally different. We enjoy a mature relationship; we are secure and confident together. We are a team and I know I can rely totally on his support. If we begin an argument or a heated discussion, he senses it immediately and will change his tone to take the sting out of the words. Because he has this great ability to keep our relationship a peaceful one, I never feel he is goading or provoking me.

But when Richard and I were discussing our reunion, the old resentments arose. He could not see that, much as I loved him, I could not give up the horses. It was not the cause of our real problems, and the horses weren't relevant to our marital problems. If I gave them up, I could see Richard becoming more involved in his commentary work, taking on more writing commissions as time went by, and leaving me to my own devices once again. I could very easily be back to the 29 Tubbs Farm Close days: frustrated, bored, and back on tranquillizers. My solution to the problem, therefore, was that Richard should become more involved in the yard. But he didn't agree with me. I believe, looking back, that he felt it was too much *my* yard, and that he wouldn't be an equal partner in the running of it. Perhaps he saw himself as working *for* me, and not *with* me. He was unwilling to help me train, because he saw himself in the role of my assistant. I saw us only as a team, working together for the same end, as David and I do today. It seemed logical to me, and I simply couldn't understand why he felt otherwise.

However, for all this, we decided that we would give our marriage another try. The Church of England vicar persuaded Richard to return home, and my husband went to Mark and Paul to tell them of his decision. He said he was sorry for what had happened, what they had been put through, and how they had been hurt. He promised that it would not happen again and they, being children, cried with relief that Dad was coming back again. I was pleased for them, and only hoped Richard could keep the promises he was now making to the boys. I was concerned not for myself, but for them. Even when he returned, some six weeks after we had moved into Weathercock House, I still had a feeling – which I took great care to keep well hidden from both Richard and the boys – that somehow it would not work. Nothing had really changed. But I was prepared to try, because I wanted my marriage to work. Maybe things might change. I was not going to stand in the way of any efforts Richard might make.

Since the house was diabolical when we saw it, and not much better when we moved in, Richard agreed to plunge what was left of his £20,000 from the Parva Stud sale into the renovation work. The house needed it, desperately, and I watched the builders work all the hours God sent to make sure the roof was fixed back on in time for Christmas. Everyone worked like slaves so that we could spend our Christmas together, a family once more, in warmth and comfort. To begin with, it was idyllic.

Before Richard's return, I had advertised for a housekeeper. Judy Trout joined me, and Bryan Smart took up temporary residence in the spare room to help fight off any intruders who might break in. The boys had begun to board at Pinewood, since they were growing up, and being away from home would not harm them. Judy continued to live in after Richard's return, though Bryan vacated the spare room and went to live outside in the caravan. Bryan and Judy were good friends to me at that time, and would be invaluable again to me later on, when Richard eventually left us for good.

The horror story that was Weathercock House was gradually transformed. The fencing was erected, the family of rats which had inhabited the house was banished, and the stables and yard were cleared of their waist-high weeds and nettles. The yard had had no drainage at all and became a quagmire whenever it rained. The water didn't actually run into the stables, but I had always been worried, just in case. The house's old beams were cleaned up and restained dark, the outside walls were painted contrasting white. Inside, we put down carpets, papered and painted, and with some help from John Francome's father Norman, and Baker Brothers from Lambourn, it became a home. It proved wrong all the pundits who'd criticized me for buying such a wreck. I recalled Tony Stratton-Smith's very amused reactions upon inspecting it: 'Jenny', he had joked, 'I think you're very brave to live here. Wouldn't you be a lot better off sleeping out in one of the stables with the horses? They'll be a lot safer and warmer than you!' I also remembered Frank Archer's contrasting words: 'Even if the building falls down tomorrow, you've got a building plot worth £25,000'. The value of the land alone would have repaid all my debts.

When Richard returned home, full of good intentions, he took me to a sale of household effects at Cheltenham, and bought me a range of built-in wardrobes of lovely old wood which he wanted me to have. They are beautiful and I still have them today. We started trying to pick up the threads of our marriage where we had left off in the summer, though somehow I felt things could never be quite the same as before. I never felt totally off-guard with Richard again, and I was never really relaxed and happy after his return. I still had a nagging feeling that somehow nothing was going to alter, much as I wanted it to. I knew, deep down in my heart, that I had begun to recover from the shock of our first separation. I had learned to adjust to life without Richard in the end, and was now very wary of putting myself once more in a position where I could be hurt again. However, I did not wish to face the desperation of loneliness again and I was constantly watching for signs that it all might be going wrong once more.

There was nothing I wanted more than for the Pitmans to be one big happy family once again. I wanted us to be normal, loving, squabbling occasionally as do all caring families, enjoying lots of laughter. But from time to time a small event would set off a warning bell in my mind. Nothing specific, nothing I could really put my finger on; but the odd impression, from an occasional remark, gave me doubts. For one whole year I tried everything I knew to restore that old magic and to hold things together, but somehow, once again, my faith in our relationship began to waiver. The more I felt the disillusionment returning, the more I withdrew into myself, putting distance between me and Richard. I did not wish to be hurt again, but I had once made a vow before God that in marrying Richard I would stand by him through thick and thin. Marriage vows are to me most sacred and I did not wish to break them. They weren't made lightly, only to be broken when, after 10 years, the thing wasn't working as wonderfully well as we had hoped. How *could* they just be shrugged off and kicked into touch?

A few days before Christmas 1977, we arranged to go to the Jockeys' Annual Christmas Dance, held at Newbury racecourse. We were to go in a crowd: Richard and me, Bryan Smart and his regular girlfriend Debbie, as well as the owners of a horse called Canit, Keith and David Stait, and their wives. The day before the dance, however, Richard and I finally parted. He left Weathercock House for good. It was a saddening moment, but I suppose I had been expecting it. I believed in marriage, particularly in mine to Richard, but my belief had been proved misplaced and, as I watched Richard's departure from an upstairs window, I knew he would not come back again.

Nevertheless, I had no desire to appear before the racing world as a crumbling wreck of a woman whose husband had walked out, and resolved to dress up and attend the Jockeys' Dance as though nothing had happened. I put on a brave face, which covered a multitude of feelings. Surprisingly, especially for me, I enjoyed the evening very much indeed!

Then, the day before Christmas, a new blow fell. Bryan Smart and I were mixing the horses' evening feeds when I felt a sudden and searing pain in my right side. It took my breath away and I sat down on a nearby feed sack to try and recover, but the pain wouldn't go. I left Bryan to finish the feeds alone and staggered painfully indoors, and crept up the stairs where I managed to crawl into bed. I hoped the pain would subside of its own accord, and swallowed two paracetamol tablets to try and kill it. Still the pain would not go. If anything, it became worse.

By 7.30 I was almost screaming out loud with pain. I heard Bryan come in downstairs, and began banging desperately on the bedroom floor to attract his attention. He rushed upstairs, and took one look before telephoning the doctor. I didn't hear his conversation with the doctor, but a few moments later he returned to my room carrying a blue Milk of Magnesia bottle. I promptly told Bryan what he could do with the Milk of Magnesia, and asked him to ring the doctor again so I could speak to him myself. This was no ordinary stomach ache, I could tell, and the doctor, though he may have secretly thought I'd started my Christmas celebrations a little too early, nonetheless agreed to come out to me.

Dr Osmond arrived at 8.45 pm, and instantly diagnosed appendicitis. Surely, I thought, my appendix could have chosen a better time to become acutely inflamed, and I begged the doctor for some sort of potion to dispel the problem until Christmas was over. He laughed, and pointed out that unless I went into hospital straight away, I would probably die right there in bed. That pulled me up sharply!

The doctor telephoned for an ambulance and I heard him say to the surgeon: 'I've got Jenny Pitman here, the racing trainer. She says she has got more than the usual type of gutsache! I'm sending her straight in!' He went to tell the children, who'd just come home for the holidays, that I was being rushed off to hospital, whilst Bryan went off to the pub to find Judy. When she returned I asked her to pack me a suitcase with the things I would require in hospital, and I lay and awaited the ambulance. When it arrived, the ambulancemen made me laugh: 'Next time you get a pain like this', they said, 'lie down on the settee and not the bed. That way, we don't have to carry you down the stairs!' By the time the ambulance drew out of Weathercock House with its lights flashing, most of Lambourn was vibrating with the rumour that Richard had left and I had tried to commit suicide! I sent a message back, when Bryan relayed the rumour to me, that I was sorry to disappoint anyone, but I would be back. My sister Jackie, as soon as she knew that I was ill, packed her family and their Christmas presents into the car and drove down to Upper Lambourn to look after Mark and Paul. I knew they would be taken good care of.

We eventually arrived at the hospital at 11 pm on Christmas Eve, and I was given two choices. I could leave the operation until the morning when the pain might have subsided, though that was unlikely; or I could have an operation right there, practically on the spot. I plumped for on-the-spot surgery, since I was in bloody agony and wanted to get it over and done with. The sooner the operation was performed, the sooner I would be out and about again.

My pre-med. injection didn't work particularly well, since there wasn't much time to leave me lying around with an appendix that could burst at any second. As I was wheeled down to the operating theatre, I recall noticing tiles missing from the ceilings of the long corridors and wondered why a hospital was allowed to have missing tiles . . . most unhygienic, I thought dopily. The first person I saw in the operating theatre was a gentleman dressed from head to foot in regulation hospital green. My mind was beginning to go: I found myself wondering if he was the cleaner. He noticed I was still awake and began to chat with me. I felt a brief prick in the back of my hand and, defiant to the end, said I still didn't feel sleepy. 'What horses do you have in training at the moment?' he asked me. Lord Gulliver had arrived in my yard and was showing great promise, and as I drifted into unconsciousness, I was apparently saying: 'Lord Gulliver is lovely, really lovely . . .' Anyone who had not understood that Lord Gulliver was a horse, not a person, might have wondered if this were the reason my marriage had broken down!

The next morning, Christmas Day, I quite naturally woke up feeling awful. I was in agony, sick as a dog, unable to keep down even a sip of water. Throughout the next 10 days, all I managed to keep down was half a cup of tomato soup; small wonder, then, that I lost one and a half stone in weight. Richard came to see me late on Christmas morning, bringing the children with him. As he sat down he said: 'Oh, I bought you a lovely Christmas present. But as I was driving along in the car, I had to do an emergency stop and your present fell on the floor and smashed. So now you don't have a present.' The words astounded me. I had not really expected a present at all. I was not sorry to see Richard leave. It was the last time he visited me during my spell in hospital, which I found slightly strange. Regardless of our differences, we had nevertheless been married for 12 years and, despite the unhappy end to our marriage, I was, after all, very ill and I was still his wife.

I did not recover very quickly, and it was 10 days before I was allowed out of hospital. I had to fight for that. It was early in the New Year and Lord Gulliver was due for his first race. I begged the surgeon to let me go in time to watch the horse run. He was my dream horse, and looking forward to his race kept me going through all the awful days and nights in hospital. When I felt really low, I closed my eyes and dreamed of him. He was handsome, strong, a good racehorse; he would win me a National one day, of that I was certain. In the end, the surgeon agreed to let me leave, provided I would consent to attend the races in a wheelchair. I didn't like the idea, but if it meant leaving hospital, I would have agreed to anything at all!

Consequently, on the Saturday morning I left hospital. I was awake at 5 am and sharing a pot of tea with a friendly nurse, who sat and chatted with me about the horses. I told her about Lord Gulliver, and in my mind I could see him, powerful and strong, striding over the gallops as I had seen him so often at home. I lay in bed until 7 am, when I could stand it no more. Two hours later I was dressed, had eaten my breakfast, and was ready to leave for home. Jackie's husband Peter collected me and took me back to Weathercock House, where Keith and David Stait, owners of Canit, called to see me on their way to racing at Newbury. As they walked into the sitting room, Keith Stait stopped in his tracks. I must have looked ghastly, for he was prompted to remark: 'You can't go racing in that condition. You look terrible!' I felt a little offended, since I had taken the trouble to put on make-up! Both Keith and David did their best to dissuade me from going to the races, but nothing was going to stop me now. I reassured them everything would be fine and told them about my wheelchair, and went off to Newbury with Jackie and Peter. When I saw the wheelchair at the course, however, I rebelled. It was made of canvas, and looked like a child's pushchair. There was no way of persuading me to sit in it. If that shock wasn't bad enough, though, there was worse to come.

Lord Gulliver had been bought in Ireland and every Irish horse running in England needs a racing passport. It must be produced for checking by the racecourse vet to verify its markings at least threequarters of an hour before the race is due to start – and Lord Gulliver's passport had been left at home. I was horrified. The horse was to race at 1 o'clock, and it was already noon. I could hardly believe this new turn of heartbreakingly bad luck. I did not see how Paul Price could possibly drive back to Lambourn and return with the passport by 12.15. However, he had already left, as he was determined to try and get back before the deadline. I sat down outside the weighing room and watched the clock. My hopes had been pinned on this horse; my recovery from the operation was largely due to the fact that he would race that day. Now, my big lovely baby of a horse might not be able to run after all. I felt dreadfully disappointed. It all seemed in vain.

Paul Price ran back through the doorway and threw the passport into the weighing room window at exactly 22 minutes past 12. The stewards deliberately did not look up at the clock, but simply handed the passport to the vet and the declaration stood. If they had looked up, they would have seen we were seven minutes overdue. Had they chosen to, they could have stopped Lord Gulliver from racing that day. It was one of the rare occasions when I have known racecourse officials to show any real signs of humanity, my other brushes with stewards being, in the main, less happy. Lord Gulliver finished third, behind two very smart horses, Gruffandgrim and Silversmith, beaten 10 lengths. It was a promising start for an inexperienced young horse and I was pleased. He had tired only in the final two furlongs. I could not complain at that performance.

Soon after returning from Newbury I began to feel very ill once more. By Tuesday I didn't want to get out of bed, and put it down to depression after the operation mixed with Richard's leaving. I just wanted to be left alone, and even though Jackie tried to persuade me to have a bath, I refused. She felt my forehead and realized I was quite ill again. She telephoned the doctor, who wanted me to get up and drive to his surgery. That wasn't possible, and when Barry Park, our vet, popped in to see me a few moments later, I explained how I felt. I thought he was joking when he told me: 'Jenny, I think you've probably got some sort of infection'. Jackie didn't think he was joking, however, and she drove me back to the Princess Margaret Hospital at Swindon, where I was diagnosed as having a deep abscess in my stomach. The pain was very intense, and when the abscess was lanced the relief was equally intense. Two or three days later I was allowed home, with a nurse to visit me daily to dress the wound. Jackie, tearful and worried at leaving me alone, went home.

I was able to get up in the mornings and drive my pick-up to the gallops to watch the horses work. I would spend the afternoons sleeping, and I didn't find out until some months later that Judy Trout or Bryan Smart would take the telephone off the hook every afternoon so that I could at least enjoy a proper rest. They became my protectors, and acted as buffers against all the small and irritating difficulties of everyday life. Without them, I would have had the greatest difficulty coping. I began to notice, for instance, that I was never left alone at night. Judy or Bryan would always have an excuse not to go out, and would spend the evening keeping me company. They were both younger than me, and I appreciated their giving up their social life for me. They carried on this way for many months and I very slowly recovered. It wasn't until I came back to full strength that I realized quite how ill I had been. Judy and Bryan were brilliant; I could not have managed without them.

The boys, Mark and Paul, were also marvellous. Mark has always had an adult head on his young shoulders and, the day after Richard left, Judy fetched them both back from Pinewood for the holidays. Mark noticed immediately that something was wrong, and quite naturally asked where Dad was. I made some excuse about him being out for the day, but I didn't fool Mark. We cooked their breakfast and sat down to eat.

'Mum, are you all right?' Mark asked.

'Fine, thank you', I replied. 'Eat up.'

A few moments passed by, and Mark spoke again: 'Mum, are you *really* all right?'

'Why do you keep asking me that?' I enquired of him.

'You look different today, that's all', he said.

His perception was very moving and I had difficulty finishing my breakfast without choking. I blinked back the tears, but I could obviously not avoid telling them what had happened, since I knew they would find out sooner or later. It should be their mother who told them the truth, so I asked them to sit down, and quietly and as simply as possible, I explained that Daddy had left home again and this time he would never be coming back to live with us. Paul, just 10 years old, burst into tears. He sobbed and sobbed, and that set me off. Mark climbed up onto the arm of my chair, and put his arms around my neck. 'Please don't cry, Mum. When you cry, it makes me unhappy. We'll just have to start from the beginning again, won't we?' After a moment's thought, he added: 'When we had Daddy here, it was like having two arms and legs. Now it's like having one missing.' We dried our tears and carried on rebuilding our lives. There was no other way of handling it.

8
STARTING OVER

The decision to divorce Richard was not taken lightly. For many months after the final parting, I found it hard to shrug off my marriage vows. There had been more separations between us than had ever made the national Press, and it was largely due to the efforts of our family solicitor, Eric Smith, that the parting had not come sooner. Eric was a surrogate father to me. He reminded me very much of my own father, and would sit and listen to me, as I tried to explain the reasons for the failure of our marriage, in just the same way that my father listens to me: saying very little, not showing much emotional reaction, just quietly taking everything in before giving a carefully-deliberated answer. Throughout the spells of minor separations, he continually endeavoured to keep the Pitman family in one piece. Even after Richard had been gone for some months from Weathercock House, I still felt I was letting Eric down when I decided to go ahead with divorce proceedings.

Even though I no longer lived with Richard – for which I was glad, since relations between us had become very strained – I hated breaking my marriage vows, since I regard the word 'promise' as a serious term. It is probably the reason I have not remarried; David and I are quite happy as things are. We feel no need to legalize our deep and mature relationship with pieces of paper and signatures. We work on a basis of a lasting trust, and why change that? If I don't make any more promises to stay married 'till death us do part' then, if David and I ever become unhappy and wish to separate, I will not be faced again with breaking such a vow for the second time in my life. One day, maybe, we'll change our minds!

After recovering from appendicitis, I had plenty of time on my own to sit and think. I even went so far as to ask my parents not to come and see me, explaining the desperate need for a few quiet weeks in which to mull over the matter of divorce. It took me, I suppose, about one month to come to the conclusion that it was the only decision open to me, albeit a drastic one. And, once I had made that decision, there was never any doubt. I did not consider turning back. The last couple of years with Richard had been a misery for us both, the last weeks of our marriage nothing but discord and pain. There was nothing left between us. There was no point in holding on any more. In any event, the news that Richard had a younger girlfriend, had had one for some time in fact, reached me and the rest of the world through the columns of the daily papers. There seemed little point, once I finally realized this, in trying to pretend there was any chance of reconciliation. It would have been a farce to have tried to ignore his girlfriend's existence, and I went to Eric and told him of my decision to end my marriage, and apologized for letting him down. Since we wanted to get the nasty business over with as quickly as possible, I divorced Richard for adultery. It was sad, and I hated doing it, but I felt it was unavoidable.

I think I had always suspected the presence of someone else in Richard's life, at the same time not really wishing to believe it possible. The fact that he had actually introduced her to me after racing one evening at Hinton Parva was an even greater shock; yet again, the information came to me through the gossip columns. As these facts began to emerge and appear in print, so that the whole world knew Jenny Pitman's husband had left her for a younger woman, my telephone began to ring. It was the William Hickey column from the *Daily Express*, who wanted to know my reactions and hear my side of this unpleasant little story. Whenever the phone rang, my sister Mandy answered it, and if it was the *Daily Express* yet again, she would simply tell them I was not available. It was the only way I knew of handling the situation, for I was terrified that I should say something which, when it appeared in print, would hurt my sons. Throughout this messy time, I was trying to ensure that, no matter how much I was hurt, my sons were caused as little pain as possible. It was grossly unfair on them.

The *Daily Express* continued to telephone and I turned, as usual in moments of extreme pressure, to the fatherly advice of Eric Smith. He pointed out that my best way of handling the situation was to explain to the William Hickey Diary editor that I preferred to say nothing in order to protect my children, who were hurt enough already by their father leaving. If I continued to refuse to speak to them, they might publish something anyway, which could be even more hurtful for the boys. I took Eric's advice and, the next time the *Daily Express* rang, I spoke to the Diary editor and put my case to her in the most straightforward way possible. Her reply was equally forthright: 'Mrs Pitman, it has never been this newspaper's policy to hurt young children'. She put down the receiver and the newspaper never telephoned on that subject again, nor printed another solitary word which could have hurt Mark and Paul. Whilst people may criticize gossip columns, I can only say that the William Hickey column showed me and my children some humanity whilst we were undergoing a harrowing experience.

Whatever the newspapers may say, of course, whether it concerns us personally, or the performance and prospects of our horses, the horses have the last laugh. We use a lot of shredded newspaper bedding these days in the yard, since it is useful for horses allergic to dust, and most of what is written ends up trampled underfoot by the horses, and is eventually carted away and deposited on the dung heap! Poetic justice, perhaps?

I divorced Richard for his admitted adultery and he has, of course, since remarried. It was the most painless way to end the matter legally, the simplest and quickest way, fair on everyone. Fortunately he had no desire to take custody of the boys, which could have caused terrible heartbreak. It was understood that they would continue their education, live with me, and see Richard whenever they wished. The boys both, at this time, took the decision to become day boys rather than boarders which meant that I was alone much less. Why they took that decision has never been discussed; it will be interesting one day to learn how they came to that conclusion. I had no part whatsoever. They simply talked matters over between themselves.

I had, nonetheless, to legalize my custody, upon Eric Smith's advice. We went to the court at Andover for this procedure, and once again I was faced with a very long table – just like the one in Portman Square where I had acquired my professional trainer's licence – but this time it was a farce. It had the essence of black comedy about it. I had taken a lot of trouble to dress correctly for the occasion. Not wishing to look too smart, nor too scruffy, I had chosen a 'middle of the road' outfit, which I had thought would create the right impression about my suitability as a mother. I need not have bothered. The official reading the case did not once, at any stage in the proceedings, look up from the papers on the table before him. It was strange, and somewhat alarming, to think that the custody of two young boys, the future of two small human beings, was treated so casually. Watching the other cases coming up before mine, I thanked God that I was accompanied to Andover that day by David Stait, upon whose company and advice I was becoming more and more dependent. I would not have relished going through this farcical process alone: it was unnervingly cold and calculated. Thank goodness I was not having to fight for my sons. To have been in a position where custody of my children really was at stake would have been a horrible experience.

There was still, of course, an enormous financial mess which needed sorting out. As well as the sadness of the separation, there was the inevitable tangle of business affairs and other resources since Richard and I were, on paper at least, still business partners.

The puzzle took some careful straightening out! To begin with, I had a three-hour meeting with Eric Smith and Robin Platt, my accountant. We discussed matters for one entire afternoon, during which I became more and more confused. I was still feeling woolly-headed from my long illness and felt none the wiser after the long talks. In fact, I had to telephone Eric Smith the following morning to ask him what conclusions we had reached!

The business had to be divided fairly and evenly between Richard and myself, which was not as simple as it may sound. For one thing, Weathercock House, its surrounding acreage and the stableyard had increased in value. The £25,000 I had paid for the property in 1976 had seemed quite exorbitant at the time, considering the dilapidated condition of the place when I'd arrived, but when the house was officially revalued in early 1978 for the purposes of the legal division of property, its open market value was somewhere around £70,000. The only way I could remain at Weathercock House and continue as a trainer there was to buy out Richard's half of the house. In order to do this, therefore, I had to raise £35,000. What it amounted to was this: Richard had received £20,000 from the sale of Hinton Parva which, on his return to the marital home, had been invested in the renovation of Weathercock House. A year later, he was leaving with £35,000! Not a bad investment for him. For me, it was a nightmare of bad timing.

Eric Smith was not, of course, acting for Richard, though he had been our family solicitor when we were still together. There had been a rather embarrassing encounter one day in Eric's office between Richard and me, since we had both turned up to see him on the same day and at the same time. I was there by appointment, Richard came out of the blue. Eric was forced to explain to Richard that, since we were now going through divorce proceedings, he could act for only one of us, and that Richard would have to seek legal advice from another solicitor. I watched from the window of Eric's office as Richard walked away down the street in the pouring rain. In spite of the things he had done to his family and to me, I actually felt a strong sense of pity for him.

In order to pay Richard his £35,000, I had to find £17,000 in hard cash before our official business partnership, as well as our marriage, became a thing of the past. I would never have known where to start looking. Eric Smith, as always, stepped into the breach and he and Robin Platt set up a meeting with the manager of my bank at Swindon in order to arrange an overdraft. Rather in the way that I had worried about what to wear for the court appearance in Andover when I had acquired legal custody of my sons, I puzzled over the items in my somewhat limited wardrobe as I waited for Eric and Robin to take me to Swindon. Should I dress to the nines, wear my finest clothes, and risk the bank manager thinking I had so much money I did not need a loan? Or should I go in something rather down-at-heel, and risk creating the impression that I would never be able to repay the money? I steered what I hoped was a middle course and decided on a smart, neat suit.

On the drive to Swindon, Robin and Eric impressed upon me the need for total silence on my part throughout the entire interview: they felt it preferable that *they* dealt with the matter. Upon arrival at the bank, we were shown into the manager's office. There we found the bank manager and his assistant sitting at a table, and we sat down opposite them. The faces of the two men on the other side of the table showed no emotion whatsoever as Eric and Robin patiently and carefully explained my plight. I listened to Robin's detailed plans for the repayment of the overdraft and my reasons for needing the money. He gave the bank the name of one of my owners, who had kindly agreed to stand guarantor. Eric Smith gave a glowing account of my honesty and character, and my ability to make my racing yard a paying, viable proposition – I stared at him in some amazement as he built up a picture of a 'wonder woman'. I wondered if it was really *me* he was talking about.

I had a mortgage of £10,000 on Weathercock House, plus a hangover debt of similar proportions from Hinton Parva, and was now asking a bank to lend me even more! I did not feel exactly confident, for all Eric and Robin's joint abilities and powers of persuasion: I was hardly in the best position to win this race from in front. I was, in racing terms, well down the field. But I had every confidence in my two shining knights as I sat there, in spite of the dour-faced bank manager and assistant. I was not at all, in any sense, worried about paying back the money. If Robin and Eric said, after their careful investigations into my finances, that I could pay it back, then that was good enough for me. I could pay it back. My faith in their abilities was as simple as that, and it has always been so. Eric has been witness to some of my most personal problems, and could always be relied upon for good advice. I had even taken him to see Weathercock House before I went ahead with the purchase, and recalling his words as he looked it over still makes me smile today: 'Jenny, as your solicitor I must advise you very strongly to get a survey done on this place. However, as your friend, and since the house is in something of a state, I would advise you not to bother. A survey would only depress you.'

I listened as Eric and Robin finished telling my side of the story, and looked on, keeping quiet as instructed, as the bank manager studied the papers and notes before him. When he gave his reply,

I could hardly believe my ears. The bank would be happier, he announced, if Richard and I stayed together as business partners. If Richard remained a partner, there would be no need for me to buy him out and no need to borrow the money. That was the end of my silence. I launched, despite Eric and Robin's pleading looks, into a strongly-worded monologue.

This was my future being assessed, I told them, and I was going to have my tenpennyworth of say. There was no way I intended staying in any form of partnership with Richard Pitman, marital or otherwise. We had ended our marriage and, as far as I was concerned, any other form of relationship with Richard was an anathema to me. I was unable to live with Richard and I certainly couldn't work with him, I continued. I wanted my financial affairs, and much else besides, to be totally within my control from now on, and had no wish to be tied to anyone ever again. Once I got up steam, I was hard to stop, and I went a step further.

I pointed out that it was not just my future we were all talking about. Other people's lives were involved, other people's livelihoods at risk. I had a team of six stable lads working for me, who had taken their chances with me, and I wasn't about to let them down. They had worked night and day during my illness, to the point where I had been obliged to tell them not to be so stupid. They had mended fences, dug ditches, painted and creosoted stables, working long after hours to help make our yard successful. They had gone beyond the call of duty to put things right at my home. Their futures, as well as mine, were on the table. I ended my speech. We left the bank manager's office on a note of apparent stalemate. I was not remotely sure that this money would be forthcoming.

There was an odd atmosphere in the car, as Eric and Robin drove me back to Lambourn. I felt depressed and, by now, convinced the bank would refuse to lend me the money. Eric and Robin chatted about mundane matters, talking of everything under the sun *except* the money I needed. It was as if, by not talking about it, I would not feel so unhappy. But I could contain the question no longer: 'They won't let me have that money, will they?' Eric replied very quietly and simply: 'You can never be sure of these things, Jenny. Quite honestly, it doesn't look very hopeful.' The ice broken, Eric and Robin began to discuss a plan of campaign in the event of the bank's refusal. There were alternative ways to raise the money I needed, and they assured me there was no need for concern just yet. 'Just carry on training the horses', Robin said, 'and leave the money to us. We'll get it for you somehow, from somewhere.' Their confidence was remarkable but I had a nagging doubt. Were they just saying that to keep me from feeling more depressed? The future looked decidedly shaky.

By the time I got home I had convinced myself that the bank was going to refuse to give me the overdraft I so badly needed. Over the next few days I kept thinking how I would have to sell Weathercock House, and all the effort and work we had put into the place would be wasted. The horses would all have to be dispersed, and the lads would have to find jobs elsewhere. All the hours of hard slog, all their determination, would disappear down the drain. I had never felt so totally alone as in the days following the interview with the bank.

Ten days – a lifetime, it seemed – passed by. I had given up all hope of hearing from the bank, when I noticed a letter amongst the others bearing the bank's crest. It was postmarked Swindon. This had to be the answer. I tore the letter open, snatched it from the envelope, and began to read. My heart was pounding fiercely. This was one of the most important letters of my life. 'Dear Mrs Pitman', I read, 'whilst we have reviewed your case with every sympathy . . .' That was enough. I threw the letter on the table, not wishing to read on. The introductory words were enough to indicate a refusal from the bank. But, somehow, I knew I had to finish the letter. I picked it up and read on. '. . . it has been decided, therefore, to grant you an overdraft'. I could not believe it. They had said *yes*! I threw the letter up into the air and gave a whoop of joy, before rushing to telephone Eric Smith and Robin Platt to tell them the wonderful news. They were the only people who really knew what this meant to me; it seemed, to me, they were also the only ones who really cared.

The bank's only proviso was that Peter Deal, who had had horses with me for several years, would stand guarantor for the money. Peter had already kindly agreed to this. We were home and dry . . . I could pay off Richard and end the business partnership. From now on, it was my business. I was in business in my own right. Any mistakes would be mine and mine alone. There would be no one to share the blame – and no one to share the troubles, no one to turn to in times of crisis.

In the intervening years I have managed to clear most of these debts, although it has been a long, slow and uphill struggle. It was not the end of the story, since so much still needed to be done and, in order to continue in my chosen profession as racehorse trainer, I needed certain facilities. Whilst I was slowly paying off the borrowed money, I was also having to eke out my earnings as a trainer so that I could plough some of it back into the business. I couldn't just keep taking money out, putting nothing back, for something would have suffered and business would not have flourished. For example, there was the matter of a lorry. For years I had motored round the roads of England in a somewhat inadequate lorry which had the name 'Richard Pitman' across the front. That had to go. I needed to create the impression that I was doing well, and travel my horses in comfort, even if I was struggling. I invested £24,000 in a new, larger, cream Renault diesel-powered horse transporter – with 'J. S. Pitman' painted on the front. At Weathercock House there was still no driveway; now I put a tarmac driveway up to the front door, around the house and into the yard, so that owners could park their cars and we could park the lorry. We could now walk outside without sinking knee-deep in mud. I erected another 10 boxes so I could take on more horses. Robin had advised me that 25 was my minimum in order to keep a successful business going; these days I have 29, which I find ideal. I continued to make improvements to Weathercock House. Whilst most of it had stood for 300 years, I wanted to make sure it would stand for another 300!

I suppose some of the publicity which resulted from the divorce helped, in one sense. At least people knew I existed, that I had always been the trainer, not Richard, that I was still in business. But I did not intend to trade on that publicity: I wanted to make it because of the way my horses won races. I concentrated my attention on the effort to ensure that I was known as a trainer, not as Richard Pitman's 'ex'.

My first-ever winner, following the divorce from Richard, was a horse called Fettimist. He was a real old trouper, one of those horses I could always rely on, after a string of luckless races, to pull something out of the bag and get me back on the winning streak. He lived up to his reputation as our 'saver bet' time and time again. This is true of several horses a trainer comes across in his or her career. From time to time, you buy a horse that isn't necessarily a world-beater, but one which somehow always seems to win a race at a time when you are wondering if you'll ever have another winner.

Fettimist belonged to Peter Deal, my guarantor with the Swindon bank. Peter had instructed me to buy him a horse, with a price limit of £2,500. He had added: 'But don't lose a good horse for the sake of a couple of hundred pounds. If you see something you *really* like, you can go to £2,800.' Off I went to the Ascot Sales with Peter's words ringing in my ears and somehow, an hour or so later, I became the buyer of a horse costing £3,200! Normally I never exceed an owner's price, but this horse had caught my eye and as soon as I had watched it move, I knew it was the horse I wanted for Peter Deal. I followed the bidding to £2,800, but somehow I just couldn't stop. I wondered what Peter would say when I broke the news to him, and wasn't cheered by a passing light-hearted comment from the jockey Graham Thorner: 'What on earth have you bought that thing for, Jenny? That horse'll remain a novice all its life.' I knew he hadn't meant it unkindly, but it stuck in my mind for a long while.

Fettimist pulled like a train and was one of life's 'worriers'. A horse which worries makes life difficult for a trainer, since it loses condition (weight) easily, worrying about being trained, and worrying about its races. I had to completely re-school Fettimist before his career could begin. Fortunately, at the time I bought him, I had not moved from Hinton Parva and still had the use of the indoor school. The horse quickly proved my faith in him was not misplaced. He won three novice 'chases in a row in his first season, as well as the Crudwell Cup at Warwick, and the Robert Gore Cup – which was so huge that it took both Peter and I all our strength to carry it back to the car! Those races qualified him to run in the Grand National, and I planned to train him for that race the following season.

Alas, however, Lady Luck wasn't on his side, nor ours. He got colic during his summer holidays at grass down in Basingstoke. I drove straight down when I heard the tragic news, and I could see instantly the horse was dying. From being a handsome, lovely racehorse, he had transformed into an ugly wreck in a few short hours. The pain of the colic had caused him to roll over and over in agony, and he had banged his head on the ground. It was bruised, swollen, and a sickening sight. The vet could offer very little hope. David, with whom I was becoming friendly, had driven down to Basingstoke with me. We sat up all night together with the horse, and at one stage he seemed to be making a recovery. It was, sadly, merely an illusion. When a horse rolls about in agony with colic, he can twist his gut. The twisted section of the intestine, as it turns over, becomes completely cut off from the blood supply. After a while it 'dies' and all sensation vanishes and the horse, no longer in pain, appears to have got over it. But this is a temporary respite. In Fettimist's case, it would have been a temporary respite from a painful death. By the morning the pains were returning and the vet put him to sleep. It was a blow. Yet another friend gone.

Fettimist was also welcome evidence that my owners had no intention of deserting me just because Richard and I were divorced. Any worries I might have had on that score were swiftly dispelled and Peter Deal's request, in asking me to find him a horse, had been a particularly happy invitation. My other owners included David Stait, who owned a horse in partnership called Golden Bob, and his brother Keith, who owned Canit. Canit was a very nice type, and I had always had the famous Topham Trophy in mind for him. The Topham is run at Aintree, on the same course as the Grand National and using the same fences, but is run over a shorter distance. I felt the horse would get the two miles six furlongs, and was ideally made to win that type of race. I was to be proved right, though the horse had, sadly, been moved to another trainer shortly before the race.

My friendship with David and Keith was, at the time, a totally platonic one. When David's own marriage broke up, it seemed perfectly natural that we should spend more time together. He became friendly with Bryan Smart, and came down to visit us at Lambourn more and more often. I always insisted that he stay at the local village pub, however; I was divorcing Richard and had no desire to become the subject of scurrilous gossip. Besides, it was still very much just a friendship, with no hint of the love affair to come. He spent a lot of his time with Bryan, who was Canit's jockey, and often went out during the evenings with Bryan and his girl-friend Debbie. No one was more surprised than I, therefore, when Bryan and David came into the sitting room one Saturday evening as I sat watching television with Mark and Paul. I was pleased to see David. I liked him, though in a fairly detached way. He was always good with the children, and he had an unexpected sense of humour. He could frequently make me laugh, even at a time when there wasn't much to laugh about.

David sat down, whereupon Mark piped up: 'What are you doing here?' The reply startled me a bit: 'Actually, I'm here to ask your Mum to come out with us for the evening, provided you don't mind'. Paul cut in. 'Good idea, Dave. It's about time she went out and enjoyed herself for a change.' There was no way, however, that I was going to be pushed out of my comfortable chair to go out on a Saturday night, and I refused the invitation, point blank. But David was very persuasive. 'What about the children, if I go out? Who can look after them?' I asked. That, I thought, would foil him. No such luck: 'We've already thought of that. One of the stable lads is coming in,' he said.

It was already 8.30 pm by that time. I continued to hold out for a little longer, but by 9 o'clock I was getting ready to go to the local pub for a steak and a bottle of wine with David, Bryan and Debbie. To my amazement, as I sat with them over dinner, I heard a voice laughing. The voice was mine. I had not laughed and relaxed freely in any man's company for many months. It was quite a shock.

I had to admit, against my own judgement, that I was very much enjoying the evening and David's company.

David and I, with Debbie and Bryan, continued to make up a foursome most Saturday evenings, going to the South Marsden Country Club where David and Bryan could play snooker whilst Debbie and I sat chatting over a drink. There was a small band, with an area for dancing and when Bryan went off to dance with Debbie, David quite naturally asked me to partner him. I thought it was more from politeness, but it was agreeable enough to be asked to dance again. We enjoyed those evenings very much.

We began to go out more regularly: sometimes with Bryan and Debbie, sometimes on our own. All the while I found David nicer and nicer. He was a gentle, understanding person, and very kind. He began doing odd jobs around the house for me, such as fixing broken windows, and he made an excellent job of repairing the oven door, which had been annoying me for weeks! But our friendship did not meet with his brother's approval. David told me, as gently as he could, that Keith planned to take Canit to another trainer if our friendship continued. Ironically, our relationship was still on a totally platonic basis at the time. I did not feel Keith was justified in taking such a stand, and I had not the slightest intention of submitting to any form of blackmail. I had just extricated myself from one tricky situation, and certainly wasn't bent on becoming caught up in another. Whatever Keith's decision was to be, one thing was for certain. Canit, I said to David, might be a good horse, but could he be relied upon to mend my oven door? David and I continued our friendship, and Canit was duly removed from Weathercock House and taken to Fred Rimell's yard in Worcestershire. David was upset, and all the more so when Canit won the Topham, since he felt I should have enjoyed the horse's victory. Canit had had several problems, which we had ironed out prior to his departure. After he left my yard I wrote to Keith Stait and urged him to run Canit in the Topham. The horse had never been so well as on the day he had left us – and duly won the Trophy very shortly afterwards.

I began to look forward more and more to David's visits. Friendship started to grow into something else. I began to telephone him when I had a problem with the children, and later, with the horses. He knew plenty about betting and racing but, at the time, not so much about horses themselves, though he was soon to learn and has now become an invaluable partner to me in their training. I also taught him to ride a racehorse, sitting him up on my old hack, Black Plover, who has since gone to the great hunting ground in the sky. Black Plover was a wonderful old animal, who was quiet enough for me to ride out with the other horses on the gallops in those days. Not many horses are quiet enough to allow you to sit still on them whilst young horses are galloping all about them. Black Plover was a model of good behaviour. He used to take Mark and Paul show jumping in the summer months and was always as good as gold.

My relationship with David took a more serious turn after the divorce from Richard was finalized. I really began to care for him, and we spent as much time together as we could. I was a free woman, in the sense that my decree absolute was granted; yet not so free, since I was falling quietly in love again. What had begun as an innocent friendship was turning into something more enduring. Our love was a love born out of friendship, not mad, youthful passion. It was not a case of love at first sight, and I wish I had known earlier in my life that friendship is the most important factor in a marriage. David was a good friend when I needed one badly; he really cared for the children, and still does. They grew to love him and respect him, and we all thoroughly enjoyed our Sunday afternoon walks up on the Downs, where we would play cricket, and he and the boys teased me unmercifully about the state of my game! I began to telephone David not just with my problems, but on any pretext. I just wanted to hear his voice.

The moment eventually came when we could no longer hide our feelings from one another and, naturally, we wanted to live together. Since I was divorced, there was nothing to stop us doing so – although it was possible we might face a problem as far as the boys were concerned. Would they be hurt again, having lost their father – and having heard that he had now remarried and was the father of a young baby – if someone stepped into Richard's place? Dave was everything I needed and I knew the boys thought highly of him, but would they accept him in this new role? David had won their friendship easily, since he was always very interested in everything they did. It was not a feigned interest, it was genuine. And a condition of us living together was that Mark and Paul were made fully aware of the situation *before* it happened, so that they knew what was going on. We sat them down together one Sunday morning, and David explained. He has a brilliant way of getting through to people, and whether his audience is a king or a pauper, he can communicate with them. He was able to convey to the children that he and I loved one another, and that our relationship had developed beyond the usual bounds of friendship. In the most straightforward manner, he told them that, loving me as much as he did, he wanted to live with me. Since he wanted to be with me all the time, that included sharing a bed; and he explained that, when they were older, they would feel the same one day about a girl. I wanted the boys to learn from an early age that one should not sleep with a girl 'casually'; that sleeping with someone was a matter of loving and caring. Since we intended to live together and sleep together from now on, David said, your mother and I feel it is only fair to talk to you about it.

The boys were perfectly happy with this, and David moved into Weathercock House. There was no resentment, and gradually they became used to David always being in the house, helping me with my work, living as one of the family. One morning, Paul came into our bedroom and sat on the end of the bed, talking to us. It developed, a few weeks later, to 'I feel cold. Can I get in under the covers?' And soon afterwards, Mark joined us – and it seemed perfectly natural that we should spend Sunday mornings in this way, all in bed together as any normal happy family, sharing cups of tea and eating biscuits.

My friends ask me: 'When are you going to make an honest man of David?' My reply is simple: not being married doesn't affect our relationship in any way. Nor does it affect his relationship with the boys. It has always seemed so happy and natural. Even Richard has ventured the opinion that David and I should marry; he suggested that it might embarrass the boys when David went to collect them from school. That aspect had not crossed my mind before, so I asked the boys how they felt about it. I have always believed that questions concerning the boys should be put to them directly and honestly. I maintain that, with children, it is better to be straightforward and honest. It is pointless to imagine that you can fool them, and treat them as unintelligent beings. Mark and Paul both gave the same reply to my question: 'Embarrass us? Why should it?'

They are both fond of David and he of them. Now they are growing up, of course, there is less physical affection between them but, when they were smaller, both boys felt fond enough of David to kiss him goodnight, and throw their arms about him in greeting. David has taken on many of the fatherly roles in their life, such as willingly taking part in the father's cricket match at their school. Richard was unable to play: he was going clay pigeon shooting instead.

9
TAKING CLOSER ORDER

I won my first National by default! I should explain here, perhaps, that there are four National steeplechases run each year in Britain: there's the Liverpool Grand National, the classic jump race of them all, run at Aintree; there's the Scottish National, which takes place at Ayr; the Welsh National, run at Chepstow; and the Midlands National, run at Uttoxeter. The latter three races do not make the headlines in quite the same way as their Liverpool counterpart, but they are Nationals nonetheless and I was awarded my first at Uttoxeter in 1976. I was still married to Richard at the time.

The race was run on a Saturday afternoon and Watafella, our runner, came third. I thought little more about it, until we went to Plumpton races the following week where, upon arrival at the course, Richard and I went straight to the weighing room. I wished to check that everything was in order with my horse. Richard, meanwhile, met up with Stan Mellor and they began to chat. Richard had wanted to talk to Stan about a couple of minor matters, and was slightly puzzled by Stan, who looked alarmed and worried. Richard discussed the minor matters, and nothing further was said. Driving home in the car after the races, Richard mentioned Stan's apparent confusion and worried appearance, and added how unusual it was for him ever to appear flustered. I agreed.

I considered the matter as we drove along and, after mulling it over, I connected two ideas in my mind. Stan Mellor's horse, No Scotch, had won the big race at Uttoxeter; now, just a few days later, he looked worried when Richard approached him – there might just be a connection, I realized. I also remembered that the qualifications for entry to the Midlands National had been unusual, complicated and strange. The horses allowed to run should not, said the rules, have won a race of a particular value between two certain dates. Jokingly, as we neared home, I turned to Richard: 'You don't think, for a moment, that Stan's horse didn't have the proper qualifications for the Midlands National last week, do you?' Richard did not have an answer, but by the time we reached Lambourn I had decided to check the form books, to see if there was a connection between the qualifications for entry to the Midlands National, and Stan's manner towards Richard at Plumpton. My position, if I discovered that Stan's horse did not possess the proper qualifications, was clear. It was not only for myself that I would have to make a formal objection to the Jockey Club, it was for the owners of the horse, Watafella. Their prize money would be affected. If they were entitled to second-place prize money, instead of third-place prize money, it was my duty to ensure that justice was done.

At home, I brought out the form books and began to check them over. I looked at the records for No Scotch's most recent races, and looked again at the rules for entry for the Midlands National. There was, as I had suspected, a discrepancy. I went into the sitting room where Richard was watching television and relayed my discovery to him. 'Stan Mellor must have made a mistake about that race, and it looks as though his horse didn't qualify for entry.' Richard replied: 'Don't be ridiculous. How could Stan have made such a mistake?' I told him to take a look for himself. The rules for entry had been very complicated, and it would have been easy to misread them. Richard duly looked both at the form books and the entry standard for the race, and could only agree with me that No Scotch appeared to have been ineligible to run.

I was friendly, and still am, with Stan Mellor's head lad Eric. I decided to telephone Eric and explain my discovery about No Scotch. Eric replied, half-jokingly: 'Well, you were only third. It won't affect you very much. How would you like to take yourself off for a little holiday until next week?' Had I accepted this very considerate offer, made in jest, the two-week period permitted for lodging an objection would have lapsed! I laughed. If we were only going to move up one place and if they were prepared to make up the prize money to my owners, I was not too bothered. I put the telephone down after pulling Eric's leg while longer. But then I began to think again. If Stan Mellor's yard had made a mistake, how many others with horses in that race could have made the *same* error? Out came the form books again, as well as my pen and notepad. I worked my way through all the other horses, which took several hours. Four horses, I discovered, hadn't had the right to run. Two of them had finished in front of Watafella – they should, by rights, be due for disqualification and my horse stood to be awarded the race. I couldn't laugh this off. My owners would lose a lot of money if I were to ignore the facts now before me.

Richard, at first, refused to believe me. To be doubly sure I paid Fred Winter a visit at Uplands and asked him to check the facts for me. He raised an eyebrow at first but, after looking through the form books, he nodded his head and agreed that I was right. Upon returning home, I telephoned the Jockey Club in London and explained the situation to a steward. I waited for the verdict, hanging on the telephone for about 10 minutes, while he went away to verify or dismiss my claim. When he returned, he said, very cautiously: 'It seems you are right. We shall telephone you later today.' The phone rang later in the afternoon and it was, as I had hoped, the steward from the Jockey Club, telephoning to confirm that I had been right. I immediately put my objection in writing and sent it off to the Jockey Club, along with my cheque. When one makes an objection in racing, it must be accompanied by a deposit in order to ensure that the objection is not frivolous. If the objection is thrown out, the deposit is lost; if the objection is proved justified, the money is returned. If the objection is thrown out *and* decreed frivolous, there is a fine attached as well. So my objection and deposit winged their way swiftly to London by special delivery.

All the trainers whose horses had not been properly qualified for the Midlands National were called before the stewards of the Jockey Club in London. I invited myself along, too, rather saucily – but I wanted to be certain of fair play! I met up with the other trainers in the Churchill Hotel before the meeting. As I walked into the bar, they began to tease me: 'We don't know how you have the nerve to come in here with us, Jenny. We're not speaking to you!' But it was all taken in good part and no enemies were made. I felt sorry for Stan, but I also felt sorry for my owners, who had been deprived of the honour and glory of winning a race which they deserved. However, the owners of Watafella ended up winning £4,214 instead of just £606 in the Philip Cornes Midlands National. Since only four horses had actually finished the race on all four feet, Watafella was officially placed first *and* fourth! The owners received first-place prize money and the trophy was sent on to Alan Phelps and Stan Ensinger, but that still was not quite the same as receiving the trophy at the moment of triumph. They, however, were pleased with my efforts and kindly donated the £606 third-place money to their trainer to thank her for pointing out the facts!

The other horses I had in my care at that time included Bueche Giorod, who won me my first 'big race': the Massey-Ferguson Gold Cup. Named after the famous Swiss watch company, the horse was a really good servant to my yard. He recently ran in the famous Newmarket Town Plate, a flat race, trained by my brother Peter Harvey.

The Songwriter, owned by a songwriter named Peter Callender, was my first-ever runner in the Liverpool Grand National: he came sixth, in 1977. A small horse of not quite 16 hands, he was a cracking little jumper and went round Aintree like a bird. I was really thrilled, since his performance made fools of everyone who had been unwise enough to laugh when I entered him for the race. I had known, from the first time I ever saw him school over fences, that he would get round Aintree: he had legs which worked like pistons. He was made for jumping.

Benghazi Express I bought for a mere £1,200 at Ascot Sales . . . and he subsequently won 10 races and was placed 17 times! He more than paid his way, and was the first horse ever to win three in a row for me. He was a funny character, a bit like Monty Python, his stable companion. They could both run a brilliant race on one day, and an absolute stinker the next, for no reason at all. Every time Benghazi ran badly his owners used to throw their hands up in the air and threaten to send him off to the sales. I would persuade them to give him another chance, and I swear the horse could understand English: I would always tell him 'This is your last chance' before he ran – and he would go out and run a blinder. The owners would then swing their opinions right round, and promise never to sell him. Michael Reay, one of his owners, stood guarantor for my mortgage on Weathercock House.

The same owners had Glasgow Express, a very nervous animal. He couldn't bear a stick being waved near him, and he loathed having a red underpad beneath his saddle: the colour seemed to frighten him. John Francome rode him at Fontwell Park and carried out my instructions to the letter, sailing round perfectly clear, coming to the last well in front – but tiring slightly. I remembered, too late, that I had not warned John about Glasgow's fear of the stick. I yelled 'Oh no' helplessly from the grandstands at the top of my voice, but John was too far away. Everyone else in the grandstand heard my cry. John took out his stick to give the horse a quick reminder and the inevitable occurred. Glasgow crashed, as feared, into the roots of the fence. Next day I received a very charming fan letter, which said that in view of Glasgow Express' running at Fontwell I should be publicly pole-axed!

My great white hope of that time, however, was Lord Gulliver, the horse I had been so anxious to leave hospital to see. His first race at Liverpool was the Maghull Novice Hurdle over two miles and five furlongs, where he finished third, beating some good horses including Colonel Christy, and from that moment on I maintained he was the answer to all my prayers. He was such a good horse I believed he would one day release me from all my debts. I nicknamed him 'my slave' or 'Toby', after watching the television serial *Roots*. Toby, like The Songwriter, was owned by Peter Callender.

In October 1979 we ran Lord Gulliver at Ascot in the Embassy Premier 'Chase qualifier, over two and a half miles. Carrying 11 stone 7 pounds he ran well, particularly since he had an abscess in his foot which we did not discover until afterwards. When that burst two days later, our vet pronounced he would run a stone better next time, and he was right: in the Britax Chase at Wolverhampton Lord Gulliver won very easily indeed. He beat Snow Buck and Kas, and the victory qualified him to run in the Liverpool Grand National. This is it, I said to Peter Callender, we're on our way at last. I was convinced that this horse was a superstar. Nothing that was said could convince me that we didn't have Aintree sewn up and in our pockets.

I sent him to Cheltenham for a novice 'chase, where he was placed third to Lacson, a good horse, and the Queen Mother's good animal Special Cargo. That was on 8 December 1979 – and it turned out to be his last run of the entire season. He developed a difficult leg problem, and required a long rest. I was disappointed, but confident that he would soon be back on his way to the top.

It was January 1981 before he raced again, at Ascot in a handicap hurdle. John Francome rode him for the first time, aware that Lord Gulliver needed an easy race: he'd been off the track a long time. However, he still came back after that race with perfectly sound legs, and the object of the exercise had been achieved. Nottingham was our next venue with 'my slave', where Phil Blacker rode him, and where they won very easily, carrying 12 stone in a handicap 'chase. There was eight lengths back to his nearest rival; Lord Gulliver was never out of a hack canter. Then, after another period of rest, ordered as a result of a blood test that showed he had anaemia and required a course of vitamin injections, he ran in his first Liverpool Grand National. Colin Brown rode him, and they were prominent until baulked at a jump by a loose horse. Lord Gulliver couldn't see the fence properly, made a hash of jumping it, and fell. Then, like an idiot, he got to his feet, shook himself, and galloped off after the field, minus his jockey! He flew round the rest of the course jumping like a stag. He never missed a single fence and enjoyed every moment of his solo adventure! I remember thinking that I couldn't wait to take him back to Aintree the following year. After that race, Lord Gulliver went off for a summer holiday with the rest of the horses from the yard.

He was unplaced in his first run of the new season, at Kempton Park in October 1981, but came third in his next outing to Cavity Hunter at Leicester, over three miles, and beaten only three and a half lengths – a cracking good run. Then came the 1981 Corals Welsh National at Chepstow, run a few days after Christmas. The going was very soft; Toby always liked the top of the ground and Ben de Haan pulled him up, which was disappointing. A few weeks later, he went to Nottingham, was ridden by Phil Blacker and came fifth to the strongly-fancied Grand National runner Lucky Vane. He ran well and we looked forward to his next race: the 1982 Grand National in Liverpool. Sadly, it was not to be. Nottingham was, unbeknown to us, the last race of Lord Gulliver's life. One February morning, he had a heart attack on the gallops, crashed into a concrete post, and died. My hopes of winning the 1982 Grand National died with him. . . .

A friend called Jeremy Norman had, by this time, become a regular visitor to Weathercock House. So much so, in fact, that my stable lads regarded him as something of a threat to David, and each weekend as Jeremy appeared, the lads ran a book on whether he or David would end up with Jenny! But Jeremy remained firmly a friend, nothing more. He enjoyed coming down on Saturday mornings to ride out with the string and, since I had a fair opinion of his knowledge of horseflesh, I agreed when he suggested that I go over to Charles Ratcliffe's yard near Oxford to look at a young horse. The horse, it transpired, *was* rather special.

10
CORBIERE PREPARES

I liked the two-year-old chestnut gelding immediately I saw him at Charles Ratcliffe's yard at Bampton. He impressed me with a body which was both big and strong, but not too heavy; and legs that were clean and stocky, with plenty of bone. A trainer of jumpers looks for a minimum of nine inches of bone, a measurement taken around the horse's leg just below the knee. Less than nine inches is regarded as unsuited to the rigours of life as a steeplechaser; more than that may make the animal appear carthorse-like and can have a slowing effect. This horse had a frame, I decided, that would carry any penalties which might be imposed on him throughout his career as a jumper, which was a vital factor in my consideration. The better horses are, the more weight they are given in the racing handicap system. This gelding with the broad white blaze would, I was certain, stand up to weight and was an animal to win races. There was a further element I liked about this horse, in addition to his physique. It was his eye: a kind eye, full of courage and honesty. Just as one can tell a lot about a human by the eyes, so it is with horses. He was altogether a nice-looking animal, and Jeremy Norman, who had asked me to accompany him to the Bampton yard, duly purchased him.

Alan Burrough, a businessman relative of Jeremy's, later bought a half-share in the horse, and gave this half-share to his son Brian as an eighteenth birthday present. Later still, Alan purchased Jeremy's share as well, and the Burrough family owned the horse entirely. There was a rumour, at one stage, that Fulke Walwyn liked the horse so much he wanted to buy it for the Queen Mother. Since Jeremy had already purchased the horse, we replied that the Queen Mother was welcome to a half-share, provided the horse still came to Upper Lambourn for me to train! We heard nothing further on the subject. As it was, having agreed to buy the chestnut, we left him at Charles' farm for a year to grow on. It was important that he should mature at his own pace for the next 12 months, on good grazing and with good food. If left to his own devices he would develop properly between the ages of two and three, when he would come to us at Weathercock House to begin his life as a racehorse proper.

It was no exaggeration to say that, in the year spent with Charles, the horse grew at an alarming rate and, when David went to collect him from Charles in 1978, he had a shock in store. The horse had been a big two-year-old, but as a three-year-old he was massive. He was like a baby elephant and David wondered if it was the same horse! As the ramp of the lorry into which they loaded him to bring him home was seen to sag visibly under the horse's weight, one of Charles' lads said: 'That horse can already jump a five-bar gate. You'll win a National with him, if you can keep him sound.' They were prophetic enough words.

The Burrough family chose to name their racehorse after the lighthouse near their home in the Channel Islands. Corbiere, or Corky as he was affectionately known both to the family and to everyone in the yard, had already been backed and ridden when he arrived at Weathercock House – that is, he had been taught to accept someone sitting on his back and had been given some quiet hacking – and my task was thus made easier. The process of breaking in and backing racehorses can be time-consuming and difficult, and it was a relief that we could start working him fairly soon after his arrival. It was the Burrough family's first venture into racehorse ownership and they were naturally anxious to see their horse running. I remember our first morning on the gallops with the animal, when I wondered for a moment what we had bought. It crossed my mind, when I first saw him work, that this animal might never make a racehorse, he was so *slow*. It was almost painful to watch him, and it made me doubt my first instincts about him. He was like a big roly-poly pudding and my honest feeling was: just how slow can a horse be? Corky just rolled and lolloped along like a big fat puppy, and my heart sank.

Nonetheless, after some muscle-building walking and trotting on the road, a couple of months spent cantering, and a few weeks of work upsides some of my faster horses, Corky began to sharpen up his pace. He sharpened up enough, in fact, for me to feel confident enough to race him, and we selected a National Hunt 'bumper', or amateur and conditional jockeys flat race, at Nottingham. The ground was heavy, Paddy O'Brien rode him, and to everyone's surprise he romped through the mud and won very comfortably. I was both pleased and rather worried. Worried because it was the first time the Burrough family had ever been racing, let alone owned and run a horse . . . great for them, but it put me under pressure to find as successful a follow-up. It causes the trainer problems when an owner buys a racehorse and wins with it straight away, since even the greatest racehorses get beaten sooner or later in their career. No horse can win every race it runs and the trainer is acutely aware of this; the first flush of success may be followed by a long string of disappointing runs. But nothing could take that happy day away from the Burroughs or their horse and, after a memorable celebration in the box with Peter Marsh, who sponsors this series of bumper races, we all went home well pleased.

Inevitably, in the horse's next race, a bumper at Chepstow, Brian Burrough was fully expecting his horse to repeat the Nottingham feat. But he was, as I feared, to be disappointed and Corbiere could make only eighth place. Probably it was because he became over-excited prior to the race, which was understandable. At his first outing he had not known what to expect and had gone out onto the track and raced with the other horses, and simply enjoyed himself. The second outing was rather different. Corky knew what was coming, and sweated up in his anticipation of the fun and games to come. It was a characteristic of the horse's younger days, that he would sweat and become over-excited before racing.

Since the ground at Nottingham had been heavy, and at Chepstow was on the firm side, we quite naturally jumped to the conclusion that we had a soft-ground horse in Corbiere. That assumption was not entirely wrong, because when Corbiere runs on soft ground he simply isn't anchored by the going. He runs just as brilliantly over the top of the ground, like any champion racehorse should; but the speed merchants find it easier to catch him when they are not bogged down in bottomless mud. When mud does take the edge off their speed, Corky just keeps on running forever. The further they go, the happier he is.

The final of the Peter Marsh series was held at Warwick. This series is for young National Hunt racehorses, and events are held at courses throughout the country and culminate in a final at Warwick towards the end of the National Hunt season. At Warwick Corbiere redeemed himself and ran second to Esparto, beaten a length and a half, and Esparto went on to become a rather useful horse in time.

These three bumper races comprised Corbiere's first racing season, since I considered him too young as yet for hurdling. He was, by the end of that season, into his fourth year. He had learned something of the art of racing, and deserved a summer holiday. The real tests, the real opposition on the racetrack, could wait until the new season began in the autumn. In the meantime, the late summer found us doing our best to remove some of Corbiere's excess weight. National Hunt racehorses live a hard life between August, when the season starts, and June, when it ends. They live a regulated existence, and have a regulated diet to keep them in ideal racing condition. So their summer holidays, their weeks at grass in

June and July, are their annual playtime – and they make the most of it.

One of the antics Corbiere enjoys, if ever he is out in the rain, is to find a patch of mud or a big hole in the field, and roll about in it on his back until he is satisfactorily covered from head to toe. If there isn't a muddy patch available, he will dig his own. Mrs Burrough came down to have a look at Corbiere during his summer holiday, when he was turned out. She was quite shocked at the difference in his appearance. No longer the smart, well turned-out animal she had become used to seeing in the yard and at the races, he was now a mud-bespattered animal with a tangled-up mane and tail. 'Oh dear!' she exclaimed, her illusions somewhat shattered by the spectacle before her. 'It's a bit of a shock to see him like this, all covered in mud – I'm only used to seeing him with a shiny coat and painted toenails!'

After the initial cavorting for joy round the paddocks, revelling in their freedom, most horses want to get down to the very serious business of consuming as much grass as they can in the time allowed. The grass is possibly at its best in May and June – though this point is a cause for endless argument in the horse racing fraternity – and at its most nutritious. Not only is the horses' freedom from routine important, so also is this chance to put back any weight lost through a hard racing winter, and the horses enjoy it wholeheartedly. It is as important to the racehorse, this kicking-up of his heels and the return to a natural way of eating and living, as the average hard-working businessman's fortnight in Sorrento or Majorca. And the net result of the holiday is frequently the same, for horse and human: the need for a bit of swift dieting.

After his summer break, Corky was brought up from grass in early July to prepare for the next step in his racing career. Our plan was to start schooling him more seriously over hurdles once again, in readiness for what lay ahead. He had, in fact, already been given an introduction to hurdles whilst working on the gallops at home during the previous winter, but this time we meant business. Now, rising five years old, he needed careful and thorough tuition so that, by the time he arrived at the racecourse for his first run, he would know what a hurdle looked like, how to jump it cleanly and swiftly with an economy of effort, and gallop away from it without breaking his racing rhythm.

In November 1979, at Nottingham on a day when the ground was declared good, Corbiere ran for the first time over hurdles in public, and he did not make a spectacle of himself or his trainer. He finished a fairly respectable seventh over the two-mile course. Considering his age, and that he was immature and still a bit on the burly side after the summer, he disappointed no one. Everyone felt they could look forward to his next run, the hunters' novice hurdle over two and a half miles at Worcester where I felt the extra distance might suit him. Remembering Nottingham, the crowd backed him down to 100–30. It was an optimistic price and Corbiere did not justify this popularity. He ran perfectly happily until the third hurdle from home, when the edge went off his speed and he began to 'go backwards' through the field. I was as disappointed as his owners and the backers, since I had felt sure he would improve after his first run. I could not blame the jockey, Phil Blacker, who had given him a nice ride at both courses. Had I run him too soon after the first race, perhaps? I always try and find a way to blame myself for my horses' poor running, and I set myself the task of finding another race for Corky.

I found the Philip Cornes Novice Hurdle qualifier. The going was heavy, he had an extra two furlongs – this time the distance was two miles six furlongs – and the testing ground was likely to suit him. I was proved right and, although Wayward Lad, a future Gold Cup third, won the race, Corbiere, with Graham Thorner up, was beaten only five lengths to come in third. It was cheering to all concerned that the pointer towards his liking for heavy ground was proving accurate. There were still more mysteries left to be uncovered, but that factor, at least, was now clear. The formbook gave a further clue; it read 'Every chance two out, one pace flat'. Those last three words were the most relevant and indicated that, whilst Corky had no turn of foot at the end of a race, he had one advantage over the rest: endless stamina. He might not be able to produce a fast, flashy finish but, once he was in top gear and running, he could hold his pace. Provided he could hold his pace for long enough, then the flashy finishers would be beaten long before the post arrived. Distance, lots of it, was the answer. We looked for a race where we hoped this endless stamina through deep ground could be put to good use, and found just such a race at Towcester. The Towcester finish comprises a severe uphill run of approximately one mile and, since the race was two miles five furlongs, the horses would have to negotiate the hill twice. That should find them out, we all agreed, and everyone's hopes ran high yet again. John Suthern was engaged to ride him. He came fourth, behind Prelko and Woodford Prince, and the form guide's opinion afterwards read: 'Every chance, not quick enough'. The result, though it disappointed Corbiere's following in one sense, eventually proved a pointer to his quality. No one realized until much later in the season that one of his Towcester conquerers, Woodford Prince, was himself a very good racehorse.

Since I had been at another meeting and had not watched Corky's Towcester run, John Suthern telephoned me that evening and said: 'Have you thought about running him in blinkers?' Blinkers, which are worn under the horse's bridle, have the effect of reducing his line of vision to ahead only, so that he ceases to be distracted by things to his right and to his left. They are associated with slightly dishonest racehorses. Offended by John Suthern's advice in connection with my horse, I ignored it. I knew Corbiere had it in him to win good races, and one day the Grand National, and I quietly continued my campaign of preparation for the horse's future career.

Knowing Corky was still crying out for a longer trip, I sent him next to Kempton early in 1980, to a three-mile novice handicap hurdle, where he was ridden for the first time by Bryan Smart. In a handicap race, horses are weighted so that, in theory, they all cross the line together. The better horses are given more weight to slow them down, the not-so-good horses are given less to help speed them up. However, this theory of a blanket finish in a race of handicapped horses has never yet been known to happen! That day saw the success we had waited for. Corbiere seemed to love Kempton Park, and he just bolted home six lengths clear of the field. He was racing that day against Burrough Hill Lad. The two horses were upsides as they came to the last, only Corbiere pinged it and galloped away, and Burrough Hill Lad turned himself over and left my horse in front. Some said afterwards that Corbiere might not have won if Burrough Hill Lad had stayed upright, but I don't think so.

Strangely enough, Burrough Hill Lad was later sent to me to train and is still in my yard and today, if you put the two horses together to gallop at home, Burrough Hill Lad would be half as fast again as Corbiere. But they are of a different racing 'type'. I have always seen Corbiere as a Grand National horse, since he has the build and the stamina for the Aintree course. Burrough Hill Lad is, in my book, a Gold Cup horse. Cheltenham, where the Gold Cup is run in March, has a different type of fence to Aintree and it is my opinion that a horse who enjoys Cheltenham – in itself a very stiff course and hard to win on – is not necessarily an Aintree horse. We always knew Corbiere's style of jumping would suit Aintree: the way he jumped hurdles, his stamina, his action, pointed to a horse that would jump well over those massive National fences.

Corbiere ran his next two races at Newbury, the first being a novice handicap hurdle over three miles, where he gave the winner 1 stone 8 pounds and finished second. Next was the Philip Cornes Saddle of Gold Final, where, in heavy ground, we met Woodford

Prince, our old rival. Woodford Prince won the race but this time Corbiere managed to get a lot closer, with only Wayward Lad, yet another old rival, between them. The winner was threequarters of a length up on the second, Corbiere three lengths away third. At that point we realized what a good fight Corbiere had, in retrospect, put up against Woodford Prince at Towcester earlier in the season.

The season was now almost over, and we rounded off Corbiere's first campaign 10 days after Newbury, in the Waterford Crystal Stayers' Hurdle, run over three miles two furlongs at Cheltenham's Festival Meeting in March. Here Corbiere met a top class Irish horse called Mount Rivers, which duly von the race. Among the horses which finished in front of Corky was Derring Rose: the horse that won the same race a year later by 30 lengths. Those behind us included in their ranks John Cherry, a top class stayer of some years' standing both on the flat and over hurdles; a very good racehorse indeed.

Throughout this first season of racing over hurdles, Corbiere had proved a model of good behaviour in his training. For a start, he is what is called a 'good doer' or, as we say, he 'does on stones'. This means that he always eats every bit of food put in front of him and that his system utilizes it to its best advantage. If a racehorse eats all his feed and does well on it, then he is helping you to train him. It is as much as three-parts of the way to success with him, because a horse that won't eat and goes off its food when worked hard is a real headache. Corbiere is the opposite – a bit of a pig. He also has a marvellous racing temperament. I find I can read him like an open book. If he comes quietly out of his stable in the morning, I know there is something wrong. He's not necessarily sick, but just telling me he has had a bit of a hard race. Until he once again starts bouncing out of the box in the mornings, I don't give him any serious work. He doesn't exactly train himself, but he sends me messages loud and clear that I would ignore at my peril!

The 1980–81 jump racing season, commencing in the autumn, was Corky's first as a steeplechaser. He had proved himself over hurdles, showed that he was top class when the ground and the distance suited him, and his improving conformation reinforced my first impression: here we had the true stamp of a 'chaser, typical of the Irish breeding that is responsible for so many of history's top 'chasers from Arkle downwards. Corbiere was five now, rising six, and ready to tackle the bigger obstacles. We had schooled him over steeplechase fences at home at the end of his first hurdling season and, after a summer break, we gave him further schooling before considering him ready for a public run. We felt that two and a half miles would be quite far enough for his first run over fences in public and chose a straightforward novice 'chase over that distance at Lingfield for his debut. He was running against Josh Gifford's Moonlight Express, a horse with which Josh thought he might win a Gold Cup one day. The horse never did win a Gold Cup, but on that day he ran a race good enough to beat Corbiere and echo the course betting which had made them first and second favourites.

However, I was not happy with Corky's jumping at Lingfield and I determined to revert temporarily to hurdling in public, whilst continuing to improve the horse's jumping over fences at home. He was, therefore, sent to Cheltenham for a handicap hurdle for his next race, where he ran against another very good horse, No Pardon, finishing second, beaten four lengths, over three miles one furlong. I was well enough pleased with that result and continued the policy of marking time until the New Year.

In the meantime I selected the classy November Handicap Hurdle at Kempton Park over three miles for his next outing. Kempton is a fast track, with a short run-in and no hills, and is therefore regarded by trainers as a 'short' three miles, with not particularly testing ground. Corbiere's previous success in a three-mile hurdle race had also taken place at this course on the outskirts of London, which always attracts quality runners. When Corky romped up, carrying 11 stone 10 pounds, giving weight away all over the place, there were 10 lengths between him and his nearest rival. I felt rather confused by the results. As he had been running well for me in heavy ground on testing courses like Cheltenham, I imagined that *that* was the sort of course to suit my horse. I was somewhat perplexed, therefore, when on a fast track like Kempton he beat the living daylights out of the opposition not just on one occasion, but on two!

On that winning note, Corbiere was given a short breathing space before he was despatched to Ascot in December 1980 for the very high class Long Walk Stayers' Hurdle over three miles two furlongs on good ground. That very good horse Derring Rose won the race, John Cherry was second, and Siege King third. Corbiere followed this trio of quality animals home, but the running of the race gave us another inkling of the mysteries involved in Corbiere's training and racing habits. The slow pace at which they went at Ascot seemed to point to the fact that Corbiere, if he was to win his races, needed a really strong gallop from start to finish, a pace that would accentuate even further his qualities as a class stayer. Corky can run almost flat out for an entire race. Other horses find they can't keep with him when the race is run at a *true* gallop, because he stuns them with his stamina. The reason for the successes at Kempton suddenly became apparent. At Kempton, the horses had run both races at a tremendously fast gallop, and when the fields had torn off at a hair-raising gallop in the early stages, Corbiere was finding it hard to stay the early pace. Unbeknown to us, he was just biding his time! From my place in the grandstand, all I could think was that he was running an awful race. But as they came around the turn for home, he began to revel in the speed and the distance, covering the ground like a true stayer and picking off the other runners one by one like a sniper in the trenches. He just became stronger and stronger as the race went on, until the opposition was at the end of its tether.

In spite of this happy outcome in a hurdle race, I felt it was now time to reintroduce Corbiere to 'chasing and I took him to my 'home' track at Leicester for a quiet race over fences in a three-mile novice event. To our delight, Corbiere justified the patient schooling at home, jumping brilliantly and going clear of the field two fences out. He came galloping home by 12 lengths, hardly stretching himself for a moment. I thought my prayers had been answered at last. David always says I take horses to Leicester so that, if they are beaten, I can run home to cry on my parents' shoulders! But there was nothing to cry about that day and we decided that this was the beginning of Corbiere's career as a fully-fledged 'chaser . . . or so we thought.

Bob Champion, newly returned to the racing scene after his long and courageous fight against cancer, rode Corbiere in his next race, the three-mile Mitton Novice 'Chase at Warwick. The going was heavy, which suited us, and our instructions to Bob were to take him along at a good, strong pace and beat the rest with his stamina. It was not to be. The field refused to run at a good gallop, so Bob was obliged to cut out the running. Unfortunately, he and Corbiere parted company at the fifteenth fence, just when they looked as if they might win, and Bregawn – a future Gold Cup winner – went on to take first place. Bob Champion, when he had returned from the long walk back from the fifteenth, advised us always to take Corky to right-handed tracks, as he would be more at home on such courses. This preference by a horse for running either right-handed or left-handed round a racecourse is common enough. For some reason, a horse will prefer to gallop on courses that bend round to the left, while others favour those where the running rail bends to the right. Various explanations have been sought and expounded, but none seem really satisfactory. Ironically, Aintree racecourse, where the Grand National is run, is a left-hand track, and that was where Corbiere excelled and ran the best race of his life! Horses are continually confounding humans and that is perhaps one of the reasons they are described as the great levellers of man.

However, we chose to listen to Bob's advice, remembering the poor jumping displays which Corky had given at Lingfield, which is a left-handed course, and that he had won twice at Kempton and once at Leicester, which are both right-handed. We selected a three-mile novice 'chase on Ascot's right-handed course for his next race, where he met Bregawn again. This time it was Bregawn's turn to make the sudden departure from the scene, and he fell at the thirteenth fence. Corbiere won the race most convincingly and, in the process, became my twenty-second race winner of the season. It was exciting to become the first woman in racing history to train more than 21 winners in a season. From our small yard, then containing less than 20 horses, the feat was all the more considerable. It was both an historic milestone and a personal best, and I felt particularly pleased that it should be Corbiere who helped me achieve it. We eventually finished the season on 28 winners, a record number from a small stable.

But the season was still far from over when we took our National hope to Leicester, where, starting favourite, he met Sea Captain and other good young 'chasers over three miles of right-handed track. Our belief in his ability and our supreme faith in his honesty, which others had once doubted, were once again justified. Corky sailed round, making most of the running, slapping the opposition firmly into their place, and winning by an easy six lengths.

Next stop was Sandown, another course which draws a good class of horse. The horses were running right-handed yet again, but Corbiere was burdened on this occasion with the impossible task of giving a stone to Sea Captain, who stole the march and beat Corbiere two lengths. I remember the race with a degree of disappointment – which was not the result of losing to Sea Captain! Bryan Smart had ridden Corky at Ascot and at Leicester, and we'd always been pleased with the way he'd handled the horse. But at Sandown he made me very angry, because he knew perfectly well that giving a horse of Sea Captain's class a stone was a massive task for my horse. I had already decided that the Sun Alliance 'Chase at Cheltenham in March was my prime objective with Corbiere for the season, and I really didn't want him having any hard races prior to that event. So when, in my opinion, Bryan started using his whip too freely a good mile from the finish at Sandown, I was livid. The horse went very quiet after that race. I knew that if we weren't more careful, and if my jockeys weren't more thoughtful in future, the horse would go to Cheltenham in an unhappy frame of mind.

The solution to the problem of Corbiere's sulky behaviour after Sandown was a refresher race. To the layman, the solution to a hard race might appear to lie in a rest from racing, but we applied the theory that horses, when they go onto a racecourse, tend to remember their last run. If that run was a hard one, then they will be worried about a repeat performance. If, on the other hand, their previous race was a pleasant experience, they will be quite happy to race again. It is quite true that horses have elephantine memories: a horse will remember his last race very clearly when he goes out to run his next, and that last race therefore needs to be a sweet one if the horse is to be kept happy about his work.

In spite of Corky's apparent dislike of Lingfield, I had little option but to run him there again, since it was the only suitable race before Cheltenham. Bryan Smart was given the ride, with a flea in his ear and threats of dire consequences if he so much as touched the horse with his whip! Corky ran well until two fences from home and, though he could not quicken away, he was only beaten just over five lengths. He had been given 11 stone 10 pounds to carry, which allowed the opposition plenty of leeway, but he looked a happier horse when he came back in. My prime concern had been to restore Corbiere's zest for racing. I was pleased that he had stopped sulking, and we had given his confidence a badly-needed boost and re-minded him that racing is an enjoyable occupation. Once a horse ceases to enjoy his racing, he is lost to the trainer.

The Sun Alliance 'Chase, for which we were aiming as the high-spot of Corbiere's first racing season as a 'chaser, is not only the prime annual target for every top young 'chaser in England and Ireland, but also a most valuable pointer to a 'chaser's future. It proved a significant race for Corbiere, and one in which he ran against the cream of the season's best youngsters. Lining up at the start alongside us was Wayward Lad, a horse which subsequently won the King George VI Gold Cup at Kempton Park on Boxing Day and finished third in the Cheltenham Gold Cup to his stable-mate Bregawn. Also present were Lesley Ann (who won this race and many others), Fred Winter's good young novice Easter Eel, Captain John, Pilot Officer, and a good Irish opponent called Luska. The distance was three miles, and the going for the 1981 running was officially declared soft.

Bryan Smart gave our horse a fine, well-timed ride. Corky revelled in the soft going, enjoyed the pace at which the field went along, and rose to the challenge of the demanding Cheltenham fences. Truly delighted with his second place to Lesley Ann, I felt that, with eight lengths between them after three miles, Corbiere might have closed the gap had there been another four furlongs. Had it been a race over four miles, he could have won with the greatest of ease. The further the race, the better he was; more and more keenly I felt this was our Grand National winner. He had courage, jumped his fences carefully, and stayed all day. The season had been a good one, if slightly up and down at times, and the summer holiday for which Corbiere was now due was well deserved.

After two months in the paddock from the end of May to July, he came in from grass once again looking well. He and all the others in the yard were given a good bath, and their manes were pulled – which isn't as cruel as it sounds. The racehorse does not need yards of mane when he is in work, because reins and manes can easily become entangled during a race. The last thing a jockey needs is a fight to free the reins from a long mane and so, at the start of each racing season – indeed, as and when needed throughout the season – we pull the horses' manes. A special comb, or a simple old-fashioned finger, may be used for the task and the longer strands of mane are gently tugged loose until they come away from the horse's neck. The process is comparatively painless for the horse – though some become slightly irritated at having someone fiddling about with them – and the end result is a short mane, at one level from the top of the neck down to the wither, and a much smarter horse.

Corbiere, like the others, was shod, and then given two months of road work. The first couple of weeks were spent walking, the second part of the month walking and trotting, and then he was given mostly trotting work to harden his legs off before we started cantering on the gallops. Road work is an important part of the fitness programme, and Corbiere went through these processes at the end of his summer holiday in preparation for the new jumping season. He was now well into his sixth year, looking stronger and bigger than ever. Much was still expected of him but, had we been able to see a little way into the future, our hopes might not have been so high.

We selected the three-mile Charisma Records Chase at Kempton Park on 17 October 1981 for Corky's first race of the new season. New to Corky that is, for the National Hunt season officially begins in early August or late July with the small 'country' meetings at courses like Market Rasen, Newton Abbot, and Devon and Exeter, and slowly builds up to the more serious racing and the bigger prize money in October. Most of the major jumping races are run between October and early April, including the Whitbread, Hennessy and Mackeson Gold Cups, the Eider 'Chase, the Welsh, Scottish and Liverpool Nationals, and many others. After Liverpool in April, the season tails off to its close in early June, giving us most of June and July for our summer holidays.

At Kempton for the Charisma Records 'Chase, the going was officially good to soft, and our opposition was noticeably top class, including Approaching, Josh Gifford's nice horse which had won a

Hennessy Gold Cup. There was Stan Mellor's Royal Mail, a Whitbread Gold Cup winner and third in a National. Ridden by Steve Knight, Corbiere was giving both these top class 'chasers 2 pounds. The task before him was no picnic, but since he had returned from his summer grazing looking fitter and happier than ever, we were not unduly concerned. Approaching won the three-mile race, carrying 11 stone 7 pounds, and it seemed likely Corbiere would be runner-up. But it was not so. Totally uncharacteristically, totally without warning, and for the first time in his racing career, he fell. Not as a result of careless jumping, or of going too fast: the jockey had him perfectly poised for the third last, and he took off in exactly the right place and at exactly the right moment. But, as his feet touched down on the landing side of the fence, they met a wet and slippery patch of ground and, before he knew what had happened, Corky's front feet had shot out from under him. His back legs crashed through the fence and, as we watched, horrified and helpless, he spreadeagled onto the ground. It was a devastating moment. A horse falling in such a manner can do untold damage to itself. Fortunately, and to our immediate relief, Corky scrambled to his feet and showed no sign of lameness as he was led slowly back to the racecourse stables. No serious damage was in evidence but a fall like this, coming so unexpectedly and when he had been going well, would clearly give his confidence a most severe jolt.

It was not the first time I had faced a jolt to Corbiere's confidence, and certainly not the first time that I had restored a fallen race-horse's nerve. It was desperately disappointing, however, because everyone's hopes were running so high for the season. We were already working towards the 1982 Grand National which, at the time of the Kempton Park fall, was just six months away. The fall could change the entire picture, ruin our plans, and quite a few people suffered sleepless nights over the matter. This is racing, how-ever. Right at the beginning of a season's campaigning, disaster can strike. It had happened to me before, as it has happened to thou-sands of other trainers. The usual answer to a confidence-draining fall is some careful re-schooling over fences on the gallops at home, where the horse is slowly brought back to jumping to restore his faith in his own ability. A chink had appeared in Corbiere's armour and we needed to make sure it was repaired as quickly as possible by careful handling.

It wasn't fair that we should then have further bad luck so soon, but we did. No wonder the Irish call racing the glorious uncer-tainty; all the care we took was in vain. Whilst schooling on the gallops at home a few mornings afterwards, Corky struck into himself – that is, he hit the tendon running down the back of his foreleg with his hind foot – and within 12 hours a nasty lump had developed. In spite of protective boots, the damage was done. On top of the racecourse disaster, we now had an additional problem on our hands. I was very, very worried.

For several days we bound the affected tendon with Animalintex, a marvellous antiseptic padding which, if applied to open wounds, acts as a poultice and draws out infection. It is also very effective when applied to a bruised tendon, in conjunction with many hours spent with a hose playing cold water gently on the affected part. But in this case, the leg did not respond to the Animalintex and hosing treatment and, worrying more than ever, I called in our vet, Barry Park. Barry's advice was much as I feared and expected: complete lay-off, complete rest, and no work at all for at least three weeks. We also had to continue the hosing.

Time, being the healer that it is, duly worked its magic and within three weeks the unfriendly-looking lump had slowly vanished. That was not enough, however, to disperse the cloud which I now felt hanging over our heads and over the horse's future. I spent several very wakeful hours pondering on what was best for the horse, and what was best for his owners. What was the best course of action for everyone concerned?

The stable, as it happened, was going through what is known in the trade as a 'quiet' time. An owner, one of my best patrons, had just decided to take his horses elsewhere, and no less than 14 horses had been removed from my yard at one time. It was a rather low point: not many runners, not many winners and, as a result, not a great deal of incentive. Every racing stable needs its share of runners, and share of winners, to keep up the morale of the owners, the trainers, the stable lads, and the jockeys who ride the horses in their races. It is very tempting, when a yard is having a quiet spell, to run horses that are perhaps not one hundred per cent ready, in order to keep the ball rolling. It is easy to justify yourself to the owners if you run a horse before he is ready, because the owners are invariably anxious to see their horses in action. It is more difficult to be firm, both with yourself and the owners, and to refuse to race the horse until he *is* ready. Fortunately, my owners on the whole do realize that every yard goes through a lean period, and most of them will rally round and stand by to wait for the action to begin and the winners to start coming in again.

In the case of Corbiere, I had two choices, both unenviable. I could bring him back into work, more or less ignoring the fact that the lump had ever existed, and try to race him again. If he broke down as a result of that decision, untold damage would have been done – damage that might never be repaired. He would be out of action for more than just the 1981–82 season, but would be out of work for the 1982–83 season as well. A great deal more than the Grand National would be lost. The other option was to have the horse fired. There were other possibilities, but none of these were suitable. I could consider some of the usual remedies, most of which I had used at various times during my years of looking after other trainers' injured horses, which would help the ruptured fibres of the tendon to heal, provided the damage was not too severe. And there are other, more drastic techniques available, when bandaging and massage fail, including the surgical replacement of the damaged tendon with carbon implants. This may or may not work and may take many months to heal, which is fine if the horse is not a heavy financial investment to an already hard-pressed owner and trainer.

Of the three firing methods available – line, pin (or point) and acid – I chose line firing, simply because I have found the method works. Though some vets seem unwilling to fire horses' legs, I have found that the treatment, followed by a year's rest, will usually bring a horse back. Aldaniti, Josh Gifford's horse, proved a classic textbook case where line firing and a rest brought a broken-down horse to near-normal, and his historic victory in the 1981 Grand National is proof of the pudding. Not that Corbiere had broken down in the same sense as Aldaniti, for he had not. But I decided that sensible precautionary measures taken at the time of the injury, followed by rest, would prevent a recurrence of the tendon problem in the future. If he fell again as he had at Kempton, we might not be so lucky. A second tendon injury could have much further-reaching consequences.

After a successful line firing operation and a year's convalescence, Corbiere was back on a racetrack. It was a long time to wait for the return of a horse upon whom such high hopes were pinned. We chose Uttoxeter, the undulating Staffordshire course, for his next run. It is always my policy to give horses a couple of runs over hurdles after an injury since a hurdle race is less severe than a 'chase, so we reintroduced Corky to his job with a hurdle race on 21 October. Ben de Haan was given his first race-ride on the horse, and was instructed to let the horse have every chance, but on no account to hit him. Corbiere ran as expected, and it was a joy to see him back in action again. I was happy enough watching him run into twelfth place that day, and he appeared to have bounced back from his troubles with as much zest as ever; though for the next 48 hours I kept a watchful eye on him just to make sure that the nasty lump wasn't about to make another appearance. After such a gentle reintroduction to racing, we felt that Corbiere was perfectly capable of another run quite soon afterwards, and we entered him in a hurdle at Cheltenham on 27 October. With the going good to soft, he showed all his old pleasure in racing, and ran a very presentable race before tiring. It was another step in his return to the bigger obstacles, and convinced me that our horse was good and ready to take up where he had left off at Kempton Park just 13 months before.

I could not have dreamed of a better return to the steeplechasing scene than the race Corky ran at Sandown on 6 November 1982. He was up against a classy field of 'chasers, of whom only two finished ahead: Leney Duel and Colonel Christy. Ben came back into the unsaddling enclosure and uttered the immortal – to me, at least – words: 'Mother, that horse will win you the Grand National'. I believed him. He was only telling me what I already knew. Corbiere continued to enjoy his training and his work. The success of the firing operation assured his continuing soundness, and I did not feel that two weeks was too soon for another race, since I knew he was capable of running again fairly quickly. Had he seemed remotely listless, or dull in his coat, I would have waited a little longer. But he was bouncing with health and when we took him to Newbury for the Hennessy Gold Cup on 27 November he was fighting fit. It was probably his biggest race to date; one of the most important venues of his career so far.

His fifth place at Newbury that afternoon was far from a disgrace, especially when one considered the opposition and the distance. The race was won by subsequent Gold Cup winner Bregawn, followed home by Captain John and Sea Captain, and was run over three miles two furlongs. Corbiere was just beginning to find his stride by the time the winning post arrived. I was satisfied that he had given a good account – but I wasn't so happy at his owner's next suggestion! It is very easy, when one is the owner of a good racehorse, to get slightly carried away. Brian Burrough concerned me a great deal when, after Newbury, he started to discuss the possibility of running Corbiere in the Gold Cup at Cheltenham the following spring. Fortunately for Corky, I was able to persuade the owners that Gold Cup horses and National horses are two different entities. The former needs to be a high class animal with a definite finishing speed, to whom a three and a quarter mile race is the ideal. The Grand National horse requires stamina over speed, and the ability to jump four and a half miles of big fences with painstaking care. After pointing this out, reminding the Burroughs how close the two races would fall to each other, and how unwise it would be to give Corbiere a hard race at Cheltenham so close to the Aintree event, they agreed to rule out the Cheltenham Gold Cup. Added to this, I could hardly see us turning the tables on Bregawn in the Gold Cup when he had given us weight at Newbury and still beaten us!

Once again, just as we were becoming perhaps a little complacent about Corky's health, he gave us another fright. It happened at Worcester, in the race immediately following the Hennessy Gold Cup. He was made favourite to win over this three and a half mile course, leading the betting at 5–2. But he ran too badly to be true, finished in seventh place, and was never in the hunt nor looked happy for a moment of the running. It was quite awful. What now? we asked ourselves. It was December. The Grand National was just four months away.

11
GRAND NATIONAL 1983

It was an enormous relief to us all when we were able to find the solution to Corbiere's latest problem with comparative ease. Barry Park, our vet, elected to take a blood count from the horse, and found that his troubles were not severe on this occasion. He had a low count and proved to be temporarily anaemic. He needed a course of multi-vitamin injections and we all hoped that this would put our horse right. It would be put to the test when we went to the Welsh National at Chepstow just three days after Christmas. Here all our faith was restored and the story of Corbiere once more took an optimistic turn. I was fully confident, professionally speaking, that both the ground (soft) and the distance (three miles six furlongs) would suit our horse. Personally speaking, however, I was haunted, in spite of the vitamin injections, by the memory of his Worcester form all the way from Weathercock House to Chepstow racecourse. The Worcester ghost stayed with me throughout the saddling-up procedures and followed me to the grandstand where I was to watch the race with the Burrough family.

The runners settled down for the first circuit and Corbiere found himself sitting comfortably in fourth place. He made a slight mistake at the eighth fence, and set my heart pounding again: was he now struggling to keep up with the field? I expect, deep down, I was rather unrealistically hoping he would win his race from the front! Defeated before the race was over, I turned to Mrs Burrough and told her I was sure we were about to be disappointed yet again. But I had not reckoned on Corbiere. As the field turned for home, Ben started niggling at Corky for some action. The horse responded and began to run on relentlessly. Three fences from home, he was still full of running, though Ben had to keep working on him. He cleared the last fence half a length up on Pilot Officer, and they went to the line nose to nose. But to our joy, Corky battled on when it counted the most and as the two horses went across the finishing line, he was a neck up on his rival. He had won me my second National. The mighty Aintree venue now beckoned all the more invitingly. However, there was to be an anxious 10-minute wait before we were given the all-clear: Pilot Officer's jockey, Sam Morshead, was told by Mercy Rimell to object to Corbiere for 'taking his ground'. The stewards' decision went totally in our favour, and Sam Morshead lost his deposit and was fined for a frivolous objection.

Interestingly enough, we gained another first that day. The BBC, no doubt with some trepidation since Richard was commentating on the Chepstow race, invited me into the commentary box to be interviewed on television for the first time since we had divorced. There was obviously an atmosphere of some concern among the technicians, whom I could hear asking each other in a worried manner: 'Is this Richard's new wife?' To save them further embarrassment I butted in and said: 'No, I'm the old model'. They all burst out laughing and any tension immediately disappeared! Later on in the day we were invited by Corals, who sponsored the 1982 Welsh National, to join them in their box, where the Burroughs and I had a talk about Corbiere's racing between then and Aintree. As our aim from the beginning of the season had always been the Grand National at Liverpool, and as he had worked very hard throughout the first half of the season, we decided that Corbiere had earned a break. I was certain there was still plenty of improvement in him between now and the Grand National, which, at the time of the Welsh National, was just three months off.

After an eight-week spell off the track, we planned Corbiere's comeback in a three and a quarter mile 'chase at Doncaster on 28 February. To be frank, I did not think, for several reasons, that he could possibly win this race, although he would be trying his hardest. For one thing, he had been away from the track and would *need* a race; for another, the trip was on the short side for Corbiere; and I felt Doncaster too fast a course. The opposition would be too quick for Corky at the end of the race. Once again, however, our charge showed us we could all be wrong. Starting third favourite at 11–2, he hacked around with the leaders to three out, then simply took up the running and won a comfortable three lengths from Priest Rock. The result was a little surprising to his trainer, but who was I to complain that he had won a race when everything seemed to be against him? He was blowing hard after this race, but I was certain there was yet more improvement in him.

Doncaster demonstrated another facet of Corbiere's marvellous temperament. As it was a long way north of Lambourn, the furthest that we had taken him to race, we were obliged to use the overnight stabling facilities at Doncaster. Staying away from home often upsets a horse and, because he misses his familiar surroundings and his familiar stable companions, he often frets and worries the night away before his race. The net result is that such a horse will invariably run a frightful race next day and negate the whole purpose of the journey. Difficult travellers are a trainer's nightmare. Corbiere, however, was supremely confident and made himself completely at home in the overnight racecourse stabling. He settled down as though he were racing's most seasoned traveller, and duly ran a blinder the next day.

There was time for one more race before Aintree, to act as a pipe-opener to the big event. It was the Ritz Club Trophy Chase at Cheltenham, run over three miles one furlong, where he met a good horse called Scot Lane on good to soft ground. To be perfectly honest, I did not feel, at the time, that Ben de Haan had given Corky a very good ride, and I admit to cursing roundly when I watched Ben use the longer route to take it up with the leader. I was less happy still when Scot Lane ran on and left Corbiere five lengths behind. Fortunately I managed to hold my tongue on the matter until after I left the course and, driving home in the car, I thought about Ben's riding more carefully. Liverpool was, by now, just 23 days away. Ben had not given Corky a hard race and, in any event, I decided, the outcome was likely to have been the same. Scot Lane was always going to win the race, Corbiere was always going to be runner-up. It was really only a matter of the distance by which Scot Lane won. With hindsight, I was pleased with myself for not having given my jockey a rollicking, and pleased with my jockey for being such a considerate rider!

The next entry for Corbiere in the formbook reads very briefly, and goes something like this: '9 April 1983. SUN GRAND NATIONAL HANDICAP 'CHASE. Worth £52,949 to the winner. CORBIERE 8 years 11 st 4 lb. Ben de Haan. Looked well. Always close up. 3rd Halfway. Led 21st, 22nd, 23rd. Stayed on strongly flat. Won ¾ length.' Strange that all the effort, all the worry, all the fun and the fighting which we went through to get the horse fit enough to win a Grand National should end up in almost insultingly brief telegraphic form. No one would think, reading just those few abbreviated sentences, that a horse called Corbiere, ridden by a young and comparatively inexperienced jockey, had just won the greatest steeplechase the world has ever known. Trained, for the first time in history, by a woman. And yet that was what happened.

We have always stayed at the same small family hotel, the Sunnyville in Southport, ever since I first started taking horses to Aintree. I have no liking for large impersonal hotels where, if one needs to be out working racehorses and cannot return for breakfast until 10 am, it causes havoc with the hotel management. The larger hotel takes even less kindly to the idea of a trainer, having worked her horses, bringing 14 guests back to share breakfast with her! Our little guest house is always warm and friendly and, knowing my addiction to endless cups of tea, I always receive the same welcome upon arrival: 'Pot of tea, Jenny?'

The first item on this trainer's agenda on Grand National morning is always the same. Rise at 6 am to a pot of Mrs Bramley's early morning tea – I think if I asked for tea at 3 am it would be brought to me with just as much pleasure. Having drunk that, I dress quickly, not forgetting to wear wellington boots, and we make our way down to Aintree racecourse before 7 am in order that I can have my first look at the horses in my care. The way horses appear first thing in the morning, the way they first come out of their stable, is an age-old way for a trainer to gauge horses. If a horse emerges slowly, looking neither very alert nor particularly interested in its surroundings, then it is cause to give the trainer concern. If, however, it comes punching its way out of the stable, bucking and bouncing around like a two-year-old, the trainer can rest assured: he has a fit horse. On the morning of 9 April 1983, my three runners looked very well, fit and ready for their final workout.

Our routine remains invariable on the day of every Grand National. It would be unwise to push the horses into an extended gallop and risk them injuring themselves, so after a mile of walking and trotting, they canter for a couple of furlongs with the jockeys taking them along at a steady speed, before being pushed out for a furlong at a sprint pace. They will probably cover one and a half miles altogether, as we find this is the right distance to give both the horse and his jockey a blow-through. Bearing in mind that the horses have been shut up in their overnight stables since their arrival at Aintree on the previous day – we always travel the horses up the day before the race – they will be feeling slightly pent-up and will need to stretch their legs. I usually think the jockeys can also benefit from the blow-through, since they have probably been enjoying life to the hilt since *their* arrival at Aintree the day before the race!

The morning of the 1983 National was beautiful and, as the sun shone down on the horses as they completed their morning workout, I chattered happily with the Press and television interviewers who had come down to watch us. There was an air of high excitement and, of course, the usual speculation about the state of the runners and their prospects for the race. The usual talk about the odds and the betting was flying around and I recalled the day, a month before, when I had met some workmen on the sands at Burnham-on-Sea in Somerset and had given them the tip of a lifetime. Corbiere had been taken down to Burnham for some work on the sands, at a time when the ground around Lambourn was solid with frost. Corbiere, and the five other horses we had taken, cantered steadily for seven miles along the beach before being given half an hour's walking in the sea. To Corky this was a great new sport and, much to Ben de Haan's amazement and horror, he tried to get down on his knees for a roll in the waves! When we removed Corbiere's tack, he dropped down on his knees and this time managed to get right down and roll over on his back. Between rolls he was getting back to his feet and digging deeper and deeper with his feet into the sand, and the three council workmen who were loading sand onto a trailer to put in the goal mouths of the local football pitches said that, since he was doing a better job of digging sand than they were, would he please dig a little closer to their trailer? They asked his name, and I strongly advised them to have a tenner on my horse to win the Grand National. I wonder to this day whether they took my advice.

At Aintree, it felt absolutely marvellous to watch the horses at work and to see my three charges so obviously ready for this big race. I felt supremely happy – for the present, at least. As soon as we felt the horses had had a satisfactory workout, and had been settled safely back in their stables behind the security gates once more, it was time for our traditional walking of the course. This year, travelling around the course with Brian Burrough's father and sister, who felt unable to walk the full four and a half miles, I saw the course from his car. We drew up beside each fence in turn, and the fences looked awesome. Alan Burrough, not a man who normally shows his emotions, looked pretty taken aback by their size. It was up to me to reassure him that, win or lose, we were running a fit horse; Corbiere was more ready to tackle those jumps than ever before in his life. I knew we had every chance with him to win this race. Barring any unfortunate accidents, he would most certainly complete the course; though I dared not let myself think too much about winning.

The party which walked the course that day was, quite naturally, a large one. There were some 20 people connected with our three runners who undertook the four and a half miles on foot, including the owners of Artistic Prince and Monty Python, and our three jockeys. At each fence I spent a few moments with each jockey, discussing in detail the exact point at which, if possible, I would want him to place his horse. Ben de Haan dropped out of the main party for much of this time, walking quietly on his own, sizing up the route over which he planned to ride Corbiere. He didn't get involved in the banter with the rest, but kept himself very much to himself.

Each jockey listened as I gave my opinion and judgement, and though there was plenty of leg-pulling, the discussion was basically a serious one. Each of the horses was different and needed to be taken on a route to suit its ability and stamina. The intense happiness of the previous hour disappeared bit by bit as we moved from one massive obstacle to another, and each of us became more and more nervous as the party progressed towards the end of the course. By the time we had finished our walkabout, none of us was in any doubt about what lay ahead. This was the Grand National, and if any of us had forgotten the importance of the occasion, one look at Becher's was enough to act as a stern reminder.

The waiting between looking at the course and the race itself, which normally starts soon after 3.20 pm, seems interminable. There is something like five hours to fill between leaving Aintree for breakfast back at our hotel; five hours which can seem more like five days. It's a nerve-racking time for all concerned. There are the owners, who have been paying out month after month, possibly year after year, in order to be able to bring a horse to Aintree to run in the Grand National. Apart from the cost of buying the horse – anything from £6,000 to £60,000 – there are endless ups and downs, spells of uncertainty, and only a very faint chance of recouping the costs, even if the horse wins the race. There would be people who might say that £50,000 is a lot of money for winning one race, and I wouldn't argue with that, but there are other considerations to bear in mind. The cost of the horse in the Burroughs' case was about £10,000 and, having bought him as a two-year-old, they had probably forked out some £5,000 a year to keep him in training, which adds up to an incredible £30,000. From the possible £50,000 which the Burroughs were gambling on winning with their horse, they would have to pay me, their trainer, around 10 per cent of the prize money, give the jockey his 10 per cent, and only a mean (and subsequently rather unpopular) owner would miss out the stable lad who takes day-to-day care of the animal at home. Fifty thousand is probably what it cost to get Corbiere to Aintree to run in the Grand National and, fortunately for all concerned, he won and repaid his owners in full. By comparison, the winner of a Derby would collect a figure nearer £100,000, then be taken off to stud to earn a figure which can run into several millions of pounds! Little wonder there is a racing adage which says that if you win the Derby it makes you rich; if you win the Grand National it makes you happy. It's perfectly true and makes even clearer the point that the average National Hunt owner is of necessity a very sporting man or woman.

A great deal of jumbled and confused thought may go through your mind as you whittle away those five hours. For myself, I head back to our little hotel where I know Zena Bramley isn't going to have a fit when I tell her that in addition to myself and my family, there are some of my owners and their families to feast upon her bacon and eggs. She takes it all in her stride. After breakfast, on the morning of the 1983 race, I bought all the newspapers and simply took them upstairs to read as I lay on the bed. I wasn't the most sociable person in the world. I could think only of the horses, the prize money we were running for, the hazards of the course and the danger to the horses and their riders if something should go wrong. In one sense, I would be pleased when it was all over, no matter what the outcome.

For the one hundredth time I turned to David and asked: Why do we do it? What possesses us every year to bring runners to Liverpool? Every year is a repeat of the year before: we long for the entire racing season to have a runner in the Grand National and spend weeks and months working to that end, only to arrive on the day of the race and find ourselves wishing we had not bothered. The overwhelming pressure of those hours is repeated each and every Grand National day; there's no relief from the tension of the waiting. And yet, what point would there be in training National Hunt horses, if there was no Grand National at the end of the season? There would be almost no purpose behind the long hours of work, the arduous travelling, the early mornings on the gallops in freezing rain and biting winds. The fear and the worry might disappear, but what would replace them? Some trainers may be content with a Gold Cup or a Champion Hurdle – not so me. To me, as the supreme test of courage and ability for both horses and jockeys, the Grand National was a constant quest . . . the be-all and end-all of my racing season. Nevertheless, I hated the day of the race, though I had strived so hard to be there. I would have felt worse only if I had not had a runner at all! It is the greatest steeplechase in the world, watched by millions of people all over the world, and I wanted one of my horses to win it. So there I lay, reading the racing Press and their comments on our horses, torn between intense ambition and intense fear.

The racing Press, that morning, did not seem to fancy Corbiere. The betting at the start of the race put him at 13–1, though he had been longer in the odds during previous weeks. His race at Chepstow in the Welsh National had produced a remarkable effect on his odds and put him well into the limelight, but his chances were still not best-fancied by the racing journalists. It occurred to me to wonder whether racing journalists ever realize quite how offensive and hurtful their dismissive comments on a horse's chance may be to the horse's trainer, let alone its owner. They have a job to do, and most of the racing journalists I encounter do their homework thoroughly before advising their readers where best to place their hard-earned cash. Do they care how the trainers feel when we are told that our horse isn't good enough, doesn't have the turn of foot for the race in question, and sometimes, quite rudely, shouldn't even be in the race at all! Fortunately, on that day none of my three runners was dismissed quite so brutally, and Corbiere, whilst not looked upon as the most likely winner, was given an agreeable press. I wondered how many trainers of Grand National winners had picked up a morning paper to be told their horse 'lacked experience' and would 'find the fences too big'. What pleasure it must give trainers at the end of the day, when *their* horse, who lacked experience or was supposed to find the fences too big, is nonetheless wearing the famous sash of honour and standing in the winner's enclosure?

Time crawled on and we began washing and changing. My sons kept coming in and out of our bedroom with an endless stream of questions which on the one hand were very annoying, but on the other helped keep our minds off events around us. 'Mum, seen my hairbrush?' or 'Dave, can I pinch your aftershave?', or 'Where's the hairdrier?' or 'Does this tie go with this shirt, Dave?' They irritated us intensely, but secretly I was rather pleased that Mark and Paul felt the occasion important enough to warrant dressing up. Dressing for the Grand National is to 'chasing people what dressing for Ascot is to flat racing people. Everyone concerned goes to great pains to look smart, even down to the stable lads leading the horses in the paddock. I had bought a new hat and gloves, and a dark brown suit with cream piping which I thought befitted the occasion, and with David, Mandy and my sons all looking unrecognizably smart, we trooped downstairs together to join my parents and our friends, and hence to our cars to drive to the racecourse. Some of the waiting, at least, was now over.

My first task upon arrival back at the racecourse was, and always is, to find my way to the weighing room, primarily to check that the horses were correctly declared to run. That year was more important than most, since I had three runners. Artistic Prince and Monty Python as well as Corbiere had to be taken care of, and it would have been most unamusing, to put it mildly, to find we had come this far and not declared the horses to run on the day of the race. I need not have worried, as it turned out, and everything was in order by the time I reached the course.

Robert Stigwood, Artistic Prince's impresario owner, had kindly given us the use of his box for the day. Mr Stigwood's manager, Rod Gunner, was host to the various members of my family as well as my owners, and it was a relief to have a refuge away from the crowds in the stands and the public enclosures. This was especially true of my parents who, both being in their late sixties, would not have taken kindly to being jostled about for the rest of the afternoon. I stayed with my family in the box for about an hour. There was a delicious spread of food and everyone about me was tucking into the goodies, but not the trainer. All the trainer felt capable of consuming at that moment was a large brandy with a liberal quantity of lemonade and several cigarettes to accompany it. I'm no great drinker, but at that moment I needed something stiff to calm the inner woman.

Feeling brave and more secure for having had the brandy, I went to the weighing room to seek out the jockeys who were to ride my horses. Ben was riding Corbiere, Colin Brown was riding Artistic Prince, while Paddy O'Brien had the mount on Monty Python, leased to Top Rank, who had held a raffle amongst their club members so that one of them would have the pleasure of 'owning' a horse on Grand National day. I have never forgotten the lesson that my former husband Richard was taught at Fontwell Park, when he was weighed out incorrectly by the clerk of the scales. I was determined that this should never happen to a jockey riding one of my horses and the visit to the weighing room was mainly to ensure that the clerk of the scales and I saw the same reading on the scales!

My next task was to saddle up the horses. Tack is all-important, and tacking up a horse for a race is a job which demands a high standard of thoroughness and care. Because the correct tack is so vital and is the only thing that holds the jockey to the horse during the race, and enables him to steer his horse and regulate the speed, I always saddle up my own runners. This means that, in the event of a piece of equipment breaking or coming adrift in running, there's no one but myself to blame. The order of saddling the three horses was decided entirely by their weights: Artistic Prince and Monty Python, both with 10 stone, were saddled up first; Corbiere, with 11 stone 4 pounds, was next. I checked and double-checked each horse and, feeling satisfied that everything was in order, I knew I would be able to relax – on that score at least – when the race was in progress.

Tacking up a horse for racing requires a special 'running order', as it does for any other competitive occasion, such as driving, horse trials or show jumping. It is not a question of simply slapping on a saddle and throwing on a bridle. The horse's breast-girth is put on first. It runs, as you would expect from its name, around the horse's breast, and is elasticated to allow freedom in running. It is held in position by a strap over the horse's neck, whilst the two ends of the breast-girth attach to the main girth on the saddle. Following the breast-girth, a large, slightly-dampened piece of chamois leather is laid on the horse's back which, being shiny from all his recent grooming and care, could cause the saddle to slip. The leather helps prevent this. A pad is laid over the leather, which acts as a buffer to the saddle and prevents saddle sores developing. This pad may be made of polystyrene (for horses carrying light weights) or from foam-filled cotton (for heavily weighted horses), and is then covered with the light cotton cloth bearing the horse's race number. In the case of Artistic Prince and Monty Python on Grand National day, all that remained to be put on was their special lightweight racing saddle, held in place by a girth and anchored the more firmly by a webbing surcingle which runs around the top of the saddle and buckles under the horse's belly. The girth on the saddle has a special non-slip rubber lining which acts as a further safety measure.

Corbiere, since he had 11 stone 4 pounds to carry, wore a special cloth under his saddle. Known as a weight cloth, it contains small pockets where lead weights are stored. Since the jockey and his saddle together weighed only 10 stone, over a stone of lead had to be added to Corky's weight cloth. Hence the expression 'lead weight': the jockey's weight is a moveable feast, which can be placed forward in running to help keep the horse balanced, and can equally easily be placed back in the saddle if a horse pecks or stumbles. But the lead weight, which in the case of some horses may amount to as much as two and a half stone, is fixed firmly on his back and will not obligingly shift around to help him. This is why, when a horse is given top weight of 12 stone 7 pounds in a race, a heavy jockey who can ride at that weight is preferable to the lighter jockey who needs a pile of lead to help him make up the weight.

With the horses tacked up, time moved slowly on until, at long last, the parade began. Horses always parade in the paddock before a race, from the smallest country courses like Folkestone and Fontwell, to the class tracks such as Ascot, Cheltenham and Sandown Park. From this moment onwards, privacy is gone. This is the moment the public has waited for, when the horses, owners, jockeys and trainers are on view to the world at large. If anything has been overlooked, until this moment it may be retrieved. But with the exception of emergencies, such as a horse spreading a plate (losing one of his special lightweight racing shoes), or tack snapping and breaking, you are now in the hunt and, provided your horse goes to post and consents to race, there's no turning back.

For the trainer, this is yet another of those more stressful moments. Having been busying oneself around the horses in the privacy of the racecourse stables, where security ensures that no strangers can pry into one's activities, suddenly life is a goldfish bowl. An added worry to me that day was a television camera hidden in a flowerbed. I had agreed in advance with the BBC to meet my three jockeys beside the flowerbed in the parade ring, where I would give them their riding instructions prior to mounting up, for the benefit of the cameras and the television viewers. In fact, terrified of fluffing my words before the camera, I had already drummed my riding instructions into the jockeys' heads well beforehand and I warned them not to take any notice of anything I might blurt out in front of the television microphones. Later on, after the race, it would not matter what I said in front of a television crew . . . just before the race, it was crucial!

I knew how each of my horses was to run that day. I had already instructed Colin Brown to take Artistic Prince, along with Ben and Corbiere, on the inside of the course. Both were to run on the inside track – but not too close to the wings! – and both could be relied upon to jump their hearts out, come hell or high water. The fences are more severe on the inside of the track, but this has the effect of persuading more jockeys to ride nearer to the outside of the course. The result is a clearer run on the inside, with only the very good horses and very brave jockeys for company. I preferred Monty Python to run on the outer track, because he can run a terrible race one day, and slaughter everything in sight the next. When he races well, he can be brilliant; when he runs badly, he is unbearable and I'm frequently to be seen jumping up and down in the grandstand at race meetings, tearing large chunks of my hair out at the roots, simply because Monty Python is doing something awful in a race! He was capable of cruising round Aintree like a Rolls Royce, but he was just as likely to take each fence by the roots and turn himself upside down. As it happened, he did neither. But if Monty was going to get up in front of a fence and do one of his famous 'Ali Shuffles' before deciding which way to jump – if at all – I didn't want Artistic Prince or Corbiere to be in his slipstream getting caught up in his antics.

The horses began parading around the paddock and, gradually, one by one, their trainers and owners joined them. I was in a slight dilemma with three runners and three sets of owners, each of whom would want my undivided attention during these moments before the race. Fortunately, all three sets of owners realized the problem and very considerately all stood together in a most sportsmanlike fashion. One by one we mounted up our jockeys and, seconds later, they left the paddock and disappeared from our view to parade before the grandstand on the course. This parade is a feature of many bigger races in England and, whilst it might entertain the public at large, it gives the trainer something else to worry about. Many horses become particularly anxious before a big race. They have a sixth sense which tells them that this is no ordinary occasion.

The size of the crowds, the general air of excitement and tension about them, are quickly picked up by sensitive horses. A nervous animal can boil over completely during the parade before the grandstand and it's a moment which I'm always pleased to see out of the way.

The route to the parade is a hazard in itself. Some members of the public take it upon themselves to get up to all manner of tricks, and I have heard of horses coming back with large chunks cut out of their tails by souvenir hunters! But more worrying to the trainer is the problem of dope. Racecourse security ensures that there is little chance of anyone 'getting' to your horse to feed him undesirable substances – at least while he is in the stable area. On the advice of Barry Park, our vet, who told me that some substances can be absorbed by the horse if rubbed onto his coat, I instructed two lads to go down to the parade with each of my three horses. Not a single soul was to come into direct contact with any of them since, according to Barry, any doping substance rubbed onto the horse's coat in this manner would take only 15 minutes to become effective. Six eagle-eyed lads therefore accompanied my three runners through the crowds and kept potential dope fiends at bay!

None of my horses threw a fit during the parade; nor indeed would I have expected it of them. They were all seasoned campaigners, with Artistic Prince at Aintree for his third Grand National, Monty Python for his second, and Corbiere, whilst taking his first tilt at the race, no longer an over-excitable animal. I watched the horses closely as they went back to the start, following their inspection of the first fence. Three of my stable lads were ready and waiting at the start to tighten up the three horses' girths a hole – in cantering to post the tack settles down on the horse's back, and a girth that was tight when the horse left the paddock can be dangerously loose by the time the race begins. The starter and his assistants usually undertake to check horses' girths, but in the National, with 40 starters milling about, I prefer that my own lads are there to make doubly sure.

We returned from watching the start to the television monitor, since it is the best way to watch the Grand National. Whilst watching from the grandstand or from the box may give a sense of atmosphere and excitement, it cannot match the view obtained through the television cameras, which are strategically placed at the fences to catch the action at every jump. This gives me the chance to watch the race for every second of running, though I was not to know, as I glued myself to the monitor that afternoon at around 3.20 pm, that it would be one of my horses filling most of the frame throughout the race. At that moment, however, I was chiefly concerned that no one should be hurt: none of the horses, none of the jockeys, and especially not my three.

Suddenly, the waiting, the anxious preparations, were all over. The starting official climbed onto his rostrum and raised his red flag and, with a roar from the crowds, it dropped. No turning back now. They were *off*. I felt incredibly sick with fear and wondered how I would get through the next 10 minutes of my life. The field was running, apparently at one million miles an hour, towards the perilous first fence. This always happens, and has become a feature – albeit a dangerous one – of every Grand National. Every year the clerk of the course goes into the jockeys' changing room before the start and utters the same warning: 'Boys, the ground is fast. Don't be in too much of a hurry.' And always, without fail and despite the warning, the field heads at a flat-out gallop to the first fence! Safely up and over, and I could see Corbiere striding away and on towards the second. Artistic and Monty were lost, temporarily, in the mêlée. A few seconds later, as the field swept over the third fence, the haze began to clear, the field spread out, and I was relieved to see them reappear. Artistic was around 12 lengths behind Corbiere, and Monty somewhere behind Artistic. But Corbiere's jumping was a sight to warm any trainer's heart, let alone mine. This was how I had always pictured him in my more optimistic moments: flying the fences, picking up and galloping away from them as though they were no more than a foot high. But I kept my thoughts to myself as the field went over the fourth and fifth. The sixth fence was Becher's, but there was nothing to fear: Corky flew it with almost contemptuous ease. That was fine, but a horrid nagging thought crept into my mind: had Ben taken Corky to the front too early? They were up with Delmoss and had been galloping along just in behind the leaders almost from the start of the race. How many times in living memory had the Grand National been won from in front? Crisp had run from in front, with Richard, and look what had happened to them. . . .

I could not, however, fault Corbiere's jumping and though I dearly wanted to turn to my family and say so, the superstitious side of me took over and I refrained. I was certain that the moment I said 'Look how he's jumping', it would have put the mockers on him. Whenever one of my horses is going well and I say as much, it seems to have an adverse effect! I contented myself with watching and waiting and trying to keep calm. It was beginning to look very, very good to the Corbiere supporters and they were beginning to rumble with excitement in the box all around me.

All appeared to be well, though Ben told us later that he had one anxious moment. Although Corbiere didn't give him a second's concern, at one point Delmoss and Bill Smith galloped off in a different direction. Ben had to make a split-second decision. Should he assume Bill Smith was going the right way and follow suit, or should he carry on his own way and trust his own judgement? It was an agonizing moment, but Ben kept his head, young though he is. He stayed on course, but it must have given him a few nasty seconds and he handled it beautifully. Bill Smith was soon back on course and upsides of Corbiere.

The first circuit was complete. Of my three runners, Artistic Prince was still in contention, but Monty Python had been obliged to bring himself to an abrupt halt when the horse preceding him to the Chair had slammed on the anchors and Monty had found himself with no room to manoeuvre. He was by now most decidedly the happiest horse at Aintree! Artistic Prince, who would not have felt so pleased as Monty at being forcibly withdrawn from the hunt, met with the same fate at the eighteenth fence when baulked by a refusing horse. It was now all in Corbiere's hands, and those of his young rider. The mad gallop of the early stages was over. They were going along at a more sensible speed, and all the horses and jockeys were giving themselves time to approach the fences with more care, and jumping as a result with a greater degree of safety.

A loose grey horse now began to haunt us. It poached Corky's ground, and was giving him little freedom and space to jump. It dithered about in his path for a few seconds but, to my relief, it ran out and left Corky in peace.

As he came to Becher's the second time around, I began to pray for dear life. Just let him jump this safely, I begged my Maker, whilst I closed my eyes for a second. I promised I would do almost *anything* if Corky could just get round safely and win the race. Fortunately, I did not make any rash promises about not telling fibs! When I looked at the monitor again Corbiere had landed safely and was galloping on to the next two fences easily. Then came the Canal Turn, at five feet, which Corky also flew. The next big worry was Valentine's, five feet six inches in height with a five-foot brook on the landing side. No problem, Corky was over. Now we were in with a really great chance. Ben proved his horsemanship time and time again. Keeping Corbiere balanced and always straight into his fences, he had the horse on the bit for virtually the entire race. Only in the dying strides at the finish, when Greasepaint was coming up and threatening to snatch victory from under our noses, did he finally let the horse come off the bit.

By now the entire box was adamant that nothing could beat Corbiere. But close behind and moving with obvious ease was the bay figure of Greasepaint. Delmoss had dropped out and Corky was in front from the twenty-first fence. Hello Dandy, Greasepaint and Grittar, Colonel Christy and Yer Man comprised the serious opposition. I was relieved to see Grittar's jockey pull out his stick and get to work. But Greasepaint was still full of running and made my hair stand on end. It was unbearable. I felt very, very scared. Ben de Haan looked over his shoulder, which may or may not have been a good thing. I knew he couldn't hear the other horses, for the noise of the crowd was so great, but a jockey can lose his rhythm by turning his head to look behind. Ben didn't lose his stride, but what he saw was worrying: Greasepaint, slowly closing, and everything else tiring. Only Corky and his Irish rival seemed to have any gas left in their tanks.

They came over the last and the Irish horse was just down on Corbiere. At this point my sister Mandy began to cry and that was all it needed: I was soon crying with her. The rest of my family were insane with excitement, screaming their heads off all about us, but it wasn't over. Not yet. I did think, for that moment at least, that Corbiere was going to win easily. He ran away from the last big Aintree fence like a hurdler pinging the last at Kempton, and immediately put a lot of distance between himself and Greasepaint. But he was giving Greasepaint over a stone in weight and the Irish horse began to quicken after us. The trouble for me, in electing to watch the race on the monitor instead of from the grandstand, was that I could not see just how far away that winning post was! Greasepaint got to Corbiere's girth, and I think that was when Corbiere felt the challenge. It was close enough for his liking, and he surged forward yet again. Ben apparently felt the same way and between them they worked like furies, and as the last strides of the race were run, Greasepaint could get no closer. It was over. Corbiere had won. Threequarters of a length.

David came running up and threw his arms about me. 'You've done it, you've done it', he was shouting. A second later, the words sank in . . . 'Lord, we've done it'. This wasn't a dress rehearsal, this was the big performance. This was the Grand National, the race we had wanted to win for so long. We were all crying like babies, and even my father, who had stayed dry-eyed for the last 69 years, allowed himself to shed a tear or two. Suddenly I was tumbling down the stairs and rushing to see my horse come home. Could all this really be happening to me? Surely not, this must be someone else. But it wasn't.

12
CORKY COMES HOME

The road to the winner's enclosure at Aintree had been long. Many hours later, after the last echoes of the cheering crowds had faded from the rafters of the old Aintree grandstand, and the only sound which could still be heard on the Aintree turf was the whine of the night wind, I drove home to Lambourn. I reflected on the day gone by . . . thought of the people whom I knew would care . . . hoped my family would come down for the party at home next day to welcome Corbiere back . . . and reminded myself that whilst these were the early hours of Sunday morning, and Sunday would be spent celebrating, I should soon be in harness once more and back to the everyday life of a racing trainer. We could bathe in the glory and happiness of this victory for only a few short hours before reverting to the essential and strict routine of a racing stable.

We had enjoyed a celebration meal with Corbiere's owners, the Burroughs, at the Bold Hotel in Southport, leaving the hotel at midnight for the long drive home, though Corbiere stayed overnight at the course after his big race. I had checked him over before bidding him good night, thanking him from the bottom of my heart for making this dream come true for me. He would have a quiet, restful night to help him recuperate from his marathon, and to prepare him for his long journey home on Sunday. He was taken by his lad Gary for a walk round to pick at some grass verges before finally being settled in his box with a deep bed, a light feed and some hay. Gary was still in a dream world of his own. Our stable lads become very involved with their horses and it is a matter of enormous importance when their horses win races. They spend several hours of each day in the company of their horses back at home, mucking them out, grooming them, feeding them, and attending to all their needs. They travel to the races with their horses, take care of them at the racecourse, lead them around the parade ring, and are waiting – overjoyed or otherwise – as their horses come off the course at the end of a race.

Quite naturally, each of the lads wants his three horses to be the best in the yard, and win the best races. There tends to be a certain order of priority amongst the lads, and the older, more experienced lads tend to have the best horses to 'do'. As the lads become more experienced and gain, we hope, some wisdom, they are allotted better animals. One would not, quite obviously, tell a young stable lad with no experience to look after the yard's extremely valuable Grand National winner or Gold Cup winner. It is one matter for a stable lad to look after a horse which is believed by the owners and the trainer to have Grand National-winning potential. It is quite another ball-game when the horse, just a few short hours before, actually won that race and stood, feted and beribboned, in the famous winner's enclosure at Aintree. To a stable lad, it would be the highspot of his working life; it was certainly the most awesome event in Gary's life until that moment. It is little wonder, therefore, that when an unsuspecting lady, watching Gary and Corbiere as the horse nibbled at the grass, said: 'Young man, do you like your horse?', Gary could come out with only a very few short syllables: 'Like him? *Like* him? I f————g *love* him!' The lady, not realizing that she was looking at the Grand National winner, stalked off in high dudgeon, whereupon Corbiere's connections, who had been standing a few yards away and had heard the exchange, creased up with unhidden mirth.

I had been swept about for the entire afternoon, following the race, by a pair of protective and hefty policemen. If I didn't know before what a criminal feels like when he is arrested, I knew it afterwards! I was escorted between television news crews, journalists, and a host of well-wishers both from the racing world and from the public at large. The afternoon took on an air of fantasy. Rather like a character in a story, I heard champagne corks popping, people cheering, and felt the ground briefly touch my feet from time to time as I floated from one interview to another. This, then, was Fame!

Driving home down the motorway hours later, I found there was another kind of fame. My family, whose energy was spent, slept quietly in the car as we thundered towards Berkshire and continued sleeping as I pulled the car into a service area for petrol. I unscrewed the cap and began filling the tank. The attendant looked at me for a moment. 'You look as if you've had a hard day', he said cheekily. I gave him a surprised stare. 'Oh, really?' The boy laughed. 'You bet! I know you. You're Jenny Pitman and you won the Grand National today. I watched you on the telly this afternoon.' I laughed and went off to the ladies' loo. It was full of very cheerful ladies, who had obviously come from a coach party. One of them suddenly stared at me. 'Hey, girls, look. This is Jenny Pitman!' They all came and congratulated me, and we stood laughing and chatting for a long while about the relative virtues of women trainers. 'You've shown them all the way today, Jenny', they said as they headed back to their coach.

It was 1.30 am by that time. We arrived at Upper Lambourn soon after 3 o'clock, and my first desire – after a pot of tea, of course – was to sit and watch the video recordings of the day's proceedings. I had said an awful lot of things before television cameras that day; now I could find out whether I'd managed to make any sense or not! Watching the videos helped me to relax, and brought me back down to earth slightly. I had been as high as a kite from the second that Corbiere had crossed the line to win the 1983 Grand National just 12 hours ago. Was it really only 12 hours? It seemed like a lifetime.

I had been up since 6 am on Saturday morning and, having watched the video recordings right through and reassured myself that I'd said nothing out of place – though I was slightly disconcerted to hear myself announce that I was now out to beat Red Rum's record of three victories in the race – I had a bath and lay on the bed for a few hours. I felt very, very contented and relaxed and smiled happily to myself as the enormity of our achievement filtered through to my brain. It would make such a difference to us all. This race marked the attainment of a personal ambition for me, but I was not forgetful of those who had helped me. It would reflect on them, too, and help a lot of people. We were in the record books, and history had been made. Our yard would always have this achievement behind it, and would hopefully enjoy more success as a direct result. I was very much aware of this; and was proved right. The year prior to the Grand National we had 18 horses in the yard; the season immediately afterwards, we had 28. That was all to the benefit: more stable lads had employment, the yard gained a new respect, and from being a good yard, we became an in-demand yard. People who had not previously considered sending horses to Jenny Pitman suddenly wanted to send their horses to me to train. Thus, we found ourselves with some new owners to join our already-staunch team and, as a direct result, we found some new friends. Sleep finally overtook me and I drifted off for a couple of hours.

At six o'clock I was awoken by the noise of cars in the driveway. I had a quick look through the window – and was amazed to find the drive already filled with cars. There were quite a few people wandering about: some I knew, some I did not. I didn't mind at all. I felt that if people were prepared to drive to Lambourn in order to wish me well, and to share the pleasure of Corbiere's homecoming, that was fine by me; they were all welcome. David made me some tea and brought me breakfast in bed on a tray. I was not hungry, though I usually relish my first meal of the day, but since David had taken the trouble to make it, I ate it all to please him. Then I had a bath, dressed, and went downstairs – to find the house like a miniature version of Piccadilly Circus in the rush-hour. I was quite unprepared, I realized, for the vast numbers of people who were arriving to wish us well. I telephoned my friends Marcel and Janice Klien at the Rose and Crown, our 'local' pub at Ashbury, and they, fortunately, stepped into the breach to cater for the endless stream of visitors. They arrived with trays of food and crates of drink, and we spread out the goodies on the dining room and kitchen tables so that everyone could simply help themselves. I was moved and touched that so many people, both those I had never met before and will probably never meet again, as well as old friends, were prepared to go out of their way to join in the celebrations.

All we needed now was the hero himself, Corky. He was travelling, at that moment, in the 'J. S. Pitman' cream lorry on the road between Liverpool and Lambourn. He was accompanied by Artistic Prince and Monty Python, and our team of lads, who had agreed to telephone me from a call box before reaching Lambourn so that I could be ready for the horse's return. Corky didn't know what was in store for him! All the way back to Lambourn, the lads driving Corky home were tooted at and waved at by traffic they met on the roads, who could read 'J. S. Pitman' on the front of the lorry. They felt very famous at all the unexpected recognition!

The police were, all the while, being marvellous. They organized the cars pouring into the tiny hamlet in which we live, and they helped keep the crowds out of the stables as I arranged to unload Corbiere from the horsebox in David Nugent's yard close by. The police agreed they would hold back the crowd as the horse emerged from the box, since any sudden or startling noise might cause him to rear up and smash his head on the roof of the box, or fall off the ramp. It was going to be a pretty hair-raising experience in any event. The cream lorry pulled into David's yard just 10 minutes after the lads' promised telephone call came through, and Corbiere came down the ramp and back into his own stableyard at Weathercock House to a tumultuous reception. He positively bloomed as the cameras clicked, and the crowds cheered and called his name. He was very quick off the mark in realizing that he was, quite suddenly, a superstar . . . and he has not forgotten it yet, I might add!

We spent the day in a whirl and the hours flew past. We can hardly recall any particular individual incident of that Sunday since, yet again, our feet hardly seemed to make contact with the ground all day. The telephone rang continuously and the platefuls of food on the dining room and kitchen tables slowly vanished until there was one crust of bread and a small section of Stilton cheese remaining. David and I suddenly realized that we had fed the world and his wife but, apart from my luxury breakfast in bed, we had not eaten a morsel ourselves.

BBC Breakfast Television and TV-am asked me to make an appearance on their early morning shows next day, but I could manage to do only one. Thanks to my neighbour Malcolm Wetherill stage-managing matters for me, it was agreed that the BBC would pay my expenses and that I would drive up to London on Sunday night and stay at a hotel near the studios so that I would not have a 4 am start on Monday. David and I consumed the crust of bread and the small wedge of cheese before setting off down the M4 motorway towards a very smart and expensive London hotel. I looked forward with relish to arriving in a luxurious room, unpacking at my leisure, having a hot bath and then perhaps enjoying a large rare steak and a bottle of good wine to wash it down. Daydreamer that I am, I had forgotten the limitations of what are loosely described as luxury hotels. Our hotel that night did nothing to change my opinion of such big hotels. They are impersonal, and very often positively uncaring in their attitude towards the guests. Considering the exorbitant rates they charge, their service often leaves something to be desired. Give me the cosy familiar guest house with chintz curtains and a permanent tea pot, any day of the week!

We checked into the room and unpacked only what we needed immediately. Recalling films I had watched on television, and conjuring up notions of a romantic dinner for two in our suite, I telephoned room service to enquire if something could be sent up for us to eat. No such luck. 'We have no room service', a prim voice admonished me. 'There's a bellboy in your room from which you can obtain your requirements.' Duly put in my place, I turned to the bellboy. Now, I am not a computer expert; I was not brought up in the age of data processing and, at that moment, it showed. It needed a microcomputer expert's mind to unravel the complexities of the bellboy operating system. Nonetheless, we fiddled around as best we could with the buttons until, hey presto, the bellboy spurted forth its goodies. Our tongues were hanging out. It was now 14 hours since either of us had eaten, apart, of course, from the tiny piece of dry bread and cheese before leaving Lambourn. When we feasted our eyes upon the two tiny packages that the bellboy produced, we weren't quite sure whether to laugh or cry. Each packet contained a miniature Kit-Kat and a slice of crispbread and salami. That, with two cups of tea which the bellboy also kindly consented to produce, was the steak-and-wine dinner of my earlier dreams. How odd, I reflected. Yesterday the Grand National and the world at our feet; today crispbread, salami and a cup of tea. Exhausted, and beyond caring, we fell into bed.

I enjoyed the television interview on the Monday morning, my eyes propped open with imaginary matchsticks, but was glad indeed when David pointed the car once more towards Lambourn. I was gladder still as the car pulled into Weathercock House. I was naturally very anxious to see how Corbiere had fared after his long race and his journey home, not to mention his amazing and noisy reception committee! I need not have worried. The horse was fantastically well and I knew I had been right when I had told Alan Burrough, as we walked the course at Liverpool on Saturday morning before the big race, that the horse was as well as he ever could be for the Grand National. He had, admittedly, looked tired on the previous afternoon when he had returned home, but he was so well that, by the Wednesday after the Grand National, he was being so ridiculously naughty, kicking at cars, that we had to give him a sharp short canter on Thursday and Friday to settle him down again. He came right back from that four and a half mile race as though it had been a two-mile hurdle round Kempton. I had never seen a horse look so bright and well, and he quickly dispelled any fears that the race had taken too much out of him.

That same Monday morning, two days after Corbiere's victory, the post arrived and it took four hours to open all the letters and read all the cards from hundreds of well-wishers. Tuesday morning was the same, and post began coming in from all over the world. The greetings were from people that I had never met, and never would, and their generosity of thought was very moving.

Corbiere then began a slightly different career: that of making personal appearances. He began with a few charity functions to raise money for the Grand National Appeal, although some money also went to cancer research, some to the famous hospital for spinal injuries at Stoke Mandeville, as well as Riding for the Disabled. The Burroughs, most generously, have paid throughout these charity functions for Corbiere's travelling expenses. None of the money which was paid for Corbiere's personal appearance at an event went into their pockets or ours: it was all sent to a charity. If his services were required by a commercial venture, such as a betting shop which he and I would be asked to open, there would be a fee payable to the Grand National Appeal or to charity. If, on the other hand, Corbiere was asked to a fund-raising concern, we would not charge at all. One way or another, he helped raise several thousands of pounds.

Any idea that I may have become an overnight millionairess through winning the Grand National is a myth, and my fee from the race – approximately 10 per cent of the winning prize money – was spent mostly on celebration parties for either the owners, my family or friends – or used to continue the improvements to our home. Apart from the small items of jewellery I permitted myself, the winnings were not spent on luxuries.

I held a party at Lambourn for my owners, staff, and all our supporters, to which I was able to invite some of my best friends, such as Bill and Pam Shoemark who were so good to me during the unhappy times with Richard, and my very great personal friend Mary Corbridge, who lives nearby in Lambourn. Mary has always been a terrific pal, the nearest thing to a fourth sister I could wish for. She has always stood by me, and though she leads a busy life of her own, she will always come and lend a hand if I am ill. If I am in need, she is the person I can always rely on to help. We held a second party in Leicester for my family, organized by my sister Jackie – to which she also invited five of my old schoolfriends. Three of these friends arrived at the party dressed in their old uniforms from Sarson Girls' School, which made me laugh even though it reminded me that I could no longer get into mine! Let's hope you win again next year, they all said, then we can have another party!

13
THIS TRAINER'S LIFE

I look to the future of my training career, and that of my yard, with what I sincerely hope is a balanced view. I have been in the business too long to be affected by one big-race victory, or even two or three big-race victories. Horses are the greatest levellers known to man: they can put you on top of the world one day, and cut you down to size the next. I enjoyed winning a Grand National, and I wouldn't be normal if I didn't occasionally ask myself if we can win it again. I have a lot of good young horses in the yard, and plenty of good owners, and I look forward to the years ahead. A further ambition, if I were asked to name one, would be to train the winner of a Grand National for my son Mark to ride. Eventually, of course, I would love him to take over from where I leave off . . . he is going to be a good jockey and I hope his career will be as successful as that of his father. But it would be nice to think, when I'm ready to retire – though it seems a little early just yet to talk of retirement! – that Mark will be my successor. I doubt that it will be my younger son, Paul, who at the time of writing is more interested in becoming a professional cricketer.

Mark, by the time he reaches an age where he might consider training instead of riding, will be under no illusions as to the life of a racehorse trainer. At present with David Nicholson at Stow-on-the-Wold, Mark works as a pupil/assistant, and is given the occasional ride in public for his own stable, as well as for other trainers. He has also ridden several for Mum – including Queen's Ride at Nottingham, his first winner, whom I trained as well. He also gave Artistic Prince a beautiful ride round Cheltenham last year to come fourth in a good race won by Greasepaint, the horse who gave me such a fright in the Grand National.

Mark knows what a tough routine he would face: he is already aware that this trainer's life is no picnic. Constant early morning rising is probably the most notable regular feature of life as a trainer. Apart from Sundays, the day when the horses rest and when we like to have a rest ourselves to turn our days into 'family' occasions, every morning begins at Weathercock House at precisely 6 am, when my automatic teamaker, a present from Mark and Paul, sounds the alarm that is David's signal to wake up and pour the first cup of tea of the day. Before David came to join me, I would be straight up, out of bed, and into my clothes ready for the day. Since David came to live here, however, I confess life has been made easier, as he takes quite a load of the immediate day-to-day worries off my shoulders. We are a team, partners; we work together, side-by-side, to keep the yard running smoothly, keep our team of owners in the picture regarding their horses, sort out the lads' queries and problems, and ensure the horses' continued welfare. Because David is with me now, I can lie in bed for a while longer . . . just long enough for him to have a shave, fetch *The Sporting Life* from the village, and make yet another cup of tea.

David leaves the bathroom heater on, so that when I get up, the room is already lovely and warm. Weathercock House is a rambling place and difficult to heat in winter, even with central heating, so I am always thankful that someone has used the bathroom before me each morning.

Earlier still, our head lad John Ricketts has risen from his bed and dressed, and gone down to the stableyard. The yard comprises a square of 19 stables with a feed room and a saddle room, with another 10 stables backing onto one side of the main yard. These stables, which were built after we moved to Weathercock House in 1976, face towards the little lane which eventually runs up to the gallops on the Downs. John begins his day by mixing up feeds for the 28 eager inmates of the boxes, whose acute hearing has told them that he is measuring about 3 pounds of high protein racehorse nuts into individual feedbowls. Having had only hay during the night, most of the horses will be keen as mustard for their breakfast and eagerly consume the nuts. Occasionally, an individual horse will not like the taste of this 'all in one' balanced feed, and that individual may be given a bowl of oats instead. At one time, for the morning feed, we used to mix a variety of feeds, using bran (for digestion and for certain minerals), oats (for energy and flavour) and other additives. Today, the advent of the high protein all-in-one nut has relieved us of this extra chore, and the nuts are quick, as well as nourishing and tasty. Each horse is given its feed and, by that time, the other stable lads will have arrived to begin mucking out their stables.

When I was at Chris Taylor's yard and at Major Champneys', a stable lad had two horses each to 'do' – that is, muck out, groom, and prepare for work. Nowadays, the economic situation demands that each lad has three in his charge. But stable lads today are much better paid than I was at the age of 17, and receive many perks, such as travel allowances and tips, that I never dreamed of. So it has all evened out in its own way. I used to earn £3.22 a week. My lads' average weekly wage during 1982–83 was £112!

Mucking out is a job which gets easier as time goes by. To begin with, a lad may be very slow, as I was when I began. But as you get used to sifting out the clean straw or shredded newspaper, removing dirty and unwanted matter onto a large flat mucksack outside the stable door, you get faster and more adept at the job. The stable lads pick up all four corners of the sack, and cart it across to the space allocated for manure and dirty straw. Sacks are quicker and easier than wheelbarrows – wheelbarrow handles can be very hard on the hands of a stable lad on an icy February morning – and are lighter, cheaper and more wieldy, too. The stable floor is swept to remove stray bits of unwanted straw or droppings; and the bed of clean straw, which has been piled neatly into one corner of the box, is left there during the horse's exercise period, allowing the stable floor to dry and air.

It is, by that time, almost half past seven, when I expect the first lot to be saddled up and ready to pull out of the yard. I keep a riding-out board in the kitchen and, last thing every night, I work my way through it. It contains the names of every horse in the yard, written in two columns. One column is the older horses, who comprise the first lot to be exercised. The second column lists the youngsters, who go out later in the morning. There is a red plastic name tab for everyone who rides the horses, and I can slot the red tabs into the board beside the horses' names. This board is collected first thing in the morning from the kitchen and put in the saddle room so that, as each person arrives, they can see which horse he or she is due to ride.

This method ensures that the same horses and riders are not always paired up together; it gives the horses an opportunity to get used to changes of jockey, and it gives the riders a chance to learn the 'feel' of a variety of horses. There are several reasons why I will put a particular lad on a particular horse. For example, I might plan to work a slow horse next morning upsides a fast one, in which case I will put the heavier jockey on the faster horse, and the lighter jockey on the slow one: which means I can gauge the horses' individual improvement (or otherwise) on the gallops. If the slow horse were given the heavy jockey, and the fast horse were given the light jockey, it would tell me very little. The result of a work-out between the two would be totally predictable, even to the most ignorant horse-person! The exception to this rule would be a case where a particular horse and lad get on very well, where that horse is unhappy to be ridden by anyone else. For a horse to win races, it must be happy at home and must enjoy and appreciate its work on the gallops. If an animal will only work well at home for one special lad, I will not separate them and risk making the horse unhappy. A good relationship between a horse and his lad is priceless although, fortunately, only one or two horses in my yard are notably choosy about their jockeys. Most will go well for all my lads.

The lads start to tack up at 7.15 am and, as each horse is ready, it is ridden quietly in a circle on the tarmac surrounding the house. One by one the string comes together in this manner and, hopefully by 7.30, everyone is ready. David will have checked round the yard at about 7.20 to ensure that everyone is ready to go, and will satisfy himself that any last-minute decisions we have made about particular horses have been carried out. I may have asked that one animal be given brushing boots, for example, since horses are prone to 'knocking' themselves on the gallops. Brushing boots fit neatly around the horse's lower cannon bone and over their fetlock joints (known to laymen as 'ankles'). These boots have a padded patch for extra protection to the fetlock joint, which is rather prone to knocks, and are usually made of either leather or tough material with Velcro self-adhesive fastenings. We never, in our yard, use the old-fashioned variety with four or five thin strap-and-buckle fastenings, because you can rarely ensure that all the buckles are fastened with the same amount of pressure. One buckle may be too tight, another too loose, whereas with Velcro every fastening can be adjusted perfectly and evenly. A too-tightly fastened boot on a horse's leg causes blood supply and tendon problems; a loose boot can slide down and cause the horse to trip up. In an emergency, the Velcro fastenings can be quickly ripped apart and the boot removed in seconds; with straps and buckles, the boot takes several minutes to remove and several minutes may be too late.

Our work plan for each weekday is different. On Monday mornings, for example, the horses go up the roads. On Tuesdays, the older horses may have a steady long-distance canter of about one and a half miles, though the youngsters will do less. On Wednesdays, the older horses will, provided they are fit, be given a sharp gallop to open their windpipes. This is the day when, if necessary, the second string of young horses will be given some schooling work. The young horses are worked after the older ones primarily because, if they misbehave and fool about on the gallops, there is more time to give them special attention. The older horses need less schooling, and therefore less time on schooling mornings, than their younger counterparts. Schooling includes, for the youngsters, being taken out with an older 'lead' horse, who will teach the youngsters the ropes. They may also be given work with an older horse on either side. This way, the young horse in the middle learns not to be afraid to gallop 'upsides' another horse. It also teaches him not to be afraid of going for gaps on the racecourse . . . many a race has been lost because a horse was not bold enough to go through a gap between his opponents. If the horse is afraid to take his chances on the race-course, and is unused to going through a gap to take up the running, he will hang back and lose his race. Equally, once he is in front, he must learn to carry on galloping. Just as many races have been lost by horses who hate being in front as have been lost through lack of speed – so taking the lead on the gallops is another part of every young racehorse's training. If horses are allowed to follow each other along, like a string of sheep, they will not know what to do on the racecourse when faced with an open stretch of turf before them. They must, at the same time, be taught to gallop straight, so that when they hit the front on the racecourse they will remember their lessons at home, and gallop along happily in front of the field, keeping a straight course and not zig-zagging all over the place to let something else go through to win. Of course, there's always an exception – some horses, in spite of a proper education, can still do the unpredictable!

The work period for the first string lasts until around 8.45, and each horse, as it returns from exercise, is walked for the last half-hour. The lads dismount, run the stirrup irons up the leathers so they do not bang about against the horse's sides and scare him into galloping off loose and, taking the reins over the horse's head for firmer control in the event of emergency, they lead them home for the last stretch. If they wish, the horses are allowed to pick at the grass verges to help them dispel their nervous energy. This way, they return from exercise in a cool and calm frame of mind, rather than sweaty and hot from work. Only in exceptional cases is a horse so nervous that the lad has to dismount on the gallops and lead his horse all the two miles back to the stable.

My former ride on the gallops was Black Plover, the horse which taught both my sons and David something about riding racehorses. He was what is described as a hack – an animal ridden by most people for the common purpose of 'hacking', as opposed to com-peting, on horseback. These days I drive up to the gallops in my Land Rover. I watch each animal most carefully, assessing in my own mind how much each one needs in the way of work. If a horse blows hard after a gallop, that horse is not yet fit enough for a race. If, however, it pulls up after a gallop and does *not* blow too hard, then maybe I'll give it an extra furlong or two and know that it is what we call 'looking for a race'. Some horses, however, blow purely because of their nerves, so each one must be judged on its own personal merits, and needs every ounce of concentration – which is why the Land Rover is so ideal. It goes in all ground, what's more! It also gets me back to the yard in advance of the horses, so that I can watch them come in. You can tell a lot from the way a horse comes back from a work-out. I can pick up a tell-tale sign, here or there, as I watch them file back in.

By nine o'clock, each horse from the first string has had its feet picked out, so that any stones or other small objects can be removed from between the shoe and the soft 'frog' in the centre of the foot. The horses' legs and feet are washed clean, then the hooves are brushed over, inside and out, with a special oily preparation we use which contains Stockholm tar. Stockholm tar is known for its anti-septic properties, as well as for its protective way of coating the hoof. The oil in the mixture helps keep the hooves supple; hoof is like fingernail, and breaks easily when it becomes brittle. The horses are then brushed over, and any sweat marks or saddle marks removed. Saddle marks form on the horse's back in the area where the saddle rests, and where sweat naturally tends to accumulate. The horses are rugged up in their 'day' rugs, which are lighter than the night rugs, and are then given hay and water and left to settle.

Hay is somewhat therapeutic for horses. Not only does it contain nutritional qualities, it also serves to occupy their minds during the long hours between their morning exercise and afternoon stables. Horses can become bored and miserable easily, and having hay to pick at and chew over gives them something to think about. It helps stop them from developing stable vices, caused purely by boredom, such as weaving (from side to side at their stable door, causing loss of weight and leg strain), crib-biting (hanging onto their mangers and stable door tops and eating them away), or wind-sucking (holding onto the top of a stable door, gulping in air and making belching noises). All these vices are infectious; a yard which has one 'weaver' can end up with several more, since a horse watching another weave will tend to copy. All these vices can be prevented with careful attention, and hay provides an excellent diversion. This all shows just how important a summer break is to a racehorse, a spell when he can indulge in all the more normal horsey pursuits, such as rolling, digging, galloping and generally kicking and bucking for freedom – and, most of all, grazing. The horse loves something to chew at, be it grass or hay (which is, after all, dried and baled grass).

Our horses' shoes are changed very regularly. All the horses work at home in safety shoes, Adgrips, which are a great help on slippery roads. The Adgrip shoe gives the horse's foot more grip, or bite, on the road surface, containing a substance in the groove of the shoe which has a rough surface. Since we started using Adgrip shoes two years ago, our record of horses slipping in the road and injuring themselves has dropped very considerably. The everyday steel exercise shoe is worn for 90 per cent of a racehorse's working life. For the other 10 per cent, assuming that to be his racing life, he is shod in a special aluminium lightweight racing 'plate'. This type of special shoe would last precisely two days on the roads, since it has very little substance. The day before a horse is due to run, after he has had his morning's work, the blacksmith will 'plate' him ready for the following day. After racing, the shoe will be removed and re-placed with a normal exercise shoe. With shoes being frequently changed, the oil applied to the horses' feet becomes even more essential. The racehorse's hoof is even more prone to breaking and cracking than that of his fellow, the show jumper or event horse. The average hack or riding horse will wear a shoe that lasts up to about six weeks. In comparison, a racehorse's Adgrip exercise shoe will last about three weeks, while an ordinary shoe will last only 10 days to a fortnight.

That is why, quite naturally, the blacksmith is as regular a visitor to our home as the postman. Most afternoons there will be some job for him to do: a nail which has come loose, one which has sunk too deep and is protruding from the outer edge of the hoof, or simply a change of shoe for racing. The only day we don't see our blacksmith is Sunday, unless there's an emergency or a runner early in the ensuing week. The lads check their horses' feet twice daily, and we rely on them to tell us what needs doing. There is a board in the saddle room, and, if a lad notices something wrong with his horse's shoes, he jots it down on the board for the black-smith to take note of in the afternoons. The blacksmith can then look at the horse's feet, and he will gauge whether the horse needs shoeing again immediately, or whether or not the shoes will last for a day or two longer.

At about 9.30 am, the lads have finished doing the horses over, and they will sweep the yard. At this time, David and I sit down to a good breakfast, bacon and eggs usually, with Mandy and any of the other jockeys who have ridden work that morning. The lads have their breakfast and I make a giant pot of tea which John Ricketts takes outside. Sometimes we may be joined for breakfast by owners, who may or may not have arrived in time to see their horse work that morning. I appreciate an owner driving down to be with us by 7 am or so, and I like them to take an interest in their horses. It helps them to appreciate *our* problems if they can come up on the gallops and watch the horses working. I particularly like it when they come on very cold, wet and windy mornings, so they see the less glamorous side of the job! Alternatively, some of the braver owners, who may ride themselves, will come down at week-ends and ride out on their horses. Jeremy Norman, who introduced us to Corbiere, was just such an owner.

On days when we have a runner, particularly in the middle of winter when racing begins early (at 12 o'clock on occasions), we have quite a mad rush to get the first lot exercised, have breakfast eaten and out the way, whilst our runners will have been loaded and taken to the racecourse a lot earlier. Most meetings are at least one hour away by car, and I like to be there well before racing starts. If the race meeting is more than two hours away, then we'll be putting our foot down a little harder than usual on the accelerator! Racing people seem to spend half their lives driving to or from race meetings; there never seems to be quite enough time, and consequently they do twice the speed of most motorists. Our mileage can be phenomenal; my Datsun, purchased in 1981, had nearly 70,000 miles on the clock before it was 18 months old – and most of those miles were at full racing speed!

Because of the hectic rush in mid-winter, the horses which have races will leave the yard very early in the morning, sometimes at 5 or 6 am. We like the horses to arrive at the course at least three hours before the first one runs, so that they have a minimum of two or three hours rest at the racecourse stables prior to racing. This is important, and it also gives them time to spend a penny. A horse which runs with a full bladder cannot hope to give of his best. A good straw bed is important for this purpose: for some reason a horse will invariably spend a penny when put on fresh straw bedding! The lads then have plenty of time to prepare, plaiting up their horses' manes neatly before it is time to saddle up and go to post. Occasionally you have a funny character, like Lord Gulliver (and Bonidon before him) who needs a goat living with him. You must remember to tell the lads to take the goat to the races with the horse! If Gulliver arrived at the course without his goat, he would throw a minor fit and break out in a sweat. We always maintained that he would lose the equivalent of one hard race in sweat, simply because that goat wasn't around.

If a trip to the racecourse takes longer than three and a half hours, such as those to Doncaster or Liverpool, then the box will take our runners to the course the day before. Most horses settle down in racecourse stables, though you find the odd one or two that refuse to accept their new surroundings, and these horses may sweat and pace the box enough during the night to 'run their race before the start'. It is sometimes a problem with racehorses, and can be serious enough, in certain cases, to prevent a trainer taking a particular animal to a particular course. The horses travelling to an overnight stop will be accompanied by their stable lad, and by Stephen Fox, who drives the box and also acts as my travelling head lad. Some bigger yards, those with 50 or more horses, will have a permanent travelling head lad whose job is solely to go everywhere with the horses when they travel to racecourses. When Stephen gets to his destination the night before a race meeting, he will telephone me to assure me that the horses and the lads have arrived in one piece, and that the horses are eating up and content. If there are any problems, he can always let me know. He may telephone me first thing in the morning, just to put my mind at rest once again.

David and I take turns to drive each other to racecourses, in view of the long distances involved. I confess that Dave takes the lion's share, which gives me more time to think about my runners in advance. There was a time when I drove everywhere; when I first began training, I always drove the horses. Nowadays, that's not necessary and I can travel in comparative comfort. David and I will chat most of the way about the horses' morning work-out, what we feel is a solution to one particular horse's problems, or how we feel a particular animal's problem has responded to a remedy we have devised. I might ask him if he agrees that a change of work rider gave one of the horses any special benefit, he might suggest to me that a certain horse could do with some more schooling – here again, our teamwork comes into play. We discuss all these things together since two minds are surely better than one. Mandy is also most useful in this respect, of course. As well as being the yard's secretary and chasing me up with the entries each week, she rides work first and second lots, and is very much aware of what each horse in the yard is doing. She can also keep a weather eye on the staff and any problems they may have. Mandy rode a winner for Paul Mellon when she worked for Ian Balding, and is a very astute judge of a horse's ability.

Sometimes we take owners or jockeys with us, or we may travel in a car with an owner or jockey; it is an advantage, whatever the situation, to share the costs of our petrol and help cut down the mileage on all our cars. It is particularly helpful if you are taking along the jockey who will ride your horse since you can then pool your thoughts and ideas and discuss the race in advance. The sharing idea also applies to travelling the horses. We have an agreement with Fawley Transport at Wantage: if they have several runners, and we have one, we will pay them to take our horse to the races. If the situation is reversed, and we have three runners and they have just one, we take our lorry and charge them accordingly. This usually works out most fairly; we have a standard charge for each horse, so that no one ends up out of pocket at the end of the day.

My first job upon arrival at the course is to go to the weighing room and check that the horses have been declared to run. In so doing, I can also assure myself that the horses actually did arrive –

and aren't sitting in a broken-down lorry somewhere along the road
– and I can ask Stephen Fox whether there have been any problems
en route. Then I walk across to the racecourse stables to ask the
individual lads how things are, and check each horse over carefully
to make sure they haven't had a knock during travelling, which can
happen quite easily if the lorry has to do an emergency stop for any
reason. We then find the tea bar and meet up with the owners, who
naturally want to discuss their horses' chances in the race ahead.
There are always plenty of people that you know, with whom you
exchange all manner of conversation, ranging from idle gossip to
valuable snippets of racing information. But there's little time to
waste, since there is still plenty to be done before the race.

Threequarters of an hour before the start of a race, I go back to
the weighing room to watch my jockey weight out correctly. If we
have had a runner in the immediately preceding race, there's also a
mad dash to collect the tack from the first runner, to prepare it for
the next. In any event, I always insist upon saddling the horses myself wherever possible: I feel I owe that to the owners of the horse.
If I am unable to be present at one meeting because my services are
required at another, David will stand in for me. If there are three
meetings and I have a runner at each, Mandy will saddle the third
runner on my behalf. It is unfair on owners, who support us
throughout the year, if we do not, in return, support them at race
meetings. It takes some careful organization at the peak of the
season, when we do have three runners at three separate meetings –
but I always make sure someone represents me.

This is not, of course, the only reason for being present when a
horse runs. Far from it, because from watching a horse run a race,
I can learn an awful lot about it. Watching from the grandstand
through powerful binoculars, I can see the race as a whole, watch
the other runners, and though the jockey can tell me a great deal
about the horse's run afterwards, I can probably tell him just as
much, if not more. He is involved only in what is taking place in his
immediate vicinity, but I can see what is happening behind him.
Later we exchange ideas about the horse's next run as a result of
what we have learned from the present one. I always listen very
carefully to what my jockeys tell me, whether I think they rode the
horse well or otherwise. Driving home later, I can put two-and-two
together and form, quite possibly, a completely revised opinion
about the jockey's riding of the horse. What might have seemed to
me to be a bad ride can, in the light of the jockey's information, look
quite different.

Another reason for being present is, of course, the possibility of

an accident. Fortunately – touch wood – we have a very low record
of fallers and most jockeys, if I assure them that a novice 'chaser is a
safe ride, can afford to believe me, since they know we spend a lot
of time schooling our jumpers on the gallops at home. But, in the
event of a serious accident, someone must be present to take the
decision to put the horse down. Generally, if a horse is badly injured, for example if he breaks a leg, the trainer will have to take the
inevitable step of calling in the racecourse vet to check the severity
of the injury. If a horse suffers a severe injury and the trainer is not
there, it will be shot in any case. However, occasionally what appears
to be a break may be a severe case of breaking down, and a trainer can
get the horse loaded up and taken home, to try and repair the
damage. Artistic Prince, having broken his leg, normally a cause for
almost instantaneous destruction of the animal, had his bones
pinned and screwed together and ran round Aintree held together
like a bionic man!

When we give a jockey his riding instructions, we try to include
the disadvantages of riding the horse, as well as the advantages. I
may say 'This horse will get you round safely, but don't take him
too close to the wings of the jumps'; or words to that effect. Hopefully the jockey will bear the words in mind in the heat of the race.
When we do have a horse that is a tricky jumper, then my course of
action is always to go back to basics. I return to early groundwork,
starting off as with any youngster by making it jump over bundles
of birch faggots provided for that purpose on the gallops. When
they are jumping those correctly, without spooking at them and
without kicking them down, we progress to bigger obstacles.

Schooling the horses at home is, in my book, the most important
part of training and I am always present at schooling sessions. I
won't only school a bad jumper three or four times and hope for the
best, either; I'll school it and school it until it is going right, and
until I am entirely satisfied that it will be safe on the racecourse.
Some of my owners, when watching me work a slightly difficult
jumper on the gallops in this manner, wonder at my endless patience
with horses. It is true, I do have endless patience with horses: not
so much with humans, I might add! Horses cannot understand; you
must teach them slowly and carefully. It is important that they like
what they are doing. Humans *do* understand, and if they choose to
ignore my words I cannot help but get annoyed! You can get 'thick'
horses that simply won't learn, with whom one must be eternally
patient. Alternatively, some horses have natural ability and are a
joy to work with.

We school our horses in draw reins at home, in the same way as
most equestrians use draw reins. A draw rein serves the purpose of

bringing the horse's head down so that he bridles better. It is helpful in bringing a horse up together with his hocks underneath him. In other words, they are an aid to collection in the early stages of a horse's training. The rein runs from the girth, directly up to the bit-ring on one side of the horse's mouth, then to the rider's hands, back through the other bit-ring and down again to the girth. We regard draw reins as an excellent schooling aid in the right rider's hands, but they are an absolute horror story if used by a clumsy rider. I will always ask Mandy or John Ricketts to school horses which need draw reins, since I know they have the light hands required for the job. The rider must have a great deal of consideration for the horse's mouth, since hamfisted use of draw reins gives the horse a lot of pain and a hard mouth.

Draw reins also help make the horse more attentive to his rider's requirements, as well as assisting with balance and manners. They encourage the horse to form a nice strong muscle along the top of the neck. You will see horses, both on the racecourse and off it, carrying their riders along in an unbalanced way, their heads stuck firmly in the air, and a strong column of muscle down the front of the neck which is the result of years of bad schooling – or none at all! The horse with the good top muscle can flex its head and drop it, and in doing so forms a nice outline along his back and quarters. I had not seen racehorses ridden in draw reins for some years, though we have always employed them for schooling. Lately, around Lambourn, I have noticed more and more yards using them to school young racehorses.

The bit which we invariably use, both on young horses and old, is the plain jointed snaffle. This type of bit, whilst it can have a 'nut-cracker' effect if used on a particularly sensitive animal, is generally thought to be safe in the hands of most riders. On the more sensitive-mouthed youngster we will use a French-type snaffle, which has a flat lozenge-shaped centre section that lies flat on the horse's tongue; when the rein pulls on the bit-rings, the flat section prevents the bit poking up into the soft roof of the horse's mouth. The snaffle can act as a lever on a horse's jaws, and the pointed section of the ordinary snaffle can cause quite severe pain. A young horse needs a great deal of care when it comes to his mouth – that, after all, is the only means of steering on a racecourse. If the steering mechanism fails, the horse and jockey can end up just about anywhere!

I prefer, whenever possible, to buy unbroken young jumpers rather than horses which may have been broken badly and ruined by ignorance on the part of the person breaking them. The breaking process takes time, but at least I know it has been undertaken correctly if I do it myself. Most horses, of course, by the time they reach the sale rings, will have been well handled, and will be accustomed to having rugs and rollers put on. The saddle is only one step further on. They will all be used to headcollars, the stage which comes before the bridle. We give all our horses plenty of cantering work in circles and figures of eight, which is unusual for a racing yard. I find it helps the horses to carry themselves in a balanced way, and makes them a pleasanter, safer ride on the racecourse. It also helps horses to learn to respond to the rider's leg, so that they need less nagging with the whip when they are running.

Back at the racecourse, having instructed my jockey and assured him that he is riding a safe and well-schooled jumper, we have some polite chit-chat and may exchange jokes and gossip in the parade ring whilst our runners are walking round. If the weather is cold or wet, the horses will wear a warm rug over their saddle until the jockeys mount up. Once the jockey is on board, his instructions hopefully firmly implanted in his mind, the rest is up to him. The horses leave the paddock one by one, and disappear at a canter to the start. They are permitted a look at the first fence, so they have an idea of what they will be facing when the tapes go up.

Sometimes an owner will also tell the jockey how *he* would like to see his horse ridden; usually, however, we have discussed it in advance of the race and arrived at a generally satisfactory conclusion for all concerned. Some trainers take absolutely no notice of their owners' opinions, preferring rather pigheadedly to stick by their own beliefs. There is some virtue in that, but I believe there is something to be learned by listening to the person who wants the horse to win as much as the trainer does: his owner. I like to feel that jockeys, owners and trainers can pool their knowledge, and from that information we'll decide how the horse should be ridden. My jockeys, fortunately, such as Ben de Haan, Colin Brown and Malcolm Bastard, think along the same lines as me. We've 'grown up' together in racing, so to speak: we all came into training or riding at approximately the same time, and we have worked together a lot. All this is not to say that I don't have firm opinions of my own! Make no mistake, I say what I think, but I also listen. And I will berate a jockey, however much of a good personal friend he may be, if I feel he has let my horse down.

While the jockeys go to post, we take ourselves up into the grandstand, where with our owners we can watch the race from the comparative warmth and comfort of the members' stands. I watch carefully how the horse canters to the start, since it often gives an early clue as to his general, overall state of health and mind. If he goes down like an old slug, I'm a worried lady! If, on the other hand, he bounces down with his ears pricked, I'm well pleased. At this point, it matters not whether my horse is a 100–1 outsider in a selling plate at England's most distant and least important racecourse, or whether he is Corbiere lining up at Aintree. As the field comes under orders, the palpitations start. It's a special feeling that comes to me before the start of every jump race in which I have a runner, and I never have quite the same feeling if it's a flat race. It's a magical, exciting moment. Then they jump off and are running. I become critical and watch eagerly through my binoculars throughout the entire race; only as they reach the final run-in, as the runners come up past the stands, do I take the binoculars from my eyes. I am constantly looking for small, tell-tale signs. If the horse runs badly, I will need to analyse the signs later. If it ran well, we all run joyfully down to welcome it back to the unsaddling enclosure. There is much back-patting and happy laughter – there is no feeling quite like watching a horse which you have trained or owned, come home in front.

I then have a short chat with the jockey, either to congratulate him, or to ask where he thought we went wrong. He might, for instance, suggest the horse was a little short of work and could use another couple of gallops before his next run. But I have usually watched the race carefully enough to draw my own conclusions before the jockey and I even speak about the race; being in the same profession, and having worked in racing for so long, we both tend to come up with a similar prognosis. If not, we can exchange points of view and, hopefully, I can form a final opinion and can give the owner a valid explanation for the horse's possible poor performance on this occasion. Fortunately, my owners are very understanding. They know horses cannot win races every time they run. Horses, like humans, have good days and bad days.

After his race, my horse will be taken back to the racecourse stable to be washed off (since he will have been on the receiving end of a lot of flying mud and water on a wet day), cleaned up and, provided he has not sustained an injury, will be prepared for his journey home. If the horse *has* sustained an injury, or is an animal with a history of leg trouble, I treat it personally. If it is a serious injury I call the racecourse vet, but if it's superficial – fortunately, most are just minor knocks or cuts – I can deal with it. All my horses are rested for at least an hour before travelling home.

After racing, I think it imperative that the horse's legs are given some support. This is because a horse becomes 'leg weary' in a race, especially in the first couple of runs of the season, and if a supportive bandage isn't put on after the race, the horse can have a 'bowed' tendon by the time it reaches home. First, we apply a wet pad of Animalintex to the leg, covered by a gamgee padding and a bandage to hold it in position. The bandaging is important since, if the bandage is made of elastic and becomes too tight, it can cause more problems than it cures. Bandaging a horse's legs correctly is an art. Bandages must be firm enough to give support, but not too firm; and if they are not firm enough, of course, they will slip down. I bandage a horse's leg, if it has experienced previous problems, from behind the back of the knee to below the fetlock. I never let inexperienced lads apply elasticated bandages: if they aren't allowed to do it, they cannot go wrong. I tend to apply this policy to horses quite a lot – if I have done a job personally, then I have only myself to blame if it goes wrong.

Support bandages are made from a stretchy, elastic substance. Travel bandages, on the other hand, are made of wool, are about four inches wide, and are virtually impossible to apply too tightly; though, having said that, someone will one day probably prove me quite wrong! They are used to protect the horse in the event of an accident whilst travelling, such as a sudden stop, which may cause the horse to knock himself. An important factor in the tying of bandages, whether for support or for travel purposes, is that when the tapes – fixed at the end of the bandage – are finally tied, the ends must be tucked neatly out of sight and out of the reach of the horse. Many horses take pleasure from playing with the ends of bandage tapes, thereby either tightening the bandage too much, or simply undoing the knots. You then have yards of loose bandage around the horses' legs, which can be dangerous and cause them to trip.

The horses are not given much water too soon after racing. Once washed down and cooled slightly, they are given what is known as chilled water. This is a misnomer, since the water is, in fact, lukewarm. The expression probably arose from an old-fashioned method of taking the chill off when a red-hot iron poker was plunged into the horse's water to warm it slightly. The horse will then slake its immediate thirst, but will not drink a bellyful, as it might if the water was cold. This could cause a colic; if a horse drinks a large quantity of cold water after a race, it will end up with a severe stomach ache. If, on the other hand, it drinks too little water, it would be liable to choke when it next ate food.

The horses are then taken for a walk around in a 'cooler' or antisweat sheet, which most people who watch racing will recognize as resembling a string vest. It has the effect of keeping the horse warm, whilst allowing the body to dry freely at the same time. On cold days, a second rug is thrown over the cooler, since it is imperative to keep a racehorse warm – how would a human athlete react if he were allowed to become very cold after he had run an arduous race?

It was the importance of keeping horses warm that lay behind one of my most serious brushes with the stewards, not long after I received my professional training licence. It happened at Leicester, where the stable had runners, including Gylippus, whose value could then have been estimated at approximately £20,000 to £25,000. I realize that stewards have a job to do, and most of them do it admirably; but sometimes I wish they could be just a little more *human*. On that particular day at Leicester it was very cold, the rain was lashing almost horizontally, and the mud was feet deep. As the horses returned from the racecourse, they and the jockeys were plastered in mud from head to toe. It was impossible to see which colours the jockeys wore, still less the colour of our horses' coats.

During the course of the afternoon, I overheard two stable lads getting a rocket from an official for washing their horses down inside the racecourse stables. I immediately joined in the heated discussion, for I had a vested interest: Gylippus was due to run in the next race. I would not have wished to see him being washed down afterwards in the freezing rain. I wanted this valuable animal – indeed any of my runners – washed down in the dry warmth of the stable. Each horse would need at least two bucketfuls of warm water to remove the mud from its coat, and I failed to see that it should be a cause for concern. I asked the official if he had an alternative suggestion: was there another area which was dry, which we could use for washing down the horses, to save our valuable animals from catching severe chills and possibly developing pneumonia? I was stunned and speechless – though for only a second or two – at the answer I was given. What could possibly be wrong, the gentleman concerned enquired, if we washed our horses down outside the stables? We could do the same as trainers at Newmarket: *they* always managed to wash horses down outside.

'For a start', I advised him, trying to control my temper, 'this is not Newmarket. Racing at Newmarket is invariably held on warm sunny afternoons; today is neither warm nor sunny. Horses do not often come in from Newmarket racecourse totally plastered in cold wet mud as they are here today. At Newmarket in July, the dangers of pneumonia are slight; at Leicester in mid-winter, the dangers of pneumonia are incredibly high. So what is wrong with washing down *inside* the stables, away from the wind and rain?'

'The bedding', came the reply, 'costs 50 pence to replace'. I could hardly believe my ears. 'But my horse will cost £25,000 to replace if it dies of pneumonia', I insisted, imagining he would see the irony. Apparently not. The answer was still 'no'. I tried one further tactic: 'How is one stable lad supposed to hold his horse still outside the stables and wash him down at the same time?' 'Tie him up', came the reply. I knew about tying up racehorses, and I knew about tying up Gylippus in particular. Gylippus would stay in his box at home only with special security arrangements. If I risked tying him up, he would have been on the other side of Leicester town, never mind Leicester racecourse, before anyone came near him with a bucket of warm water.

'Do what you used to do', suggested the official finally, 'when you went to point-to-points'. That was the last straw, and I almost exploded. I reminded him that this was a *professional* race meeting, not a point-to-point. My owners had paid out entry fees to bring their horses to the course, and if that entry fee couldn't include the cost of 50p for bedding, then something, somewhere, was in need of reorganization. The official walked away, and we all washed down our horses outside in the relentless rain as best we could. I assumed that the matter was at an end, resolving not to come back to Leicester racecourse in a hurry. Not so. A letter from Captain Nick Lees arrived through the post shortly after that race meeting. The letter required a personal appearance by Mrs Jenny Pitman before the stewards at Leicester racecourse at the next race meeting to be held there. I was, apparently, to receive a firework for having washed my horses down in the racecourse stables. Fortunately, I knew that the lads had washed the horses down outside, as requested, in spite of my angry exchanges with the official. On the other hand, even if they *had* washed the horses down inside the boxes, I would still have defended them! But they reassured me they had obeyed the official, and my stable lads are not in the habit of lying to me. Any water to be found in the stable at Leicester after one of my horses had occupied it was due to more natural causes. Richard, to whom I was still married at the time, warned me against using crude expressions to indicate the nature of the liquid on the floor of the stables. He advised me to tell them the horse 'staled', 'stale' being another word for 'pee'. The latter word just was not professional, Richard decided.

He may have well been right, but by the time I had stood in defence of my stable lads, and assured the stewards that no horse of mine was washed down in its stable after racing, I began to feel the irritation rising in me. One of my boxes, said the stewards, was particularly wet. Now this box, I knew, had been occupied by a horse called Solvilation, who had a lot of nervous energy and relieved himself frequently when put into a new stable. Upon returning from his race, being still very keyed up, he would have wished to relieve himself again. No wonder the box was wet. Under severe pressure from the officials I was now facing, I forgot all Richard's well-intentioned advice. 'My horse', I assured the stewards, 'was not washed down in that box. The horse pee'd, wee'd, staled, call it what you like. That is why the box was wetter than the rest!' There was a stunned silence. I was asked to wait outside. When recalled I received a formal reply. After duly considering my explanation, the stewards reminded me that I had not long been granted a training licence, and I should be careful as to my future behaviour. The way I was going on, it seemed, I was going the right way to lose it. I was, needless to say, livid.

These events took place some years ago, of course, and in fact Leicester racecourse has since allocated three or four stables at each meeting where horses may be washed down. It does not solve the problem entirely, but at least it goes some way towards recognizing the trainer's need. There is always a queue, if more than eight runners take part in a race, since whilst the first four may finish washing down fairly swiftly and not keep the *second* four horses waiting too long to use the stables, any more horses waiting after that will be cold and very uncomfortable by the time the first two lots have finished washing down.

There exists, among some racecourse officials, a petty kind of tyranny and it is difficult to get past the red tape surrounding certain racecourse regulations. Washing down horses is only one of the many – and it would, perhaps, be easier to accept some of these regulations if the racecourses would only meet the trainers half-way. There is the matter of cleanliness at some racecourse stables, for example. Some courses never completely change the stable bedding from one meeting to another. The same bedding is used for one set of runners after another, and becomes a breeding ground for infection. No one might notice if a horse carrying a virus uses the box, because the carrier may show no sign of infection, though the next horse to use the box will fall victim to the virus. Yet trainers must produce vaccination certificates for every horse in the yard to prove that it has been protected against influenza. If the vaccination is out of date, we are fined £100 and the horse may not run. Some racehorses using racecourse stables may have run in France or Germany the previous week, and may be carrying a virus infection against which our vaccinations are useless. It makes a nonsense of the system. Stable bedding in training yards is mucked out every day, and a new horse coming into the yard will be housed in a freshly-disinfected box on bedding that no horse has used before. Why, then, should the same standards of hygiene not be applied by racecourses?

14
EPILOGUE

Our relationships with our owners, as opposed to officials, David and I treasure very carefully. Whilst some trainers tend to regard owners as the people who cough up the training fees every week plus expenses – which, of course, they do – David and I look upon all our owners as personal friends. We enjoy their visits and welcome their telephone enquiries. I invite their opinions, listen carefully to their ideas, and encourage them to take as great a part as possible in the training of the horse or horses they have put in my care. I would not enjoy sitting in an ivory tower, training horses in an imperious manner, permitting my owners to call on Sunday mornings to see 'my horses'. They are 'our horses'.

After Corbiere won the Grand National, one of the loveliest things an owner said to us was: 'Congratulations, Jenny. We are so proud to be associated with you. It is so lovely to be a small part of the yard which won the Grand National.' I hastened to reassure the owner, who like many others had sent beautiful bouquets of flowers after the race, that he was not a *small* part of the yard by any means. Every owner is of equal value to me. Some of them don't own brilliant racehorses, some of them own Grand National winners! But to David and I they are all alike, and their horses are given equal treatment both at home, on the gallops, and in racing. The owners all play a *large* part in the yard because, without their support, the yard would cease to exist. The owners and their horses are all equally important cogs in a wheel, and without them, it would all grind to a halt.

I like to think my owners know what they mean to us; I want them always to realize how we value their custom. There was an occasion, for example, when a reception for Corbiere was being held by the Burroughs at Henley-on-Thames, shortly after his Aintree victory. I would, quite naturally, have loved to attend. However, I had Queen's Ride running in the Haig Whisky Final at Newcastle. The race had been postponed due to bad weather on two previous occasions, which accounted for it being run on a day when we had planned to have no runners. Much as I wished to go to Corbiere's party I felt that, in my professional capacity as the trainer of Queen's Ride, it was more important that I should be at Newcastle to saddle the horse. I had, as the trainer, to give the owner my time rather than attend the social function. David went with Corbiere to the party, and a good time was had by all. But I would not have liked Queen's Ride's owner, Mr Hill, to think his horse was less important than Corbiere. The owners of selling hurdlers and Grand National winners must, I feel, all be treated alike.

Corky is no superstar at home. He may have been a little over-indulged by the stream of visitors he received after the Grand National, when he was given lots of Polo mints and apples and carrots by his well-wishers – but that doesn't make him the stable's most important consideration. To us he is still 'Corky' – one of the boys, so to speak. He is a racehorse with a job of work to do, the same as his fellow stable mates at Weathercock House. Mind you, he needs reminding of this sometimes. Since he won the Grand National he has become a trifle more aware of his importance, and at social or charity functions he plays to the gallery for all he's worth. He bucks and prances around, showing himself off, pricking his ears and standing to attention for the photographers – you have only to point a camera in his direction for him to look round as if to say: 'You want me to smile?' And he will duly pose until the camera has taken its pictures.

On one occasion he became so bumptious, receiving all this acclaim and attention, that he took it upon himself to refuse to leave the party. When the time came to go home, Corky decided he had not had enough fun yet, and refused to enter the lorry. We tried all the usual methods of persuasion: buckets, cajolings, words of endearment and the like. All to no avail. Corky knew he was one up on us . . . we were hardly likely to give him a whack on the back-side with all those people looking on. 'Right', I said to Gary, 'The Broom'. The broom, the common-or-garden yard and stable broom, is one of the most excellent loading devices I know. A quick jab in the area of his hocks will usually work where all else has failed. Gary went into the lorry and fetched the broom. Corky took one look, and he knew! Thinking the better of any further shenanigans, he obediently consented to be led up into the lorry and be driven home.

We rarely have to resort, of course, to severe measures with our horses, since none of them has any really unpleasant habits such as kicking and biting. With a yard of 28 horses, that is a good record. I think it stems from the fact that I love horses as characters, as individuals, almost regarding them as people. This transmits itself throughout the whole yard and all the lads, from John Ricketts to our most recent employees, love their horses and care for their welfare. The horses sense it, and respond. There isn't a horse in the yard which can't be approached by anyone. Caring for horses this way does, naturally, have many advantages, but it does tend to have slight disadvantages, too.

Being very involved with them means that when you lose one, whether it be through the horse retiring and leaving the yard, or through it being killed on the gallops or the racecourse, you feel the most dreadful sense of personal loss. It is quite indescribable unless you own a horse yourself, and can understand the unique feelings which evolve between horse and man. We have had five horses killed in the years I've been training – Stan's Boy, at Ascot; Norwegian Flag and Roll of Drums, at Sandown Park; Deep Sunset at Worcester; and Lord Gulliver, on the gallops at Lambourn – in each case I have been heartbroken. After Stan's Boy went, I walked around in an unhappy trance for days. Norwegian Flag's accident and Roll of Drums' death at Sandown happened in full view of the racing public, which only added to the misery of the moment. Deep Sunset's and Lord Gulliver's totally unexpected heart-attacks were harrowing experiences. In every case I have held my tears inside me, and kept them for the moment when I could shed them in private. I cannot break down and burst into tears at the races when I am acting in the professional capacity of trainer. I must save my outburst until I reach home, when I can shut the door behind me and let the emotions out.

One of my favourite moments each day is evening stables. Whilst I love mornings on the gallops, and relish all the excitement involved in race meetings, there is a special hour set aside, from 5.30 pm onwards each evening, when I go round every horse in the yard. My head lad comes in to tell me when the lads have their horses ready for this nightly inspection, and David cuts up large quantities of apples so that I can take each horse a titbit. They come to expect it, and look for it as they see me come into their stable. I run my hand over each horse, checking along his back, feeling each leg for signs of heat and swellings. Cuts and bruises are treated, sometimes with a special antiseptic gel, sometimes with a purple antibiotic spray. John Ricketts brings a tray of suitable equipment round on the nightly tour, and has all these items to hand. I may find a suspect round mark on a horse's flank. That could be ringworm, a highly infectious condition which affects horses and humans alike, and it needs an instant spray of an anti-ringworm concoction to prevent it going any further. Ringworm will spread through a yard like wildfire if precautions are not taken, and as well as being unsightly, it makes the horses off-colour. Warts are another equine problem; they may need veterinary treatment.

During this hour I catch up with each horse's individual and personal problems, and can have a chat with each stable lad to find out if *he* thinks there is anything amiss with his horse. David accompanies me on the rounds as often as possible; indeed, if I'm away racing or busy elsewhere, he sometimes does evening stables on my behalf. Afterwards we return indoors, generally satisfied with the knowledge that, to the best of our abilities, all is well with the horses. John Ricketts or one of the other lads will make a late night check on each animal, straightening any rugs that may have slipped, putting back any bedding which might have been kicked about, and generally making sure all is well. I will often do a tour myself, before going indoors to make up the riding board for the following day's work.

Indoors, there is the message pad which Mandy has left for me to look over. There will have been several telephone calls in my absence, whether I've been away racing or to the sales. These will need attending to, as will any post that has arrived. We have a pot of tea and our evening meal, and in the evening I often telephone through to owners with some news of their horse, or get in touch with jockeys whose services I shall be requiring for future races. Hopefully the phone will have stopped ringing by 10 pm, so that David and I can watch the news and have another cuppa, before turning in for the night. We try always to be in bed early. After all, tomorrow starts at 6 am, regardless.

One of my pleasures on non-racing days is going to the sales at Ascot or Doncaster, even to Ballsbridge or Kill in Ireland. The sales catalogues arrive, brimful of horses for sale, exciting pedigrees, and lists of their achievements (if any). Before I go to the sales, I will study the catalogue carefully and select those I think have the best pedigree for the job in hand. Naturally I look for the 'chasing type, though I can and do train hurdlers with the same success – I had a lot of hurdlers one season, horses which came to me straight off the flat, such as French Charisma (who won five races) and Multiply (four races). They'd been struggling to win races on the flat, but hurdling often puts new zest into a bored flat race horse, and they took to jumping like ducks to water. However, I would not go out specifically to buy a hurdler. I like to think a horse I buy ultimately has a career as a steeplechaser ahead. If you buy a horse with just the Champion Hurdle in mind, then his career could end once his best hurdling days are over.

A good hurdler will not, however, necessarily make a brilliant steeplechaser. The two do not always go hand in hand. A hurdler needs careful schooling over proper steeplechase fences at home before meeting them in the hurly-burly of a race. Sometimes a horse which was a diabolical hurdler transforms overnight when introduced to fences. Pendil was a classic case in point; he was no world-beater over hurdles, but the challenge of fences appealed to him. He simply floated over the bigger obstacles and became one of the classiest steeplechasers in history.

I like to think my horses are among the best and safest jumpers in the country: they are taught properly at home and jump well on the racecourse. Safe jumping is the essence of the steeplechaser. Speed is a bonus, especially on the flat, since if a horse meets another who jumps as well as he does, the edge of speed on the flat can make the difference between winning and losing. Yet, on the other hand, speed blunts quickly in this winter game of jump racing. On boggy ground, it is stamina which counts. Corbiere is hardly the fastest racehorse the world has ever seen, yet because of his brilliant jumping and out-and-out staying power, he won racing's supreme prize.

That is why, at the sales, I will look at pedigrees first, and inspect all those horses whose pedigrees appeal. Then I sort out those with the best conformation and, from a potential 300 horses which I may have considered, I might find only 30 with the conformation for the job in hand. Conformation and make-up are preferable to a brilliant pedigree, especially for jumping. Out of that 30, I may buy one. Having taken all the right precautions, checked it for spavins and splints (bony growths which form on horses' legs), there are still a million and one glorious uncertainties about the horse you take home at the end of the day. You can see the legs, the head, the back, the chest. What you cannot see is the engine propelling the animal. Buying a horse is not like buying a car, where you can lift up the bonnet and peer inside. You buy a horse big enough to carry penalties, with a kind eye, good clean limbs and enough bone, doing your very best – but still, in the end, you are paying your money and taking your chance. It's a gamble. The horse may have a 650 cc motorbike engine, or you may be lucky. It could turn out to have a three-litre powerhouse purring quietly away inside it, and turn into a champion. Some of the most unlikely-looking horses turn into world-beaters, and the most beautifully-bred and lovely-looking creatures cannot gallop any faster than my labrador Toby. I look, in a horse, for something that *uses* itself. When you watch Steve Ovett or Sebastian Coe, you can see they have that extra ten per cent. They *look* like athletes, in the same way that I like my horses to look like athletes. Not too fat, because fat horses don't win races. A lean horse moves faster, for the same reason that a lean person will usually move faster than a fat person.

Road Race, with his long, spindly legs, was a classic example of a horse which did not look the part, and though he was not a brilliant National Hunt horse, he was a bloody fine hunter 'chaser and point-to-pointer. In his class, he was a good horse and gave several people a lot of fun, not the least of whom was his owner, Lord Cadogan. Here is a man who had owned (and still does own) top class racehorses, which had won all the big prizes for him. And yet, when we ran Road Race in the Heythrop Hunt four-mile race, no one could have been more excited than Lord Cadogan. It was the Old Etonians' race, and being an Old Etonian – his racing colours are Eton Blue – he was most anxious to win this one. Road Race jumped the last fence upsides another horse and the two ran to the line absolutely head for head, nose for nose. Lord Cadogan turned to me and, of this minor point-to-point race, for which he would receive a maximum of £40 prize money that wouldn't even cover the costs of getting the horse there and back again, said: 'Jenny, all we can do now is pray'. Road Race got the verdict. No one could have been more delighted and proud of his old horse than Lord Cadogan that day. That is why jump racing is the sporting owner's occupation.

We bracket jump racing with rugby football, as flat racing can be bracketed with cricket. One is the rich man's summer sport, the other belongs to the more elemental person who does not mind getting wet, mud-soaked and cold in order to enjoy the excitement of watching powerful, beautiful steeplechasers and their very brave jockeys take on everything that winter throws their way, as well as big fences and long courses. To those of us who make our living from National Hunt racing, it is all pure magic.

There's no big money to be made unless you own a Silver Buck or a Bregawn, when of course you will enjoy considerable financial reward. You may be lucky, like the Burroughs, and win a Grand National with your first horse; but to say that they were lucky to win £52,000 for one race is a nonsense. They bought that horse in 1977, I have trained it since 1978, and it took six years to accumulate the knowledge, experience and ability for that horse to win its £52,000 race. It can be compared to an actor who takes 20 years to learn his craft before suddenly being offered a plum role and becoming an 'overnight' success. It takes years to become an overnight success in any field.

Jump racing certainly doesn't make the average trainer rich. My present training fee of £90 per week may sound a lot, but you have only to look at what *one* horse eats to see that £90 in a racing yard does not go very far, with Thoroughbreds to feed, lads to keep and house, and much else besides. Remember, if you will, that one racehorse consumes something between 18 and 20 pounds in weight of expensive corn, let alone hay – not each week, but every single day of its working life! A selection of expensive delicacies including oats, bran and nuts, well-soaked sugar beet pulp, molasses and tick beans are also required. Tick beans are not commonly fed to race-horses. They are grown by farmers, and we have them dried and 'kibbled', or split; they were the feedstuff for working horses in days gone by. My own father fed them to his working horses; we fed them to Dan Archer, our old point-to-pointer, when he was in training. People who feed their horses tick beans maintain that the horse will always come out of the stable with his tail in the air!

There are, naturally, a million other small things to remember about horses' welfare in the yard. All our horses' teeth are rasped annually, some more frequently, to take off nasty sharp edges. Worming horses is vital to their health, since a wormy horse cannot function; indeed, it can even die if the worms are left to flourish for long enough. We worm each horse every three months, which prevents the worms getting a hold. We also, naturally, must vary the variety of worm medicine used, since it is said that worms become immune to one variety if that brand is used every time. We do not worm a horse which is due to race within a week or so, since the medicine can show up on a routine dope test.

On the basis, as with worming, that prevention is better than cure, all the horses are given an influenza vaccination and anti-tetanus jab in a combined dose every summer. Flu is rarely fatal, but tetanus invariably kills. Our stables are steam-cleaned thoroughly every year; we also spray the boxes with an anti-virus spray, and all the rugs are treated with an anti-virus powder. Despite all these expensive precautions, we still occasionally have horses developing colds and coughs. We have tried all sorts of preventative measures, but we can never seem to win entirely. We are fanatical over hygiene, and that is one reason why I get so incensed by race-course stables which are careless. We disinfect each horse's bit and bridle every day, dipping the bit into a bucket of disinfectant so that the next horse to wear it won't pick up any germs from the previous one. We have to take the greatest care possible at all times, but when a virus spreads round the yard it is almost impossible to stop. One just has to sit back and wait for the virus to run its course while, in the meantime, thousands of pounds' worth of horseflesh sits idle, keeping everyone waiting. The owners, fortunately, realize that we cannot run sick horses: not only is that totally unfair on the horse with the infection, but it only serves to spread the infection at the racecourse.

I also feel annoyed by racecourses which don't provide electric lighting in their stables. Trying to wash off a horse in a semi-dark stable after an evening meeting can be a problem, especially with a youngster who may kick out unexpectedly at a shadow caused by the failing light. Kevin Evans, one of our promising youngsters, struck into himself very badly one night at Taunton races under these circumstances, and we had to stand outside with a torch in the pouring rain to strap his leg up.

Life as a trainer has, of course, a million compensations. The moans and complaints are far outweighed by the amusing and, occasionally, unexpected incidents. Some time back I trained a horse called Norman Bank for Mrs Stanley Yassouckovich. He was a horse that had shown a lot of promise, and had run some notable races at Newbury and other good tracks, before we took him to Stratford for the Southern Cross Novice Hurdle, a race worth less than £500, run over two miles. The date was 17 November 1977 and the race was due off at 3.45 pm, the last of the day. I knew the horse was likely to start favourite, since his previous form was very good; he looked very well, and in good condition. During the course of the afternoon, a vaguely familiar face loomed into view. Sidling up to me, the owner of the face said: 'Do you want to do any business?' I was somewhat taken aback, and the idea flashed briefly through my mind that he was attempting to acquire services of a rather unmentionable nature.

'What on earth do you mean?' I enquired, somewhat haughtily.

'*They* want to know if you are interested in doing any business', he persisted. The meaning of his words slowly began to sink in. I had not been training professionally for very long, and was un-accustomed to such approaches! It dawned on me that I was being asked, for the first time, to become involved in a racing 'fiddle'. Purely as a matter of practical interest, since I was naturally curious to know what sort of price I could raise by stopping a horse, I asked the obvious question: 'What's it worth?'

'Five hundred', said the man.

'For five hundred quid, in fact for five hundred thousand quid, you can tell your acquaintances to get lost', I answered. In fact, those were not my exact words, and modesty forbids me to recount the precise nature of the reply. The man disappeared and presum-ably he told his friends – the mysterious 'they' – what I had sug-gested they do!

I was never approached by these people again; as I later recounted the story to Norman Bank's jockey, Graham Thorner, he threw his hands in the air with horror and told me: 'For God's sake, Jenny, don't ever do anything like that'. I had advised him of the matter simply so that, should the man have approached my jockey with a similar proposal, the jockey would be good and ready with his rebuff.

The story had an ironic ending. Norman Bank was favourite as expected and ran quite brilliantly, going clear at the last. Then he fell. It is just another of racing's glorious uncertainties: had he won, my percentage of the winnings would have been 10 per cent, or about £50. It is the only time I have ever been professionally approached to stop a horse, and I would never stoop to that level, for any price on this earth. I think it might be tempting for a trainer, who was going through a really bad season and running very short of money, to be tempted to earn £500 to hold a horse up, rather than let it win to collect a mere £50. Remember that the Norman Bank incident took place in 1977: it would probably be worth £2,000 today for the same thing. My reply would still be the same.

The National Hunt trainer is the poor relation, in effect, to his flat race counterpart. The average jumper is gelded prior to his career over hurdles and fences, and his value can be gauged only on what he can win in prize money. The flat race horse which is sent to stud is not, of course, gelded, and his value is not based on prize money alone: his value may be in excess of millions, both for his stud fees and for the sale ring prices of his progeny. If the progeny win races and are successful, the horse's value increases accordingly. You can have a horse like Red Rum, who has a certain value (rather like Corbiere) as a 'business venture', which one might describe as having curiosity value. That value, quite naturally, lasts only as long as the public's ability to remember the horse's name and the public's wish to see the horse at various social functions and charity events. The two sports, flat racing and National Hunt, are in essence miles apart. Compare Corbiere at eight years of age, winning the world's most prestigious jumping prize of £52,000. His value after winning would be in the region of £100,000. The Derby winner, Shergar, at the age of three, was syndicated to stud for several millions of pounds!

I would not, personally, enjoy running an all-flat yard, which doesn't mean that I don't send the occasional horse out to win a flat race. The owners I have are sportsmen first and foremost and, in that capacity, enjoy having jumpers in training. I have said that ours is a friendly yard, and when I am out and an owner calls, he or she will always feel perfectly free to go indoors and make a pot of tea while they sit and wait for me to return. They may also, on occasion, find themselves roped into other tasks if we are busy. One afternoon, whilst I was indoors working on this book, Kevin Evans' owner George Bigglestone arrived with a huge bag of wind-falls for the horses. Not just for his horse, note: for *all* the horses. David had just taken all the stable rubbers from the washing machine; the rubbers being the cloths used under the saddle to absorb sweat, and part of the grooming equipment to help rub the horses' coats to a shine. Since George was in the kitchen at the time, he was inveigled into assisting David hang the rubbers out on the washing line to dry in the brisk afternoon wind. 'If I had known', I overhead George complain to David in a joking manner, 'that I would be asked to help hang out the washing when I came to visit you, I think I might have considered taking my horse to Fulke Walwyn instead!' George is a good friend, and I knew he didn't mean it . . . at least, I hope not!

This may not be the flashiest yard in the whole of Lambourn, but it is well cared for and well run. We may not all walk about in brogues and tweeds and talk in cut-glass accents and high falutin' terms about our horses and their abilities, but we mean business and we win races. There is a line in a book on the subject of Lambourn village which describes it as 'oozing breeding'. Well, breeding is fine in horses, but it isn't necessarily a barometer of success and racing business acumen. I had an assistant trainer here, in fact, called Chris Ireland. I discovered that in my absence at the races he was upsetting my lads slightly. It required a little more than breeding to put the matter straight, and I felt obliged to put up a poster in the saddle room for all to see: 'Actions Speak Louder Than Accents'. Dear Chris soon got the message and we got along a whole lot better as a result and remained friends for many years. I was dreadfully upset to read that he had been tragically killed in a car crash, with Sir Edward Hamner's son, Edward. I wrote to Chris' mother, and received a very touching reply from her in return. As I read the letter, I recalled her son's final day at my yard. The lads had, in good natured fun, covered Chris in white flour and brown sauce and dunked him in the water trough. Chris took all the lads' tomfoolery in good part. For the trainer, it was a case of looking the other way and pretending not to notice what was going on!

I look forward now to a new season, with some new young horses. Who knows, Corbiere may yet win a second Grand National; and there are more horses besides Corky, such as Burrough Hill Lad who won the 1983 Corals Welsh National, lined up for some good races. I believe I even have a couple of future Champion Hurdlers in the making.

But I'm in no rush to meet the future, for one can never tell what it may hold. I'm in no hurry to rush my young horses, since I have no need to try and prove any points. I'm not out to conquer the world. I always have the knowledge that this yard sent out the winner of the Grand National. With that knowledge, I can work for the future with a certain peace of mind. I'm not *building* any mountains to climb, but I'm prepared to meet those that come my way.

INDEX

The Songwriter, see Songwriter, The
Thorn, Rose, 64
Thorner, Graham, 9, 10, 111, 126, 186
Tozer, Peter, 58–59
Tregonning, Chris, 64
Trout, Judy, 95–96, 98, 101

Venn, Tom, 36, 38, 39
Vigors, Nick, 64

Walberswick, 86, 88
Walwyn, Fulke, 50, 122, 188
Watafella, 116–118
Wayward Lad, 126, 128, 132
Weathercock House, Upper Lambourn, 22, 41, 44, 60, 82, 85–86, 90–91, 93,

95, 96, 97, 98, 100, 103, 106, 107, 109, 110, 113, 115, 119, 121, 122, 123, 139, 156–157, 159, 161–168, 179–182, 185, 187–188
Weldon, Frank, 13
Wetherill, Malcolm, 158
Williams, Michael, 70
Willmott, Norah, 81
Willow Red, 42
Winter, Fred, 3, 44, 45, 46, 47, 54, 56, 61, 62, 68, 70, 76, 79, 81, 84, 117, 132
Woodford Prince, 126, 127–128

Yassouckovich, Mrs Stanley, 186
Yer Man, 153